The Secret Language
of Eating Disorders

PEGGY CLAUDE-PIERRE

The Secret Language of Eating Disorders

The Revolutionary New Approach

to Understanding and Curing

Anorexia and Bulimia

RANDOM HOUSE OF CANADA

No book, including this one, can ever replace the services of a physician in guiding you toward recovery from an eating disorder. Use this book as a tool for improving health and to help you work more effectively with your doctor and other health care professionals.

Copyright © 1997 by Peggy Claude-Pierre

All rights reserved under International and Pan-American Copyright Conventions. Published in Canada by Random House of Canada Limited, Toronto, and simultaneously in the United States by Times Books, a division of Random House, Inc., New York.

Grateful acknowledgment is made to the following for permission to reprint previously published material: Alfred A. Knopf, Inc. and The National Committee of Gibran: Excerpt from "On Children" by Kahlil Gibran. Copyright © 1923 by Kahlil Gibran. Copyright renewed 1951 by Administrators C.T.A. of Kahlil Gibran Estate and Mary G. Gibran. Rights throughout Canada and the British Commonwealth are controlled by The National Committee of Gibran c/o Colucci & Umans. Reprinted by permission of Alfred A. Knopf, Inc. and The National Committee of Gibran. • *Lowell House*: Adaptation of story of Buddha and the bird from *Disciplining Your Preschooler and Feeling Good About It* by Mitch Golant, Ph.D., and Susan K. Golant. Copyright © 1989, 1993 by Lowell House, a division of RGA Publishing Group, Inc. • *The Society of Authors*: Four lines from "A Shropshire Lad" published in *The Collected Poems of A. E. Housman* (New York: Henry Holt & Company). Reprinted by permission of The Society of Authors as the Literary Representative of the Estate of A. E. Housman.

Canadian Cataloguing in Publication Data

Claude-Pierre, Peggy
The secret language of eating disorders
ISBN 0-679-30874-1
1. Eating disorders.   2. Anorexia nervosa.   3. Bulimia.
I. Title.
RC552.E18C53 1997   616.85'26   C97-930727-9

Random House website address:
http://www.randomhouse.com/

Printed in the United States of America

9   8   7   6   5   4   3   2

First Edition

Book Design by M. Kristen Bearse

With love and respect
to my darling daughters
Kirsten and Nicole,
who trusted me with their lives

We are all angels with but one wing,
And only by embracing each other can we fly.

—LUCIANO DE CRESCENZO

Acknowledgments

CERTAINLY ANY AUTHOR writes through the lens of her own life experience. I have been most fortunate to have been helped and influenced by many extraordinary individuals.

Thank you:

To my parents, who have always shown me the courtesy of respect and encouragement even when they may not have understood; for the platform of gentle wisdom.

To my husband David Harris, for his love, patience, vision, and valuable insights in the formation of this book.

To Mischa and Darius, for bringing such sunshine and joy to all who know you.

To Terry Almeida, for her brilliance and years of dedication, giving back always to the children in need.

To the three Maggies who have been in my life at one time and always: my aunt Margaret McGill, my dearest friend Maggie Kalyk, and my invaluable colleague and friend Margaret Dobson.

To my wonderfully diverse siblings who taught me much that I needed to know about human nature.

To Howie Siegel, for believing in me.

For their unfailing support, optimism, and compassion: Celine; Sarah; Irma; Karim; Noah; Alison; Diana; Sonja; Gerry; Colin; Mona; Corrina; Chahalis; Agnes; "Erin," John, and

Paulo; John Pyper; Brenda Loney; Val Williams; Sam Travers; Bill Naughton; and the wonderful, unselfish staff of the Montreux Clinic.

In memory of special angels Ennis Cosby of New York, Christy Henrich of Missouri and Kathy D'jaime of Australia.

To some individuals of our time who exemplify humanism: Alfred Adler, Abraham Maslow, Carl Rogers, Teilhard de Chardin, Mother Teresa, Elisabeth Kübler-Ross, Jimmy and Rosalynn Carter, Bill Cosby, Pierre Elliot Trudeau, Marie Campion of Ireland, Dr. Gerald Russell of England, Dr. Keith Karran of Utah, Dr. Charles Brooks of Virginia, Dr. Craig Pratt of Ohio, Dr. Dan Smith of Illinois, Dr. Edward Feller of Rhode Island.

For an unusual level of integrity and sensitivity in journalism: Jan van den Bosch of Dutch National Television, Hans Hubner of Spiegel Television (Germany), Alan Goldberg and Lynn Sherr of 20/20 (ABC) and Oprah Winfrey.

I owe a debt of thanks to writer Susan Golant, who came to the rescue when I needed her most.

To everyone at Times Books for their unbridled enthusiasm, patience, and humor: Peter Osnos, Peter Bernstein, Carie Freimuth, Carl Raymond, Mary Beth Roche, John Rambow, Don Bender, and especially my editor extraordinaire, Elizabeth Rapoport; thank you for your insight and brilliance.

Special thanks to my agent, Beth Vesel.

Contents

Author's Note

THESE WRITINGS ARE SET FORTH without arrogance or exclusivity with the hope that someone, somewhere, may glean meaning from them and effect positive change. I have no pretense of superiority, only a passionate desire to communicate what I have learned through my personal experience in order to mitigate against the self-destruction of those in our society with eating disorders. I hope that what I have learned in working with these individuals can be used to increase our understanding of the true nature of these insidious conditions and serve as a catalyst for positive change in others as well

I have written this book in the hope of helping victims of eating disorders everywhere. It has been my privilege to work with wonderful medical doctors, psychiatrists, and other therapists as we have struggled together to cure these devastating conditions. I wish to emphasize that I am not myself a medical doctor and I do not intend the advice I give in this book to replace the advice of a doctor. Particularly in the case of eating disorders, which have taken the lives of so many, I believe that it is absolutely essential that victims and their loved ones work closely with caring physicians and other members of the health care community who can monitor their health and progress. I hope that this book will help sufferers build a stronger, more effective partnership with their doctors as they work toward wellness.

You will note that throughout this book I refer often to the "victims" or "sufferers" of eating disorders. Some people have told me, in this welcome era of patient empowerment, of their concern that these terms connote weakness and passivity. This is not my intention. As will be explained more fully later, I believe there is an essential difference between those people struggling with eating disorders and those battling physical illness such as cancer or heart disease.

The people in these last groups are often told that they have an important role in their own recovery. They may be told to refer to themselves as, for example, "cancer survivors" to emphasize the progress they have already made toward wellness. They are encouraged to take responsibility for many aspects of their recovery, to be more assertive with their doctors, to actively seek out the support of others, to do everything they can to favor their return to complete health.

In contrast, people with eating disorders, while equally blameless for their condition, generally have enormous difficulty asking for help. They wish desperately to be able to be assertive, to demand support from others, but for reasons I will explain shortly, they do not feel themselves worthy of help, and in fact their own minds usually prevent them from requesting it.

I believe that in the initial phase of treating an acute eating disorder, it is imperative to remove all burdens and expectations from the patient. In this case, making the ill person responsible for his or her recovery can be a recipe for failure. It is their inability to ask for desperately needed and wanted help that makes these people true victims.

You will note that I frequently refer to the victim of an eating disorder as "she." I do this because eating disorders affect females disproportionately; of the estimated eight million people in the United States with this affliction, one million are male. I have treated more girls and women in my practice than boys and men. However, I wish to emphasize that eating disorders are no less cruel in males, and I suspect that many men and boys suffer even more because they feel they are an almost freakish minority and because the sensitive natures that predisposed them to the eating disorder in the first place make them lifelong targets for social embarrassment. I want this book to reach out to them as well and have included stories from many of the boys and men I've treated.

I have had the good fortune over the past twelve years to learn so much from the hundreds of patients I have helped reverse their anorexia and/or bulimia. Many of them have been gracious enough to allow me to include their stories, artwork, and personal communications. I wish to note that I have changed their names and identifying characteristics to respect their privacy. I have done the same for the numerous letters I received from victims, their families, and their friends.

They are my inspiration. I am devoted to them with every cell of my being.

The Secret Language
of Eating Disorders

Introduction

FOR MOST PEOPLE, eating disorders are a great mystery of our time: an enigma to the medical and psychological professionals as well as to those who have had to live with the bizarre and often tragic behavior of its victims and the sufferers themselves who cannot explain their actions. Paradoxically, much of the mystery has arisen less because we lack the knowledge or wisdom to understand what drives people to destroy themselves, but because we are all too ready to explain their behavior in some of the most authoritative and misleading clichés of our culture.

In a world so fixated on images, so prone to reward selfishness, so ready to equate success with self-promotion, it is hardly surprising that eating disorders are often construed as simple vanity taken to an extreme.

In a society so aware of the violence of everyday life, of the victimization of women and children in particular, we are easily misled to the simplistic conclusion that eating disorders are, at least partly, the result of childhood trauma (sexual and otherwise).

In an era in which the triumphs of medical science have encouraged us to use a pill for every physical or emotional disorder, we readily expect that eating disorders also will eventually yield to medical progress and medication.

In this book, I intend to examine these and other powerful beliefs about the true nature of eating disorders.

I have spent over a decade, both personally with my daughters and in professional practice, struggling with the conundrum of eating disorders. I now believe that these conditions and the behaviors they engender can be fully understood, provided one takes the necessary steps to look beyond the obvious. Because I have been able to intervene successfully in many apparently hopeless cases, I have begun to articulate, first to myself and now increasingly to others through the work of the Montreux Counselling Centre, what I have come to call the secret language of eating disorders. I have gleaned a deep understanding of how the interplay of social situations and psychological dispositions lead people to this particular "rational irrationality."

This book seeks to explain the origins of eating disorders, what I have come to call Confirmed Negativity Condition (CNC). Then I will elucidate the therapeutic process I have developed that enables victims to create a new interpretation of their world so that they see that self-destruction—the unconscious impulse toward suicide that lies beneath the symptoms of eating disorders—is no longer a necessary response to their misperceived role in society.

The true dawning of my understanding of eating disorders began with my struggle to save the life of my daughter Nicole. I recall sitting on the bathroom floor, counting the one-inch black-and-white tiles to distract myself. My back was—literally and figuratively—against the wall; fear and helplessness numbed my mind. I held a pen and notebook in my hands. Although I could feel the cold from the tiles seeping through me, I was relieved because it kept me awake. I knew that if I fell asleep, my daughter's life could slip away.

For three days I had known that, according to all the statistics on anorexia, Nikki would not survive. I had read every book

I could find on anorexia and had a good grasp of how mainstream medicine understood it. Many, many professionals had told me that anorexia could not be cured, that my child would have to live with it to the end of her shortened life. I had read that it most often affected intelligent, gifted people. After desperate months of searching, I finally understood that no one I had contacted or interacted with could offer a viable solution to reverse Nikki's condition. I knew that Nikki would almost certainly die.

Somehow, I realized I had to divorce myself emotionally as a parent from my daughter and develop a clear mind in order to sustain a positive and unconditional caring toward her. A parent is naturally anxious and emotional under these circumstances, but I knew that Nikki had no strength to accommodate anyone's perceived or real emotions. I knew also that I could not present a false front, because Nikki was too intelligent and would see right through it. Therefore, it was necessary to present as a whole that part of me that was objective and impenetrably calm. Given that I would have to exhibit a strong platform of unmitigated stability, I had to deny myself my humanness until she was entirely safe again.

Since I was working to complete my degree in psychology, I began a form of research paper, a diary on my observations of the peculiar behavior that had overtaken my own child. My thirteen-year-old daughter was not herself. I started to chronicle her behavior and then to compare it to the girl I knew. There was little time, and I could make no mistakes. This was a chess game in which the stakes were incredibly high—those of life and death.

With the first word I wrote, sitting on those cold tiles of the bathroom floor, I stepped into a foreign land without benefit of passport or road map—only my good intentions. As I noted the disturbing aspects of my daughter's self-negating behavior, which I will explain more fully in the next chapter, I slowly came to realize that she was driven by two minds, one positive, one negative. Intuitively, I felt that for her to survive, I had to feed the positive mind and starve the negative. This is what we do now, each day, for every one of our patients at the clinic.

For five months, I stayed awake with Nikki whenever she was awake, for fear of her loneliness and the risk of suicide. I began to realize the extent of the guilt she felt whenever she ate. I understood then that the unknown enemy she perceived was more than she could contend with on her own and concluded that in order to fight it, I had to present it to Nicole as a separate entity.

I also began to see that her behavior was in some way related to her concern for me and her sister, whom we had just brought through anorexia together three months earlier. In order to save Nikki, I had to use my own vulnerabilities as a bridge. Nikki took precedence over everything in my life except her sister.

During the following months, I realized that I had a mission, not just in relation to my daughter but to the wider public.

Today, I believe with all my heart that much of what is commonly presumed about eating disorders is largely mistaken or touches only on a superficial level of understanding. The toll of our confusion and misinterpretation has been high. Believing that theirs is a condition that can at best be managed as a lifelong scourge, we have allowed sufferers of eating disorders to die. We have been complicitous in victims' beliefs that they have no value as human beings. In one contemporary Western European country, the government has considered allowing anorexics to legally end their lives, believing—wrongly—that they need be terminal cases. What more damning statement of the worthlessness and devaluation of a human life could be made? We have compounded the suffering of eating disorder victims by holding them, in part or in whole, to blame for their condition.

Eating disorders remain the condition with the highest mortality rate in psychiatric practice. Between 10 and 25 percent of its victims die or are allowed to die. Those who do not die experience lives of almost unimaginable anguish.

Sadly, the suffering caused by eating disorders extends beyond its victims. All too often, families and other loved ones are tortured by the mistaken belief that they are somehow the cause of the victim's condition. They feel guilty, devastated. Families are destroyed, unnecessarily.

It is my dearest hope that once the wider public understands the true nature of eating disorders, this crushing onus of blame will be lifted from victims and their loved ones, freeing them to focus on recovery.

Because eating disorders appear to confirm powerful stereotypes and, in turn, provoke equally powerful eruptions of blame and guilt, these clichés, and the sense of failure they induce, prevent us from seeing the subtle, immensely consuming, but in the end quite straightforward social and psychological mechanisms that drive some people to behave so apparently deviantly and irrationally. As some of the great thinkers of our time have elucidated, apparently deviant behavior can make perfect sense to those involved.

Although sufferers of eating disorders have been subject to negative caricatures of selfishness and victimhood, they are in reality purveyors of the most positive virtues available to humankind. These are lives to be cherished. Sensitivity and caring are not new in man. Poets and artists through the ages have described and ached for humanity. What is disturbing is the frequency and intensity with which this caring manifests itself in eating disorders in our contemporary global reality.

I am humbled by the intense suffering of the victims of eating disorders and those who love them and awed by their uncommon courage against all odds. It has been my privilege to play a role in these victims' recovery, to see their personalities and sense of self-worth evolve. Every one of them came to us insisting that she deserved to die, that she was a useless human being, that surely someone else even sicker than she merited her spot at the clinic. As each person emerges, I continue to be astonished by her unique lovingness and pained by the thought that her life had been so readily discounted.

My role is to serve merely as a conduit to translate a secret language I have, by default, become privy to. Certainly mine is only one interpretation and reflects only those who wish it to; those who feel they cannot ask help for themselves.

This book is written with the optimistic belief that man is inherently good and would wish to respond to these victims from a sense of social responsibility. There is no blame to be attached to anyone in this message. Surely, we are all struggling to find the answers, we are all working toward the same goal: the eradication of Confirmed Negativity Condition and eating disorders.

My hope is that *The Secret Language of Eating Disorders* will build bridges among all of us united in this cause. I have the greatest respect for parents and those individuals in the helping professions who work in this field and the greatest belief in the commonality of our cause, the human conundrum.

The poet A. E. Housman said it thus:

If truth in hearts that perish
Could move the powers on high,
I think the love I bear you
Should make you not to die.

PART I

The
Negative
Mind

I

The Beginning
of Montreux

My journey as a therapist for eating disorders seems, in retrospect, both planned and spontaneous. I knew from a young age that I would become a psychologist. The well-being of the world's children has always been my primary focus.

As a young woman, I was fortunate enough to have two incredible daughters. When they reached early adolescence, I resumed work toward an advanced degree in psychology at the university. I ended an incompatible marriage and moved to a new town to accelerate my studies, leaving behind a comfortable home for a small apartment. I had planned to have Kirsten, then fifteen, and Nicole, thirteen, join me, but Kirsten initially stayed behind to live with my parents and finish her school semester.

KIRSTEN

It was during those intervening months that Kirsten developed anorexia. One evening, my mother alerted me to the problem of my daughter's diminishing weight. Kirsten was studying until two or three in the morning, which was not unusual since she had always been a hardworking student. But my mother had noticed that Kirsten had large dark pools under her eyes, and she had lost a tremendous amount of weight in a short period of time. Hearing this, I asked Kirsten to join me.

When she walked off the plane, I was shocked to see that my daughter, who was five foot nine, now weighed less than a hundred pounds. She must have lost over twenty-five pounds while we had been apart. Going back to school was out of the question; she needed help—now. I told her, "Honey, you know you are staying with me."

She just looked back at me and said simply, "Yes, Mom, I know."

Under the surface, I was in a state of panic. I immediately took Kirsten to a doctor to check her electrolyte balance. He was the first in a procession of professionals. They all told me the same thing: Kirsten had anorexia and there was no cure for it. At best, an anorexic lived with it—that was called maintenance.

"How serious is it?" I asked. I knew the mortality rate was high. The doctor shook his head to indicate that Kirsten's prognosis was bleak.

I started reading everything I could about anorexia. I wanted to discover how I had failed this child. "What did I do wrong to make her hate herself so much?" I asked over and over again. Until I understood that, I would not know what the right help was. Everything I read told me that bad parenting, childhood trauma, sexual abuse, and a string of other "issues" were the cause.

Had our temporary separation caused Kirsten's illness? I felt remorse and extreme guilt. Naturally, as a single parent I assumed total blame for my daughter's illness, and the ensuing parade of psychiatrists did nothing to change my mind.

However, I balked at the psychiatrists' conclusion that Kirsten was being manipulative and selfish, that she was losing weight on purpose to get my attention. I had known this child all her life; I could not accept that she could change so radically from the kind, giving person I had always known her to be. Kirsten had always been unusually sensitive to and aware of other people's needs, in fact she was diligent about attending to them.

I asked my daughter to explain what she was thinking and feeling so I could understand how to help her. She told me that there seemed to be some other louder thought pattern in her head that made no logical sense. Yet Kirsten had always been a very logical child. It became obvious that she did not understand what was happening to her and was powerless to stop it. She said she felt she was going crazy. The medical doctors told me that she could not go on much longer in this manner.

I soon became aware that Kirsten felt terrible guilt about anything connected with food. Whenever I tried to persuade her to eat, she either refused, or tears would roll down her cheeks while she struggled to force the food down to please me. I remember taking her to a restaurant for a muffin. She ate it, but as we were leaving, I could tell she was feeling immense guilt about it. As we drove away I asked her, "Kirsten, I'm good enough for a muffin. What makes you think you're not good enough for a muffin?"

We stopped at a traffic light. She said, "Mom, see that light over there? You see that it's green. Logically, I know it's green, but my head tells me it's red, and I'm not allowed to go. That's the best analogy I can make for you about something that makes no sense to me. That's why I'm doing something so illogical."

She gave me similar clues about how her head operated. Later I realized that Kirsten's traffic-light analogy first made me understand that two minds were warring inside Kirsten's head. She was a determined person, and I kept trying to persuade her to fight against whatever force was barring her from eating in peace.

The first two months were the most frightening. Occasionally at night, while Kirsten was sleeping, I would go quietly into her bedroom to check on her. Under her blankets, she was skeletal. I would slowly replace the blankets so she would not know I had been there, and she would not be concerned about my worry for her. It was hard to believe that she could survive; she was down to about eighty-four pounds. Fear almost paralyzed me.

She told me sadly one night, "Mom, you've never lied to me in your life, so I'm going to listen to you, even though the pressure is more than I can bear sometimes. Everything in me tells me not to trust anybody or anything at this point, but I've always trusted you. I'll continue to trust you, whatever it takes." To this day, I know that's what brought her through, and I stand in awe of her incredible courage against the unbelievable negativity of her mind.

In retrospect, I realize that her decision to trust me unconditionally was the turning point. She kept going to the doctors because I asked her to. Over the next six months, I worked with her every day. She even came to my university classes with me; I was loath to let her out of my sight. Intuitively I knew she should not be alone; otherwise this negativity, whatever it was, would gain strength in her mind when she was by herself.

After every meal, she would talk to me about the illogical thought patterns she could not get out of her head. She was direct about how she felt. Sometimes, she would look at some minuscule bit of food on her plate and tell me, "Mom, this hurts so much. I shouldn't be eating it. I should be eating a quarter of it. That's all I deserve." She felt almost subhuman, less than the rest of us. She never knew why she was less deserving, but she just knew she was.

In the first three or four months of her illness, Kirsten was suicidal and frightened, as if eating had some great negative consequence. I talked to her constantly. She was gentle, never abusive. Together we tried to work it out. For every illogical word or act, I responded gently with a logical discussion of the reality of the situation.

She cut off her hair and dyed it purple. At the time I did not pay much attention because I saw it as a natural consequence of being an adolescent. She dressed in layers as though she were trying to arm herself to fight the world; her natural gentleness began seeping away. It was as if she were on a search for self as she kept trying on different modes of appearance. She would wear outside what she seemed to lack inside for strength. (I would later learn that this is characteristic of many people with eating disorders.)

Since we had just moved to a new city, initially she no longer had any friends. I noticed that this normally outgoing girl did not even try to make new ones.

She became extremely agitated. She had to move all the time. If she needed to stay in one spot, she would walk in place; she could not sit in a chair without jiggling around excessively. She exercised all the time. I did not think that was such a problem, so I was not as on top of it as I might have been. Later I would know better.

Several times Kirsten made statements that told me she perceived herself to be the adult in the situation, capable of making decisions that seemed rational to her but were anything but. At other times, she would say, "Mom, just let me go, just let me die. This is too hard; I can't fight it." I never heard, "Mom, help me." She never asked for help; I gave it to her, but she did not feel she was allowed to expect it.

She would never say that she was worried about me, but she was always trying to make life easier for me.

Then Kirsten started losing the ability to make any decisions, any choices at all; it was as if she had lost faith in her ability to choose. She second-guessed every possible decision or choice. When I asked about her preferences, she would respond, "Mom, what do you think?" "What will serve other people better?" She could not make the simplest choices about the most basic issues: what to wear, what restaurant to go to, what to eat. She was unable to create any of her own structure at all.

It was such an unrelenting nightmare. Not only was I terrified that my daughter was losing her life, but I was convinced I was the cause of her torment. Everywhere I went, I felt and accepted the stigma. The public knew that someone had to be blamed—the parent, the child, or both. I was overcome by the numbness of hopelessness. How could my child be dying in front of me? I knew I had to do something, but I did not know where to begin. The information I was getting made no sense. So little of it seemed to apply to Kirsten. Certainly, I would not accept that my daughter's anorexia was incurable. On occasion I glimpsed an idea that felt right, but essentially I felt terribly, terribly alone, left to stumble along an unfamiliar road in a strange country, whose signs were in a language I could not understand.

I found myself of two minds. On one hand, I was petrified that someone could live with such agony—I was witnessing an emotional state that was unspeakably cruel on a continuous basis. On the other hand, I was irritated that I had allowed myself to see doctors as gods; I had expected physicians to have an answer for everything. Of course doctors are not wholly responsible for this deity complex; we put them on the pedestals ourselves. But how could I accept it when they told me my daughter was going to die, that she could never be cured? How could anybody give up on a psychological illness?

The doctors' explanations of Kirsten's illness were based on happenstance and theory, not on strict experience. I had so many questions: Why does an eating disorder affect one child and not another in the same circumstance? I had read that most siblings of anorexics did not get the illness themselves. Did sexual abuse cause it? I knew that Kirsten had not been abused. Family trauma was another commonly cited cause, but I knew that my daughter viewed my divorce as a positive event, not a traumatic one. I started searching for venues that would prove these issues to be the cause because I wanted desperately to find an answer that could reverse the consequences.

Never was I convinced that anorexia was primarily about weight. When Kirsten was sick, she expressed fears about getting fat, but it was not her main focus. She was much too composed to complain about her looks. She would tell me, "I need to be thinner. I don't know the reason why," and then she would start to cry.

Given the public view that anorexia attacked adolescent girls, a group famously obsessed with looking right and fitting in, I assumed—wrongly—that Kirsten's illness was in part bound up with concerns about body image. I now know that anorexia does not depend on gender, age, or looks.

I considered taking Kirsten to an eating disorders clinic. Every one that I investigated had a program based on behavior modification. The theory was that if you changed a person's actions, you would change the person. At these clinics, the therapists taught the patients that there were consequences to their behavior. They were given specific goals, such as finishing a particular dish, and told that if they did not achieve the goal, there would be a consequence or punishment. They would be prohibited from seeing their parents, using the swimming pool, or engaging in some other enjoyable activity.

I felt intuitively that I had to separate Kirsten's actions from their consequences. My daughter was experiencing such intense punishment internally already that for me to inflict more would be counterproductive to her recovery. Logically, behavior modification did not seem reasonable, at least for this child.

For six months, I talked Kirsten through every meal and prepared all of them myself. At each meal, I would distract her with funny stories to take the onus off the fact that she was eating.

Kirsten's little sister, Nicole, was an enormous help; she did everything to please her sister. She spent every spare moment sitting with Kirsten, talking and joking with her, giving her things, trying to make a difference. Nicole became a completely selfless person during her sister's illness and stood by her with every possible fiber of her being. I would later realize that she was being inadvertently set up for her own fall.

We combated Kirsten's illness with unconditional love and support. I refused to react to any rare bad behavior except with soothing statements like "I know you didn't mean to do that." I would never get angry under any circumstances. Intuitively I felt that something in Kirsten was testing me to find out how willing I was to be there for her. Kirsten was trying to let me know that she deserved nothing, but she was so gracious that the signals were not always apparent. It was a successful day if I just kept her alive.

I was becoming more and more physically exhausted. I felt it was unsafe for me to sleep. What if something happened to Kirsten when my back was turned? I had tried to engage yet another specialist for insight, but he had neither the time nor the inclination. He was probably exhausted and disillusioned himself from the dearth of answers. "You're just one of many. I have no time," he told me, and I was devastated.

I felt that I was operating on base instinct. If I could only find the cause, then I would know how to reverse Kirsten's anorexia. I used to comfort myself with this thought, but in my more selfish moments, I longed for some respite. I lived in a void of uncertainty and desperation. The most lonely thought is that there must be an answer, but my daughter might die because I could not find it in time. I fought for my own sanity during this time as much as I did for Kirsten's.

Ultimately, it was Kirsten's incredibly logical, lawyer-like mind that helped bring her through. Anorexia knows no logic, and part of Kirsten's mind would insist repeatedly that she was not allowed to eat, or that she could subsist on some ridiculously small amount of food. I would argue her through it for hours, and she generously let me.

"Honey," I would attempt to reason with her, "what would you expect me to eat for a day?" I had to explain the logic of the situation every time. "Write down for me what you eat; would you be happy if I ate only that much?"

Later I realized that asking her to write out her daily menu may have been a mistake; I know now that in creating a written table of contents, the negative part of her mind could use it to reprimand her for her indulgence. (At some point in therapy, however, this can be a positive, even worthwhile interim structure.)

Slowly she became stronger. The dread drained from me as the days marched on and she became more confident. Eventually I realized she would make it, at least this time. But almost every book I had read warned me of the high rate of relapse, so I felt I could not really relax. My aim was not only to save her life, but to find out how to prevent a recurrence. What, then, was the trigger?

I began to suspect that relapse occurred when this negative mindset was somehow ignited; the trigger was something other than the anorexia itself. It seemed improbable that anorexia was a direct result of a single issue or even accumulated issues; perhaps it was the straw that broke the camel's back. Now I know: It is not the ten issues that finally become too much, but rather one's attitude toward and perception of the issues that brings on the manifestation of the condition. A person's negative mindset becomes increasingly pessimistic and subjective so that it searches out any issue to turn into another negative to feed itself. On its hunt for confirmation, it perverts any issue wherever it can because it is so hungry for negativity.

During that year, I continued to attend classes to become a psychologist and kept taking Kirsten with me. My field of interest was children. I was engaged in a major research project that involved twenty-six countries, studying how to prevent recidivism in juvenile delinquents released from prison. Two nations, Japan and Sweden, invited me to study with them for a year each. I was finding that kindness, not punishment, worked miracles. Later I would see this as a metaphor for my own work with victims of eating disorders.

It was another six months after Kirsten's weight had stabilized and the doctors declared her out of the woods that I could begin to feel safe about her. I know she suffered more than she ever told me. She has always had immense courage. Kirsten told me later that it took her almost another year after she had regained her weight to feel she had an assured self with internal guidelines that she could live with comfortably. Even though she was over the manifestation of her condition, she had needed that year to gain strength, to become as whole as every person ought to be.

NICOLE

Within three months of Kirsten's recovery, I started recognizing the signs of an eating disorder in her little sister. Kirsten's illness had fortunately fine-tuned my antennae. Nicole began making excuses to avoid meals, subtly at first, then more noticeably. She would tell me she had eaten elsewhere and that she was just so full she couldn't eat, or that she had had a huge lunch and wasn't hungry for dinner. She began taking extended walks, sometimes disappearing for half a day; I would later discover she had been walking the whole time to burn off calories.

Even though her illness presented itself in a different way— she was evasive where Kirsten had been mostly straightforward —I began having an unhealthy fear about her. I was unable to sleep because I knew intuitively that, although I tried to deny it, Nicole too was in the grips of an eating disorder. The signs became too many, too often, to deny it any longer. I would see Nicole opening a can of tuna and pretending to make a sandwich. Later I would find the whole thing thrown out upside down in the garbage, so I would not readily notice that the can was still full.

Once I made the decision to face my inconceivable reality, I experienced again the dread I had just released myself from— dread that permeated me to the core. I was unsure if I had the physical energy to pull another daughter back from the precipice. I had been so exhausted for so long. Would I have the strength? Could I outlast this illness once more? I was frightened that I would be unable to, but certainly Nicole deserved the same efforts I had made for her sister.

Nikki's illness was a nightmare that I could never have anticipated. At the worst, I was ready for a rematch of what I had gone through with Kirsten. I now know that the severity of an eating disorder depends on the sufferer's personality. As it turned out, Nicole's condition was many times worse than Kirsten's had been. Without the work I had done with Kirsten, I would have gone into Nicole's case completely unprepared. I thank Kirsten for teaching me. I was still, however, woefully unready.

From the beginning, Nicole was intensely suicidal and she went into a downward spiral very quickly. She was in a deep depression, which I now realize is partially caused by the lack of nutrition inherent in anorexia.

From the beginning, I knew I had to be with Nicole twenty-four hours a day or she would not survive. I tried to continue with school as I had with Kirsten, but Nikki refused to come along. She did not want people to see her; she was a failure, an imposter, inadequate in every way, a fool. It was a desperate situation. I had no means to invite anybody to help me deal with Nikki's illness, no money, no confidence that anyone else would take it seriously enough to protect Nicole. I knew of no clinic that would watch my child like I would. Without constant supervision, I knew she would find an occasion to harm herself.

She hated me. She hated everybody. She lashed out while simultaneously refusing all aid. "Don't you dare help me. I don't deserve it," she yelled. Once when I was rocking her with my arms loosely around her, she cried out, "Don't ever come near me. Go away."

"You don't have to love me," I replied. "You don't need to worry about that. I will always love you."

She broke down and began to cry on my shoulder. "I don't know why I said that. I don't think it. I don't mean it. I don't know why I'm doing this. I love you so much, and I would never want to hurt you."

Shortly after that, I realized that for the both of us to survive the ordeal, I had to leave my emotional self out of the picture. I knew better than to take Nicole's remarks personally. Every night I sat up trying to devise a way to separate my emotional mother self from my daughter in order to create the objectivity I knew I needed for her survival. I decided to create concrete steps for myself to follow to keep me balanced in order to buffer Nikki's condition.

I went to town and bought myself a thick notebook of lined paper and told myself that I was doing an immense research project. My diary would record Nikki's every move, behavior, bite of food, and emotion as well as my reactions. Having a well-defined task with a beginning, middle, and end gave me some hope in a bleak situation. My rational self needed this, because my emotional self could find no end to Nicole's illness; therefore I did not know where I would find the strength to fight it. My rational self had to choke back the sobs and panic that surged through me.

At night I crouched on the bathroom floor; the cold floor tiles and the stark lighting would keep me awake. I pored over a list of everything the textbooks said about the causes and characteristics of eating disorders and compared them to what I was seeing with Nicole. Nothing in her behavior computed with the theories. I played with the "begging for attention" hypothesis for a while. The public conception was that manipulative people used self-starvation as a "cry for attention." In this sense, a cry for help was construed as futile, but why would it be? I was certainly attentive to Nikki, yet her self-deprivation continued. Anorexia was no ordinary distress signal.

Theory 2 postulated that Nicole was selfish. That certainly did not make any sense; Nikki was the least selfish person I knew. She had just helped save her sister's life, and she was just a child.

Theory 3 supposed that Nicole was another example of "the best little girl in the world," a perfectionist running herself into the ground to please me because, supposedly, that was my expectation. But how could the Perfect Little Girl suddenly turn into her antithesis, as far from obliging as she could be? I had never implicitly or explicitly demanded perfection from her. Our relationship had always been warm and loving.

I took Nikki to psychiatrists and psychologists, but they would only frighten her, telling her that she was failing fast. Before long, she was given every possible psychiatric label. Finally, the threat of their involvement would make her try to eat more than usual, but even so, she soon weighed much less than her sister had at her worst.

Every night, I continued to write in my diary, to argue the experts' theories on paper. I still assumed that anorexia primarily affected teenage girls, so I compared my own feelings at that age with what Nikki was experiencing. Like her, I remember feeling undeserving, convinced that everyone else was better; I was unworthy of being in their company. I had not wanted to inflict myself on them. Though I had not become anorexic, I could see that same mindset intensify itself in my daughter. I had had inklings of this inclination in Kirsten when she was sick.

I was becoming more convinced that there was an underlying condition that predisposed people to eating disorders, not a life issue, but an interpretation of life caused by an inherent mindset. Could this explain why many people who live apparently worse lives come through relatively unscathed? I began waiting for the moments Nikki would sleep so I could work on my theories. I started adding and subtracting. This endeavor distracted my mind from the pain and apparent futility of trying to cure Nikki's anorexia and gave me purpose.

Two months into Nikki's illness, I began to find notes from her all over the apartment in every container. Most were written in the third person: "Nicole is a fat pig." "Nicole is no good." "Nicole doesn't deserve to live." "Nicole deserves to die." "Nicole needs to be tormented." Why was she not writing in the first person, I wondered, why not, "I am a fat pig?" No sooner would I throw the notes away in horror then the jars would fill up with them again.

My own health began to suffer. I slept only an hour and a half a night. What worse torture than lack of sleep? One night I purposely disrobed in front of a mirror and looked at my reflection. At that moment, I vowed to myself that I would make sure this body would die before I would let my darling child die. It was a pledge not to commit suicide or give up for even a moment. I was truly drained, but as long as there was a breath in me, there would be in her.

I made myself the platform for Nicole's survival. Anything else I may have needed—including finishing my doctorate, which I wanted to do so desperately—I had to put aside. There was no choice. I never blamed Nikki. I never felt the need. I was not angry with her for a second. I knew my daughters had not brought this on themselves; they were as confused about their condition as I was.

Psychiatrists, however, seemed intent on fixing blame. One diagnosed Nicole as schizophrenic after a seven-minute interview. Others prescribed every kind of medication, seven or eight drugs at the same time, none of which she took—she refused them all, and I would not force her for fear of undermining her faith in me. Although I felt medication was not the answer for my child, I did not have the faintest idea what was.

Nikki's behavior became progressively more bizarre. She would throw a plate at my head after she had eaten something off it or break a window because she was so upset at eating. She trembled in fear, crouched in corners of the room. It was as if there was a presence beyond the two of us that was so negatively powerful. Nicole kept saying, "Mom, you can't fight it. It's stronger than us both." That would send shock waves of alarm through me, but I knew intuitively it was imperative that I remain composed to her, that I present only strength and serenity. I don't know where it came from.

Nikki's body somehow sensed she needed potassium, so I drove her, sometimes for hours, hunting for the "right" banana. We would stop at six or ten or thirteen stores. I thought the right banana would be medium sized, yellow, with few marks. I was terribly wrong. To Nikki, the "right" banana was unfit for human consumption: blackened, hidden under others, destined to be thrown in the garbage, with only an inch of edible fruit. She could convince herself that she was not really eating if she allowed herself to consume such a lowly castoff. It was frustrating, frightening, and exhausting.

One morning at 4:00 A.M., I was writing in my journal, sitting on the cold bathroom floor, when I heard Nikki creep into the kitchen. When I followed her, she had disappeared. Then I heard a sound. I found her under the table, eating dog food out of a dog dish. We had no dog.

I did not know where the dish or the dog food had come from. She was on all fours, weeping, as she crouched down to eat. I went over to her and held her and begged, "Don't do this, darling. You don't need to do this. We will figure this out."

She just sobbed in my arms and held on. "I don't know why I do this. I'm so bad."

"Honey, why are you so bad?" I asked.

"You don't understand. I just am."

"What have you ever done that's so bad? You've been such a good girl all your life—a wonderful child."

"I don't know the answer," she replied, "but I know it's in my head all the time."

I brought her back to bed and stayed with her. I knew I had to negate every possible bad thing her head told her. I also had to assume she was hearing negative thoughts constantly. She was obviously unable to reach out for help, even though she wanted it. Something was holding her back. Certainly she did not want to die.

At first I would wait until Nikki said something, and then I would answer her with logic. Soon I began to make comforting statements even when she said nothing. I would give her positive reinforcement, assuming that what was going on in her head was silent to me but terribly loud and powerful to her. She started letting me into her game of fooling the negative voice. She eventually realized that I was strong enough to work with her against it. Her negative thoughts became an "it," because in separating "it" from her, I could fight it: United, "it" could stand. Divided from her, "it" might fall.

I presented analogies to better explain the situation of her mind to her. I pictured "it" as a wolf stalking a flock of sheep. The wolf determines which sheep is the weakest and tries to separate that sheep from the fold. I used distraction or any other means to outsmart the wolf. I had to prove to Nikki that I could do it, that she could lean on me, that I would never give in, even as her mind bombarded her with cruelty.

One windy and blustery November day, Nikki slipped out of the house in a thin coat, telling me I was not allowed to come with her. I followed her without her knowing it, as I often would afterwards, the wind wiping away the sound of my steps. Nikki was concentrating on her forced march to burn off calories.

She hesitated when she saw a frail lady waiting to cross a major intersection. Even in her misery she tried to be kind. She tentatively approached the woman. Because the wind was so loud, the woman did not hear her coming. I knew Nikki had wanted to help the woman cross the street. She reached down to hold the woman's elbow. The woman turned and began to hit her with her purse. Nikki fell back in shock. She pushed herself even further that day because the woman had not let her help her. She must have done something wrong. On two other occasions she collapsed on the street. I carried her home, never knowing if she would still be breathing when we got there. In my head, I begged for her life: "Please, someone, anyone. Just let her live. Take me instead. She is just an innocent child."

I tried yet another specialist. I sent her up to his office. After twenty minutes, Nikki came running down to the car where I was waiting. Sobbing, she got in, slammed the door, and said, "Let's leave here, Mom."

"What's wrong, honey?" I asked.

"He wants to talk to you. He told me you were to blame for everything. He never even met you!"

In less than twenty minutes this doctor had decided he knew my child's life. "Nikki, let's go up and see what he has to say," I said gently.

"Are you sure you're strong enough?" she asked. Sick as she was, Nikki was trying to protect me! Why? Had I shown her vulnerability?

The doctor was as cold as his white lab coat. Nikki asked him, "How is my mother to blame? Tell her please, because it makes no sense to me."

I was so choked up by her pain that I could barely control myself. I asked the doctor, "Would you like to know what I think of my daughter? Would you like to know about us?"

"Not particularly," he responded. "Your daughter is sick because you haven't been able to handle your life."

"I am handling my life just fine, thank you," I said. "I need help handling hers."

"Nicole will live a subquality life," he continued. "You'll have to manage her condition, and she might die."

I told him that I had always been strong, that I was committed to curing her. I began to sound defensive, I'm sure, and he said "I'm not interested in dealing with you. I will deal with your daughter and I will not confide in you anything that goes on between me and her."

That was too much for Nikki. She raised her voice to him, "My mother has never done anything wrong that I know of. She's not to blame for this condition. You're insensitive! And you don't know me at all! It's fine that my mother knows anything you and I talk about. I am bad. Are there any secrets to be ashamed of?"

I said, "Honey, let's go. He just thinks differently than we do." I saw no sense staying with someone who was negative from the start. Who would be her structure if she were separated from me? In any case, Nikki refused to go back to see him.

After a while, Nikki's negative thought pattern, though cunning, became predictable, and I could fool it relatively easily. And so I began to trick what I had come to see as "the mind below the actual mind." I realized Nikki could not allow herself to eat if she had a plate of food in front of her, so I would take her out to dinner and order for myself. Everybody must have thought I was crazy, but I was conscious only of the task in front of me. I would cut chicken, her favorite, into small pieces and put them on a side plate under my left elbow so nobody else could see. I was not admitting to her negative mind that food was in front of her. It was "mine," and she did not have to take responsibility for it. I would look the other way as she slipped tiny pieces into her mouth. If I covered everything with a napkin so only one piece was visible at a time, she would take it. Slowly, ever so slowly, I was feeding her.

I looked for other strategies. I started saying, "Darling, while you were out for a walk [she would never admit that I had followed her; we both pretended I had stayed home], somebody called [nobody had, really]. Some friends want to come over for tea. Would you mind coming with me to buy ingredients for a cake?" I am sure she became the best baker in six counties. Everybody started sending her cookbooks. (I later learned that anorexics "eat" vicariously; they pore over cookbooks all the time, watch cooking shows, and cook food for other people without consuming any food themselves.)

I would never actually make the tea—no one came—but my ruse gave Nikki a reason to bake. When the batter was ready, she would allow herself to eat a little of it (which wasn't, technically speaking, "cake"), and fool the negative that way. Later, I would ask her if she would cut the cake so when "people came," we would have ladylike finger slices. That was a way for her to eat some of the crumbs—those were not "cake" either—without her negative thoughts making her responsible for allowing herself the favor of eating.

At about the same time, I also realized I had to weigh Nikki backward and never divulge her weight, although she would demand to know. Nikki was less able to respond to logic than Kirsten had been. I could not reveal her weight because no number would be good enough; she would always have to be less than whatever she currently weighed. When she was sixty-eight pounds, I tried to reason with her. "You know that you're in an impossible physical position. You can't last like this. You thought you were low enough at eighty. Now you're sixty-eight. Logically, you know better."

"I don't know anything," she replied angrily.

"If you have to be lower than eighty, are you satisfied at sixty-eight?" The negative condition was caught red-handed. "If you weighed only twenty pounds, would your negative condition be satisfied?"

She started to cry. "No. Only if I'm dead."

That night in my journal, I wrote that I knew this was a track to death. I began to question the famous myth that being model thin was the anorexic's ultimate goal. We were not dealing with a fashion statement here.

So much repetition. So much reiteration. So much counteracting the negativity inside Nikki. So much reinforcing that small kernel of hope I knew was there. In some moments, Nikki was desperate to respond. I could often see the pleading in her eyes. Through the small bits of food, she would have occasional bits of joy. The day she "graduated" from 1 percent to whole yogurt, she was laughing and crying at the same time. Everything was a baby step, because there were only baby steps. It takes incredible patience in a society that has no patience. I wrote in my research journal, "The turtle wins the race. . . . It takes time, but you'll only get there with patience."

One day when I was near the breaking point, I left Nikki with a dear friend for a half hour, just to do something "normal" for myself. It seemed a long time since I had interacted properly with society. I took my newspaper and went out to a restaurant. It was three in the afternoon. I imagined the place would be reasonably empty. In fact, a few people were having coffee there.

One of them, a woman whom I knew only slightly, came over to me and asked, "Could I talk to you for a moment? I want to ask you something." I told her I did not have much time. She pulled down my newspaper/shield and asked, "Don't you feel like a total loser, having two out of two daughters anorexic and you a counselor?" I cannot remember my response, but I do recall feeling the world did not understand us. I spent a few more nights pondering how I might have failed my daughters. Poor mothering genes?

But then I began using the notion of guilt for my research. If I felt guilty and I could not find a clear reason for it, then how could I wonder at my daughters' guilt? Both were equally unreasonable. My children could not tell me why they felt guilty; they just "knew" they were because somehow they were bad. That week I let go of guilt. I found it useless except as a motivator, and I was already quite motivated!

My journal became my best friend. It was my only sanity. It cherished my fear and pain yet nurtured my logic. Without its comfort, I would not have survived. It heard me and forgave me everything. In it I set out a long-term plan for how we would get through the next six to eight months. They were the roughest of my life.

One particularly exhausting day, after Nikki had been yelling obscenities at me, she demanded plaintively, "Mom, what do you see that I don't see?"

God, I thought, she is giving me an ultimatum. "Nikki," I replied, "give me your happiest moment ever."

She remembered it easily. It was walking on the boardwalk in Montreux in Switzerland. "The sunlight was shining through the leaves in the trees and the boardwalk was all mottled. I felt such a complete peace and understanding with myself and everything." Nicole felt honestly that if happiness were related to peacefulness, that was her best moment.

This gave me insight: Nikki was striving for peace and contentedness. She wished she could bring that moment and that feeling back. I held that thought. I presented a dream to her that I was certain, if I could get her better, I would make a reality. I was desperate, so what might have seemed extreme did not seem so then. I told her that, as I had told Kirsten, I was going to get her better. There was no alternative to that. I was uncertain how, but I was beginning to get a good sense of it. Then, after she got better, I would develop a practice that would get other children better. I told her that I would get my doctorate in psychology so people would believe us. I told her we would call the practice Montreux.

Nikki was wonderfully excited about that and held on to my dream; it distracted her. I used it as a continuing theme in her care, by presenting concrete hope. It would give her something to live for. I told her that eventually we would be in a position to open a clinic. When we knew we could do it, we would open clinics all over the world so children and parents would no longer be blamed. Everyone would finally understand. I told her it would take me ten years to convince the world, and that somehow things would fall into place. People would need and want to learn so children wouldn't die.

That became Nikki's structure. I continued to feed her with several small meals at home or in a restaurant, where she was both too embarrassed to overreact and distracted enough to eat. I knew she was not allowed to say she was hungry ever, so I would say I was hungry. We ate six times a day. Slowly, slowly, I brought her back to health. During this time I sought other help as well, because I was terrified that I would be unable to pull her through despite my efforts. But these experts were either negative, apologetic, or benign at best, which at least was inoffensive, but unfortunately offered no insight or relief.

It took me a year and a half to turn Nikki around. After ten months, I knew she was going to recover. So that she would not feel like an outcast and to prepare her for reentry in society, I started a group at my home for any child or teenager who felt dysfunctional. I wanted Nikki to realize this was a common plight of the human condition; she had not been singled out for negativity. One of my patients was a recovering heroin addict, several others were anorexic or bulimic.

Doctors who had heard of my experience with my daughters began to refer patients to me. I received calls asking if I would consider talking to this mother or that child. Within two years, much to my dismay, I had a lineup of patients I could not contend with. More than anything, I wanted to get my doctorate before I buried myself in my practice. But each life placed in front of me was someone for whom I felt such compassion and understanding—I could never allow myself preference over any one of them.

MONTREUX TODAY

Montreux Counselling Centre began as an outpatient practice in 1988 as more and more referrals followed reports of my success with my own daughters. I did not put my name or number in the phone book because I did not want to invite more patients at this point. At some level I felt terribly burdened, because I had not had a gasp of air between treating my two daughters and the rest of the world's patients, and it was essential to me that I finish my degree.

I stuck to my plan and was halfway through when desperate parents placed a young anorexic child in front of me. The parents had exhausted every other viable option. Nothing was working, and their daughter was very ill. I had to make a conscious choice, once again, between my education ambitions and the life of a child. Naturally, the child was the only option. It was well worth it—what an angel this incredible child is.

As I confronted cases of increasing need, I began taking other patients into my home (and the homes of others) in order to create a more consistent atmosphere for them. Some of my early patients, and later my own daughters, became my co-workers in implementing these "localized environments of unconditional support" for dying patients. This experience helped me devise the medically monitored, one-on-one, twenty-four-hour-a-day individualized care plan from which we work with acutely ill patients today.

The Montreux Clinic opened in 1993 in order to meet the requirements of those individuals in extreme need who, generally, had been through many other programs and who were frequently labeled "treatment resistant." The clinic offers outpatient services as well.

Now, four years into our residential operation, we have been particularly encouraged by the emerging eagerness of professional colleagues to embrace more positive treatment modalities. We have been fortunate to work closely with excellent treatment teams in acute care hospitals where patients must often be stabilized before they are able to travel to us.

Health care insurers are realizing the highly cost-effective nature of our work and a number of companies have funded treatment for patients in our program. (Though the treatment terms called for are longer than those of programs that concentrate merely on feeding, the per diem rate is 25 to 50 percent less than the cost of treatment at acute care hospitals; moreover, when patients recover completely, they have no need for further treatment.)

We have successfully treated hundreds of people with eating disorders.* I have counseled patients as old as sixty-four and as young as three. Our clinic offers a practical application of the theory elucidated in this book.

In several ways Montreux can also be seen as a social laboratory for positive change. If victims of what we call Confirmed Negativity Condition are indeed an altruistic segment of our society, then the gifts that they have to give the world are readily evident in the Montreux community. Their altruism is reflected in the wish of many recovered patients to become care workers themselves. (We encourage recovered patients to investigate other avenues for several years in order to explore their own

---

*It should be noted that while the vast majority of the patients who come to us for treatment do achieve complete recovery—they have completed the program—there have been a few who have left the program, of their own volition, prior to the point at which we felt it was appropriate for them to do so. We therefore do not claim, nor have we ever claimed, to have a 100 percent success rate. Rather, we have shown that 100 percent recovery can, and should, be achieved.

needs before working with patients themselves; currently approximately an eighth of our care workers and counselors are former sufferers.)

For incoming patients, the possibility of spending time with fully recovered former patients helps create a bridge of hope, which is most helpful in plotting a course for the new patients' recovery. Our other care workers come from a cross section of the professional spectrum. They are chosen for training based on their ability to provide unconditional support to those in need rather than achievement in any particular discipline; we search for qualities of kindness, compassion, vision, and patience that go beyond the expected "norm." Most feel that the work itself, performed in an atmosphere of positive encouragement, provides immense rewards in terms of self-development and the motivation to surpass self-expectation.

We find Montreux an incredibly inspiring environment, a testament to the capacity of the human spirit.

2

Confirmed
Negativity Condition

Every day I receive letters from Julie, a young woman with severe anorexia. They are heartrending missives, and her words tear at my soul.

"*I am a bad person,*" she writes. "I hate myself when I eat. I don't want to live because I'm too ashamed. I want to be small. . . . I want to be little, please let me be little again. I'm too afraid to live, I'm too embarrassed to be seen. I want to hurt myself. I'm no good. I'm a terrible, evil person. . . .

"It helps so to be punished; it feels so kind, like the only gift I have to offer. I don't deserve to live and I want to show you I know that. I need you to see it on my face so you can receive some assurance, some inkling of my regret, some idea that I am sorry. There is no way to tell you, no way to express my sadness, no means to make obvious the guilt in my heart, the knowledge of my evil, the compassion you deserve, the pain I have earned. Let me hurt myself, let me do good. . . ."

Another day, another note: "I wish my mind would turn off and rest. I am junk and honestly, I deserve to die. . . . I feel like a hideous scar that ought to be removed, but still remains as a reminder of the damage that caused its appearance initially."

And then another note: "I can't stand myself anymore. I pray to God to help me punish myself with more pain. . . . All I hear when I do take care of myself is, 'You're disgusting. How can you let yourself be content. How dare you keep living, especially so well.' "

And still another. "I deserve only punishment, and abhor myself. . . . I am completely horrified and ashamed, repulsed and sorrowful every second I live, every moment I am."

What makes Julie, a seemingly normal teenager before the onset of this disorder, suffer such self-abnegation, such utter self-hatred? What makes her want to starve herself into oblivion? What makes her write in the secret language of despair?

It is my experiences with my daughters, patients, and thousands of letters and writings like Julie's that have helped me discover the etiology (the underlying causes) of eating disorders. I have coined the term Confirmed Negativity Condition (CNC) to define the complex thought processes that plague the minds of those with eating disorders and others. An eating disorder is to Confirmed Negativity Condition as a rash is to measles or swollen glands are to mumps; it is a symptom of an underlying problem.

The predisposition for Confirmed Negativity Condition begins early in life, but a CNC "carrier" does not necessarily have to develop an eating disorder. (On the other hand, as I see it, an eating disorder victim must have CNC.) Other possible self-negating manifestations of CNC may include depression, agoraphobia, panic attacks, obsessive-compulsive disorder, or somatic disorders (including any other way such victims may internalize their pain). An individual can have several of these manifestations simultaneously *with or without an eating disorder being one of them.* (Often they coexist with eating disorders and occasionally, when a patient is letting go of anorexia, she will attempt to replace it with another manifestation of CNC such as agoraphobia.) Eating disorders are of particular concern, however, given their debilitating effects and high mortality rate.

I have come to believe that CNC precedes the eating disorder and is at the root of these devastating illnesses. The eating disorder is the symptom; CNC is the affliction we must cure.

A CIVIL WAR IN THE MIND

As horrifying as Julie's situation is, it is far from rare. Indeed, I have found that virtually all people suffering from severe eating disorders experience similar secret thoughts about their unworthiness. They feel like insects trapped in a spider's web. Extricating themselves becomes increasingly impossible as CNC slowly draws out their lives.

Victims clearly are caught in an internal struggle which is often expressed as a dialogue between their being and their "head." One young woman wrote to me, "I'm lost, and I mean lost. It's like someone has put me on a desert island with no survival supplies. I'm the only one on the island, me and my head. Great, I'm stuck with my #1 enemy."

And another described how she was letting her "head" take over her life, slowly but surely.

> I know it's probably just in my head, but to me it feels like I am drowning. My head feels like a war zone and it just won't stop. Day after day I seem to be losing control over my life and it terrifies me. Even when friends come over, I just lay like a zombie on the couch, not talking or joining in with what they are doing, just listening to them and my head.
>
> Most of the time lately, I feel too tired to fight it so I just listen. When it gets too much I end up breaking down in tears but I try to hide it.

Another wrote of how her head terrorized her. "It doesn't matter how fast you run to escape it, you'll never run fast enough. . . . It has no features, no feelings; it is flat and lifeless yet it hates you and seeks your ruin more efficiently than anything else could. When you die, it's gone too. It just dissolves into thin air. Its only reason for existence is to wreck you."

This civil war in the mind—what I think of as a dual mindset—was made quite plain in another woman's writings. She actually gave voice to what I call the Negative Mind—the force that takes over the lives of people with anorexia and bulimia. "You're not going to get better," this inner voice said to her, "instead you'll get worse. . . . You wish someone would come along and save the day. No one would want to see you better. They'll hate you regardless. You're fat. Everyone else is tricking you. You can only listen to me and do what I tell you."

People with eating disorders are at war with themselves. They are of two minds. The Negative Mind is totally powerful when the symptoms of the eating disorder are present. What may have begun as doubting thoughts, indecisiveness, or mild self-criticism intensifies to form an autonomous voice. It is tyrannical, hypercritical, destructive, and despair-confirming. It tells its victim:

Everyone HATES you.
You only cause trouble.
There's nothing you can do right.
You are demanding, selfish, greedy, and mean.
Things will never work out for you.
You make the world miserable.
A person like you doesn't deserve any pleasure, and eating
    is pleasurable.
If you try to get rid of me, I will only go and hurt someone
    else; and if I did that, you know you couldn't live with
    yourself, so I'm here to stay!!
You're fat and gross and ugly.
Your father will die in a plane crash if you eat.
You should burn in hell.
You don't deserve to live.
You should not eat because to eat is to live.
You are a burden to society.
You should die.

Not all sufferers hear the voice as clearly as others. One woman wrote to me, "I constantly hear distant 'whispers' in the back of my mind. I cannot make them out or understand them. My thoughts run in circles, do somersaults, and sometimes just 'disappear.' At the end of the day, I am tired from talking so much—yet I have not uttered a spoken word to anyone in many days. Just myself. My head. My body."

The wish that someone would "come along and save the day" is evidence of what I call the Actual Mind. The Actual Mind is a positive force, which as the essential individual is desperate to live. It is the mind of the victim before she developed CNC and is the mind she will return to once the CNC is gone. The Actual Mind is who the patient would have been had CNC been averted and her emotional development not been arrested. The Actual Mind consists of normal reactions to everyday events.

It might be helpful to think of CNC as a parasite that attempts to consume the Actual Mind, its host. Such a parasite can seem to obliterate the true gentle nature of its host or, at least, temporarily cloud it and thus confuse it, so that the naturally caring victim behaves like her antithesis, striking out at everybody in an attempt to alienate loved ones. It will feed off the host and superficially change her behavior until its presence is diagnosed and effectively treated. The Negative Mind is the tool of CNC. It is the enforcer, preying on the host, whose potential lies hidden under the facade of her often inexplicable behavior.

As CNC develops more strength, the victim will try to bargain with the Negative Mind for small favors:

"I promise not to eat supper tonight if you allow me to have this grape now."
"I'll run for three hours if you let me have this bowl of strawberries."
"Please don't kill my sister. I promise not to be nice to the doctor."

The compromise is always heavily in favor of the Negative Mind.

Often the victim of an eating disorder, caught in the crossfire between the Negative and Actual Minds, will suffer for years without dying. It is difficult to imagine the miserable quality of life as an eternal hostage, being relegated to begging for mercy, for every tidbit, as a supplicant on the street. As Milton put it so succinctly in *Paradise Lost:*

> The mind is its own place, and in itself
> Can make a heaven of hell, a hell of heaven.

With this bargaining, the Actual Mind relinquishes its place progressively to the Negative Mind and diminishes over time. As my correspondent Julie had said, "Day after day I seem to be losing control over my life and it terrifies me. . . . Most of the time lately, I feel too tired to fight it so I just listen." As the CNC becomes more entrenched, the Negative Mind controls what little is left of the victim's identity. She is permitted nothing in her own interest.

Understand, however, that even though the Negative Mind is extremely domineering, at no point is the victim entirely without her Actual Mind. She is merely without most of its power. A small part of it manifests even when the Negative Mind is in control. In the acute stage of an eating disorder, the Negative Mind may be so powerful that the Actual Mind almost disappears. But the fact that the victim is still alive indicates its presence and, in fact, suggests the starting point for recovery. (See Chapters 5 and 6.)

When under the control of the Negative Mind, the Actual Mind is terrorized and paralyzed. It seems incapable of stopping itself from falling more deeply into an abyss of nonbeing. One of the dictates of the Negative Mind is to prohibit the Actual Mind from reaching out for help. The victim is undeserving of succor.

However, also bear in mind that the parasitic Negative Mind is able to host itself only in someone who is essentially altruistic and does not want to be a burden to family or society by reaching out for aid. It would be unusual for such a person to ask for help in the first place, even before CNC develops into an eating disorder.

When a person is held in thrall to an eating disorder, her Actual Mind is at the mercy of her Negative Mind. Still, the Actual Mind is the true potential mind of the patient. From my experience, it will exist again after the victim has reinterpreted herself and has learned to balance her perspective about her role in society.

THE SUBJECTIVE WORLD
OF THE ANOREXIC

To be subjective about a remark or an event is to personalize it. To be subjective means to translate everything through the prism of one's personal reality. In the case of the individual who develops an eating disorder, to be subjective means to pass every event through the distorting lens of the Negative Mind and to turn the event against oneself. Indeed, CNC is the culmination of negative subjectivity turned against oneself. This hypercritical subjectivity will cause the victim to interpret every comment made to her as a negative reflection on her, or it will make the victim assume blame for every event, no matter how objectively unrelated to her.

Consider, for example, the parents who may ask their anorexic son to help them babysit. "We have to go to the store now. Will you look after Tommy for an hour?"

The anorexic may think, "Oh God, they want to talk about something behind my back. They're just pretending that it's about looking after Tommy." Victims of CNC assume that they are excluded from everything because they feel unworthy. Therefore, they naturally assume that everyone else will be talking against them.

Imagine, further, the situation in which a mother complains of a headache. The child with an eating disorder will blame herself for her mother's pain and wonder what she had done to cause it. Or if someone said to an anorexic woman, "That dress really suits you," her subjectivity might prompt her to reply or think to herself, "Oh no! The one I wore yesterday was horrible." Suddenly there is no right thing to say.

On the other hand, to be objective means to interpret an event or statement realistically without assuming responsibility or a negative interpretation.

An individual who is able to take an objective perspective might respond to his parents' request for babysitting with: "How nice. Mom and Dad can have an hour together, and I'll have fun with Tommy. I haven't played with him for a while," or perhaps more typically adolescent, "Why do they always stick me with the babysitting? I'm entitled to a life too!" The headache would be met with the response, "I'm sorry you don't feel well. The aspirin is on my dresser," and the compliment about the dress with, "Thanks. It's brand-new. I love it too."

Because of the anorexic's persistently negative subjective reality, it becomes difficult for family members and society in general to find the correct language with which to talk to her. With each statement, no matter how seemingly benign, the victim gleans yet more material to confirm her negative beliefs about herself.

She becomes progressively less capable of any rational perspective or even of making choices. She will defer to others and become increasingly anxious, afraid that any decision she makes will be the wrong one. As my daughter Kirsten wrote ten years after her recovery, "I remember being suspicious and intimidated at every turn; I was hesitant and almost incapable of relating to anyone or anything."

A LOSS OF THE SELF

I sometimes think of victims of eating disorders as willow wands who bend whichever way the wind blows. One recovered patient wrote:

I changed my personality to become what I thought each person wanted me to be. I didn't think enough of my own identity to share it with others and I constantly tried to adapt myself to their needs. I imagined that everyone expected perfection from me, and I strove to become the perfect daughter, friend, student.

I have heard many people describe eating disorders as a consequence of low self-esteem. As I discuss in the next chapter, I believe the problem goes far deeper. In fact, I find that individuals with eating disorders have *no* sense of self or identity except for the fulfillment of their extremely subjective perception of other's expectations. A middle-aged anorexic told me on the phone recently, "I am weary and frightened to open the door each morning. I never know who I am or what I'm going to have to face, and I'm exhausted from trying." She later wrote to me, "I am 40 years old but I feel like I am 4. Daily I vacillate ceaselessly between wanting to live and wanting to die because I do not know how to live."

This woman has been arrested emotionally and developmentally. Psychologically, she is still a child with an unformed sense of self.

Many individuals with eating disorders will try to make themselves "perfect" solely in order to please others. Only in emotional maturity do we develop the necessary objectivity to realize that it is indeed impossible to make oneself or life perfect. Describing his relationship difficulties with friends and loved ones, Jeremy wrote in his journal:

> I try to anticipate and meet their every need before they can even so much as suggest there might be one. I daren't be anything less than a perfect friend or they will leave me, I fear. . . . Generally it is easiest to be alone because then there is no one to interrupt my quest for perfection. But in this quest I drive others away who are sensing my loneliness and want to mend it. I force my high standards on them. I expect their homes and things to be perfect. If they are not, I will clean

house for them while they are trying to just sit down with me, share a cup of tea and a visit.

Because the Negative Mind inflicts constant chaos, the victim of an eating disorder tries to grasp any sense of structure for herself. Unfortunately, she often fails miserably because she has no balanced perspective with which to work. Society often mistakenly interprets this wish to create order as the victim's attempt to control those around her. Society does not recognize that she struggles to exist in the world because she has no personal identity beyond her failure to create the perfect world for others.

ANOREXIA, BULIMIA, AND OVEREATING

Anorexia and bulimia come from the same mindset: CNC. They are merely different manifestations of the Negative Mind. Often anorexia leads to bulimia. The body can be so starved of nutrition that it develops what we term a "bodymind," which overrides the anorexic's impulse to starve herself and goes into high gear to search for food.

The bulimic bodymind veers from one extreme—starvation—to the other—bingeing—generally depending on how desperate it is to save itself. Parents of bulimics often report that the victim goes into a trancelike state during a binge. As the sufferer may later relate, she devours amazingly enormous quantities of food at one sitting or "feeding frenzy." Loved ones may watch in unmitigated horror as the victim "protects her territory." Often the family is relegated to another part of the house and the door to the kitchen is closed tightly. Parents have reported chaining refrigerators and freezers against the eventuality of such unbridled eating. The victim may then also purge by inducing vomiting and may overuse laxatives to finish the job.

There are many variations on this theme. One father wrote to me about his daughter: "Her bulimia was so bad when she couldn't get enough food that she would try to kill herself. I got an extra job to make ends meet but we couldn't meet Monica's needs. She would pawn anything that she could find to buy food, even her guitar which she loved so much. She would even take the lunches that I had packed for myself."

Another woman suffering from bulimia and anorexia wrote, "Presently I go weeks without eating, weeks bingeing, weeks bingeing and purging, weeks bingeing and using laxatives, etc. etc. There just seems to be no end. . . ."

Another way of purging can be overexercise, not allowing food to be accepted into the body without retribution. Intermittently, the victim becomes physically and emotionally exhausted with the effort and moves back to the starving mode.

Bulimia leaves its victims with a feeling of incredible self-loathing. Patients frequently describe themselves as "disgusting pigs." When an anorexic's Actual Mind becomes conscious of her body weight as it turns to extreme gauntness, she is often equally repulsed.

Chronic overeating can represent another manifestation of CNC. However, there is a vast difference between being overweight and having an eating disorder. There is a distinction between the person who is overweight but not distraught because of it, and the person for whom overeating is a manifestation of self-hatred and a lack of self. The diagnosis depends on an outside assessment and the individual's own view of herself.

A person who is miserable about overeating, who cannot do anything positive about it, and who eats out of a sense of self-loathing may well have CNC.

THE PREDISPOSITION FOR CNC

What are the origins of the Negative Mind? How does someone become hostage to a mental construct of his or her own design? I believe that it all begins with a predisposition for CNC. Those predisposed to CNC are acutely sensitive to the needs of everyone and even everything else in their environment. Whether it be in the microcosm of the nuclear family or the macro-cosm of our contemporary global reality, the potential victims of CNC have somehow come to deem themselves shepherds of the flock of humanity. These children are caring of their families and the universe. They are humanists of the first degree. As concerned environmentalists, the ozone layer, poverty, sickness, and the plight of the whales all immediately capture their attention.

How does it come about that a child should take the woes of the world on her fragile shoulders? That she should wish—in fact, see it as her inalienable duty—to parent her parents or save the world? I believe that, as infants, a number of us come into this world with the predisposition to CNC; it is therefore an inborn temperament. However, not every person with the predisposition develops CNC, just as not every person with a genetically endowed predisposition for a certain cancer, for example, develops the disease.

Often the immoderate sense of responsibility that is the hall-mark of a predisposition to CNC becomes apparent at an early age. Many parents, in retrospect, recall how their caring child was always inordinately worried or concerned about others, even at an age when most children believe they are the center of the universe. Parents have told me:

> "I knew there was something different about her ever since she could talk. She was always so helpful. She never caused any trouble and seemed to understand everybody's needs. She stood aside. She watched, observed rather than involving herself in fun."

> "She used to do vacuuming for me when she was three and four. I never asked her to; she just tried to help out where she could."

> "I got migraines all the time. He had to help with the younger child. He just did."

> "He put his small jacket on a care worker when their flight was canceled and he and everyone had to sleep on the floor of the airport. He was only three years old at the time."

"She sat by the baby's bed all night watching her breathe because the doctor said the baby was a bit congested. She was about six years of age when that happened. I couldn't make her go to bed."

"She always seemed to be more mature than she needed to be. The other children always came first. I worried about it at the time but it was a great help all the same. She never complained and never seemed to suffer. She looked after us all."

A mother recounted that her eight-year-old would not join her playmates until all the housework was done. She did not want her parents doing it all themselves. One child tried to make her house earthquake proof. Another fastidiously checked all the locks and pulled out all the plugs at night so that her parents would be safe. A six-year-old took it upon herself to toddler-proof the house. My daughter Kirsten wrote, "I remember as a child checking all the windows, doors, the stove and the toaster when my family was in bed at night to ensure that everything was secured and turned off."

Some therapists might describe such behaviors as symptoms of obsessive-compulsive disorder, but I do not perceive them that way; in my experience these behaviors disappear once the underlying confirmed negativity is treated.

After Nora recovered from her eating disorder, she described in an Assessment Testimonial, one of the gauges of progress we use at the clinic, how she had taken on the world's troubles from early childhood onward: "From a young age, I worried about everything. Were my parents happy with me? Did my brothers ever feel lonely? Did my sister hate herself as I did? I felt responsible for them and attributed any of their worries or unhappy comments, no matter how remote, to something I had or had not done. I worried about things I couldn't change—terrorism, poverty, sickness, unhappiness."

It seems as if this child's mind stands aside, watching and waiting, studying life's circumstance from another place. The child with the CNC predisposition is often described as "the best child" or the "most responsible one."

HOW THE CNC PREDISPOSITION
BECOMES CONFIRMED

CNC is the culmination of negative assumptions about oneself in the caring for and the sense of responsibility for the world. Whether CNC develops depends substantially on the environment.

It is natural for children to become concerned about life around them. But these wise souls take it past the obvious point, fretting endlessly about the ozone layer, recycling every last scrap in the house, and so on. Children with CNC predispositions are fertile ground for misinterpretation of society's motives. But given an intelligent mind—and it is a given that most anorexics and bulimics are extremely intelligent—why is it they are unable to put society's or their family's needs into perspective? The reasons for this are familial as well as societal.

The Microcosm of the Family

Parenting in the natural order is about instruction and guidance of a child's potential. Boundaries for safety and structure shape and program a child's attitude. The normal development of children goes through obvious stages of need. Healthy development depends on a generally supportive and structured family environment. Ideally, as a child moves forward from one phase of growth, she has learned whatever the previous phase could teach her. This will serve as a platform from which growth naturally springs.

However, children who develop without the proper guidance of an adult and the structure of a supportive family become increasingly bewildered. This occurs if a child grows without restrictions of structure, or without confidence in the platform from which she should draw strength.

Permit me to share an example from my own family to illustrate. Recently, my daughter Nicole spent several nights alone with her two-year-old son, Darius, while her husband was away on business. Shortly after his father left, Darius turned to Nikki and said, "Don't worry, Mommy. I take care of you now."

Had Nikki responded, "Oh, isn't that sweet. You're the man of the house," she might have inadvertently reinforced her child's sense that he was somehow responsible for her welfare. If Darius were predisposed to CNC, this could unconsciously confirm an erroneous assumption about his role in the family—that he needs to parent his parents.

But instead, Nicole wisely replied with a hug, "I'm the mommy here, sweetheart. I'll take care of you! You don't have to worry about anything." With her response, Nicole was creating a sense of structure and safety for her son. She was helping him to put his role in the family into the proper perspective—that he is still, after all, a dependent child, and that it is not his job to take care of his mother.

Parents who are afraid to set such limits for their CNC-predisposed children, for instance, who constantly ask for their children's opinion without stating what is acceptable or what is not (for fear of offending the child), who welcome their children's misguided attempts at parenting them, or who assume their children have the wherewithal to develop their own identities without their guidance, may unwittingly feed into the development of CNC by denying their youngsters the boundaries from which to develop a self-identity. This is not meant to blame parents but rather to illustrate how easily a precociously mature child can insinuate herself into a position of responsibility within the family structure. I know with my own children, I was more willing to let them assume more responsibility than perhaps I should have.

I am reminded of a tale attributed to Buddha. He was said to have given one of his talks to a group of disciples while holding a bird in his palm. The students were fascinated by the Buddha's ability to prevent the bird from flying away and were unable to duplicate his feat. Finally, they could restrain their curiosity no longer and blurted their question to the great master. "Why does the bird not fly away?"

The Buddha replied, "It is quite simple, my friends. Each time I sense that the bird will take flight, I simply drop my hand a bit, and the bird has nothing to push off from."

I wish to emphasize here that it is normal and appropriate for parents of children who do not have a predisposition for CNC to encourage their offspring's independence, ability to reason for themselves, and desire to set some of their own boundaries. Ordinary children generally respond well to this, but children with the CNC predisposition will begin to feel overwhelmed. The parents' task is to be aware of their child's innate temperament and respond accordingly, and to distinguish between developing individuality and encouraging too much independence (see Chapter 6).

If a child is unsure of the messages she is receiving from anxious parents, she, like Buddha's bird, has no platform from which to push, and consequently has difficulty creating a sense of self. This can arrest her emotional development by interfering with the growth of her identity, thus eventually leading her toward subjectivity and self-abnegation.

Indeed, as time goes by, a CNC sufferer becomes so given to the well-being and caring of the world that she spends little time developing her internal identity. This eventually leads her toward subjectivity and self-abnegation. Her external identity becomes anything necessary to satisfy what she perceives the world needs it to be. So her self-concept is based on an unhealthy, vicarious respect for others. She mentally sacrifices her need to develop her own identity for the sake of healing the world, and finally, anxiously, anticipating possible problems to prevent.

The Macrocosm of Society

I believe that today we are living in an apprehensive, unparented society. Parents are themselves anxious. The rules and roles that seemed so clear fifty years ago, even thirty years ago, no longer exist. We are always worried about something. Indeed, some of our contemporary cities remind one of a disturbed antbed: We are panicky, agitated, and traveling in all directions at once, daily confirming a hurried, stressed lifestyle.

Although we seem more electronically connected through cellular phones, faxes, and pagers, we are fooling ourselves, for we are connected only to the harried pace of society. We are actually more disconnected from the parts of ourselves that are conducive to emotional health—our caringness and concern for others. Rather than seeing life as being about survival, we are seeing it as an avoidance of the inevitable. We are too apt to castigate ourselves for our emotional problems; instead, we need to understand and accept that being human is about faltering and learning.

We seem to have become so anxiety-conditioned that we need to live as a sedated society—we seem incapable of living life without a crutch in the form of medication, be it analgesics or antidepressants. Our increasing numbness and sedation cause us to become more apathetic rather than more caring. Life is more anxiety-provoking, so we practice avoidance. But in so doing, do we teach our young, inadvertently, that there is a pill for everything emotional and physical? Do we indicate that pain, imperfection, and humanness are unacceptable elements of the human condition?

Our extended families have shrunk to near oblivion. When truncated families face serious problems such as illness, unemployment, divorce, or substance abuse, and the CNC-predisposed child has few trusted adults to turn to for advice and guidance, she may erroneously believe that the healing of her family is solely her responsibility. The more adults—family and friends—actively participating in a child's growth years, the more the child is able to grasp an objective reality, and the more the child seems to allow herself to be a child.

What do the media teach us? Violence in the media desensitizes us to others' suffering—we become helpless bystanders and we practice bystander apathy.

What do the media teach our children? Ubiquitous images glorify negativity and sensationalism while they discourage hope and instill fear. The media present a near-constant diet of pessimism, competition, contradiction, sedation, hopelessness, and doom. Given that bad news is more available and interesting, and a good news story is a rarity at most, it appears that young minds in our society, as they hurry along to keep up with the latest, are terribly vulnerable to absorbing the negative messages surrounding them.

Sensitive children with a CNC disposition are doused with pessimism and negativity that is passed through society like a contagious yawn, and they learn from society too well.

When a society's values become external, it devalues the essence of humanness. In so many ways, what the suggestible and ultimately vulnerable child will learn is mostly projected through television, tabloid sensationalism, and other entertainment and information media. These venues are available at a very early age—an age well before a child has the capacity to put what she is absorbing into proper perspective. One of the youngest patients I've counseled used to sit on his mother's lap and watch the evening news. She had no way of knowing that he took every bit of negative news deeply to heart and came to believe that it was his duty to right the world's wrongs.

Children need structure in order to survive. For their well-being it is imperative to encourage congruency with their environment, optimism, and hope despite the different perspectives in the world. If children conclude from watching the media and observing their surroundings that life is chaos, that the contradictions of doom and a no-pain existence can reside within the realm of perfectionism, this can tip them from a predisposition into full-blown CNC.

THE CONTRIBUTION OF PERFECTION

As these children struggle to create a perfect world, they become more agile at perfecting their own selves vicariously. Here lie additional tools for the development of CNC. They strive for scholastic, physical, and artistic excellence. They are the perfect students, athletes, artists, or musicians.

CNC-predisposed children excel in most venues society has provided to showcase important external values, such as school, sports, gymnastics, dance, music, and so on. In their minds, they are attempting to adhere to what they perceive as society's dictates—to please others before themselves. They do not strive to be the best because of their inherent sense of superiority and duty; they do it to try to prove their worth to others because they lack an internal sense of self.

Both of Connie's parents were lawyers, and she believed she needed to become a lawyer too. She suffered a complete collapse while in her third year of studies, not because she was incapable of the work, but because she felt she could never live up to her idea of her parents' expectations for her.

In fact, Connie's parents are wonderful people who did well in their own careers but had no wish for their daughter other than her well-being. Connie assumed that to make them happy, she had to follow in their footsteps. Subsequent to treatment, she enrolled in design school and is now an accomplished and recognized designer. I have found over and over in working with patients that the drive to create perfection for others replaces the natural maturation of self. Only when patients recover and nurture this sense can they begin to explore their own passions and loves—to discover what pleases them alone.

After working for many years with families of children with eating disorders, you realize that these children are more privy and prone to the contradictions society presents them: On one hand, it seems to them that they are obliged to attain perfection, while on the other, there is increasing unmitigated pain in the world and poverty, sickness, and death. The media make both poles abundantly accessible and unavoidable. The very language of our society depicts doom and hopelessness while subtly demanding the impossible—perfection. The child with a caring disposition, hoping to avert disaster either in her nuclear family or in society in general, runs faster and faster to appease others and prevent some potential catastrophe, because she believes she can—and must.

Sadly, the victim has no idea that all the world does not share her perspective of peace and goodwill. She has not had enough time to understand the differences between people, to perceive that humans operate within the limitations of their understanding and abilities, that offense comes more often from ignorance and unawareness than it does from intent, that just because society presents the notion that perfection is attainable, she is not solely responsible for achieving it. CNC victims learn society too well without having the maturity to moderate their understanding of it.

At the same time, however, it is important to note that many people can and do identify with the beginning stages of CNC—the desire to serve the world, the impulse to put the pleasure of others first—and have spent their lives helping others. Yet they have somehow learned to live in the world without developing an eating disorder or other self-negating condition. These individuals' lives somehow correct themselves before the Negative Condition becomes confirmed and therefore detrimental to their survival. They allow themselves the favor of being well and are able to achieve some balance in their efforts to help the world.

Ultimately, the failure of perfectionism for the CNC victim engenders a supreme sense of worthlessness that leads to the manifestation of an eating disorder. This worthlessness is expressed in the anorexic as an attempt at being the smallest and sickest and in the bulimic with ever more extreme binge/purge episodes. Both manifestations deny the victim any sense of normalcy; both are thoroughly degrading. The subtle reality of this mindset is that *sufferers need to be the best at being the least deserving.* Ultimately, they need to know: Are they the best *at dying?*

HOW CNC MANIFESTS
AS AN EATING DISORDER

Imagine someone who always places herself (or what little self exists) second, who vigilantly tries to appease others before anything else. She learns to subordinate her needs and desires by learning society's values and what she must do to live up to these values.

It is an extreme risk to lend one's identity completely to other people's needs. The victim lives through anyone's need vicariously. When the need no longer exists in the chosen person, she seeks out other people in need upon which to focus her attention, caringness, and overconcern, or she manufactures need where none exists.

When one's identity is so consumed with ministering to a certain need (real or perceived) over a long period of time, it becomes even more difficult to disassociate from it. Margie developed anorexia at age sixty-four when her husband died. She had spent years attending to his severe medical condition and she had to relearn living in order to survive. With months of intervention, she successfully reinterpreted herself to live objectively, with compassion and kindness yet retaining her newfound identity. It became apparent through counseling that throughout her life, Margie had looked after her siblings, then her mother, and most recently her husband. She had identified herself only through other people's need rather than her own individual potential.

Another patient was one of five siblings. Her mother was a highly emotional person who continually lamented her plight in life and was prone to tearful outbursts. Although Carla was different from her mother, she was unaware that human nature describes itself in many ways. She became determined to create a happiness for her mother that seemed unattainable for her and, sadly, failed miserably.

Carla's mother was just being who she was. But nothing in Carla's learning to that point made her understand that people operate from different dispositions and that it is acceptable to respond otherwise to life.

It is, of course, impossible for any one individual to achieve such a magnificent objective as to completely rid the world of its ills or one's family of its woes. Caring, empathy, and compassion are wonderful attributes in any person. However, even the most altruistic person must include herself in the well-being she wishes and works toward for others. When these virtues exceed themselves to the point of self-sacrifice, the individual finds herself lost.

When a child with CNC discovers that she cannot "save the world," that perfection is impossible, she is devastated. She feels betrayed if parents have cancer, or heart attacks, or become bankrupt, or if relationships are less than perfect. She feels horrified that she cannot rescue the whales or the tropical rain forests. Failure begets failure. She judges herself unworthy and weak because she is incapable of solving these overwhelming problems—problems that continue to challenge the best adult minds. These disappointments and traumas, although they do not "cause" the eating disorder (since the cause is the underlying misinterpretation of her role fundamental to CNC), can nevertheless trigger its onset.

The child's initial perception, that she can effect change, is coupled with the growing knowledge that she is, in fact, all too powerless to do so. The contradiction inherent in these two disparate forces leads her to believe that either she or the world is living a lie. She becomes increasingly subjective—everyone and everything around her reinforces her unworthiness, her defeat, her impotence—and she fails to advance in the natural growth toward objectivity. She falls into CNC.

As the confirmed negativity becomes progressively worse, subjectivity comes to dominate 20, 30, 50, 60 percent of her thoughts. Without early intervention, when subjectivity overbalances objectivity, when it constantly seeks ways to feed itself and becomes increasingly successful in doing so, the eating disorder manifests and quickly grows dangerous.

The CNC sufferer becomes incapable of handling responsibility for the pain in the microcosm of her own family and in mitigating what she sees as the pain of the world. Yet despite her incapacity, she still feels she must somehow be responsible. She therefore unconsciously decides to resign. She becomes despairing of survival in her perception of what society requires. She does not want to come to this conclusion but sees no recourse. At this point in her demise, she feels it is her just deserts. As the victim heads toward self-destruction, her Negative Mind grows in importance and magnitude.

Understanding the motivating forces behind the eating disorder behavior helps to translate it. It can be broken down to a relatively simple formula:

Eating means having food.
Food means having life.
I should not have life because I do not deserve it.
I do not deserve life because I have failed humanity.
Therefore I do not deserve food.

As a victim moves from CNC to a manifestation of eating disorder, her mind will increasingly deteriorate her sense of worth. She indicates her lack of faith in her identity by severely cutting back on food. She has lost confidence in herself and her decision-making ability since she has lost faith in her own validity in the world. She becomes isolated from friends because she believes she is less than they are and does not want to impose her ignorance and boring personality on them.

Victims love their parents so much that they feel guilty eating in front of them. They do not see themselves as worthy. They find it extremely difficult to allow themselves any pleasure since they have surely not protected their parents from all ills. To admit openly that they are allowing themselves to partake of life seems selfish. In the victim's mind, she has profoundly disappointed her parents.

Here is how Nora describes her slide into CNC and then anorexia: "I finally just wanted to fade away completely, to remove myself from a world that appeared to be sad and cold. The restriction of food was simply a way to make myself even more unobtrusive. It was a continuation of the punishment I would impose on myself for not being able to save everyone. . . . Inside my head there was a constant harsh voice, encouraging me in this downward spiral, telling me that I was nothing, that I was unworthy, that I was not doing as much as I could to contribute to everyone's happiness."

THE PARADOX OF BLAME

When we talk about eating disorders, the concept of "blame" seems to raise its head distressingly often. For want of a clearer answer, parents blame themselves or are blamed for being inadequate in some measure. The sufferers, already incorrigible in their own heads, are blamed for being callous enough to hurt their parents and siblings; their noncompliance during treatment is construed as intentional and volitional. But to suggest that any one person, or society as a whole, is to blame for eating disorders is an oversimplification.

Eating disorders develop unconsciously; victims are as confused as those around them when the contradictory symptoms emerge. Moreover, who is to blame if a person is born into the world highly sensitive?

To borrow an analogy from physiology, it has been determined that in any cross section of individuals, the number of taste buds in a square centimeter of tongue can range from twelve to two hundred. Some people are simply more sensitive to taste than others. Such ranges also hold true in a cross section of personalities. Some people are more emotionally sensitive than others. However, the heightened sensitivity of a CNC-predisposed individual is always directed toward the needs of others. She possesses a selfless sensitivity. Is this blameworthy? We wouldn't blame someone whose predisposition to diabetes or cancer caused her to develop the illness; why would we blame those who develop eating disorders?

Society may inadvertently contribute to the production of eating disorders, but until its members have been enlightened, can they be held responsible?

The victim is living a nightmare, internally and externally. Her beloved parents, who in her mind need support in the first place, and whose love and support she so badly needs, are in the uncomfortable throes of added chaos and distress because of her behavior. She has unintentionally made their lives a worse hell. As Julie wrote to me in some of her voluminous letters:

"I hurt people and regret the reality of what I am doing to everyone. I think of my mother and cry at the horror of creating so much misery just being alive."

"In a weak moment I confessed these feelings to my mother and have now successfully ruined her life as well."

"I cringe when I think of what I have done to my mother."

One of the most tragic facts of eating disorders is that its victims become receptacles for society's inadvertent abuse. They are accused of noncompliance when they have failed a hospital program. Rarely do we hear that a system has not worked for them; rather, we are told that they have not worked for the system. I have received hundreds of letters that reiterate this point. The following is just a sampling:

> "Please help us. Our daughter Hannah has failed her fourth program. Her weight dropped down to 68 pounds."
>
> "Celine wants to get better but she has been unable to find the solution to cure herself. She has tried and failed basically every program out there. It will come down to 1) her dying or 2) your program/miracle to cure her."
>
> "The doctor told Marci that she was a waste of his time, that she doesn't have a life. She has disappointed the doctor

because she hasn't been able to 'fix' herself, and since Marci doesn't really have a life, why should anyone try to save her?"

"I have been rejected by several hospital programs because they say my depression is so severe that they are not trained for that level. One hospital said that I am going to die from this if I keep on losing weight and then rejected me."

"My life has been one big failure. I hate myself, and have attempted suicide three times. I plan to finish the job next fall."

"I have not been successful with any other treatment programs I have tried, but that is completely my fault. . . . My family has pleaded with me to recover, but I constantly fail to put aside my own wishes and do the necessary things to stabilize my condition."

"I really hate myself for getting trapped in this disease. There must have been something I could have done to prevent it. It's all of my fault that my family is hurting. I destroyed the trust that my parents had in me before."

"I am in my thirties and have been hospitalized several times in an eating disorder unit which did not help me overcome my problem. I am not blaming them and I take full responsibility for my failure. . . . At the time of my last hospitalization, the psychiatrist said he would no longer treat me because I had let him down. He told me that I was a failure and that I would be a chronic anorexic. Everything he told me is true. I am a failure and don't deserve to live."

It would appear on the surface that these victims wish their deaths. It seems never to occur to us that perhaps that assumption doesn't make rational sense, that anyone wishing death for psychological reasons certainly must be misguided; that it is probable that, as many of my patients have said, they don't know how to live rather than that they don't want to.

What the general public most likely does not understand is that the victim may attempt suicide because she thinks there is no way she can live with the internal mental horror, the unrelenting pressure of the Negative Mind. If society continues to lay the onus of blame on the eating disorder victim, if therapists and others in the helping professions tell victims that they're failures, *if we turn on our own*, how can the Actual Mind not admit defeat?

Sometimes, in frustration and desperation or for the perceived protection of the victim's siblings, parents, often at the suggestion of therapists, throw the eating disorder victim out of her home—a Tough Love approach. With less protection and ability now to fend for herself, she somehow must, as must her siblings accept that their sister must be punished because she did not adhere to society's rules. She becomes doubly stigmatized.

One mother of an anorexic child wrote, "She finally quit going to school and just gave up. And I am ashamed to admit it, but so did I. I basically threw her out of the house because of her negative influence on our other children. I love Alicia with all my heart, but I couldn't sacrifice the other children for her."

The concept of "blame" disallows that imperfection is a part of the human condition. Rather than creating acceptance and support for unity and understanding for everyone's benefit, blame sets up corruption and division of family and eventually of societal structure.

When anyone blames an ill child or her anxious parents, they are operating out of the mindset of "authority for authority's sake." The danger is that if a therapist blames an eating disorder victim or labels her a failure out of frustration or a sense of helplessness, the family and patient may still swallow those statements whole and without question. The attitude that eating disorders are "incurable" becomes a self-fulfilling prophecy for the victim.

Unfortunately, it seems many traditional methods of treatment worldwide put the onus of blame and responsibility on a mind that is incapable, in its acute manifestation, of taking it. The translation to the sufferer is "I cannot overcome this. I am worthless and a failure." As this attitude is often repeated through many more years of treatment, the Negative Mind is only more reinforced and armed with additional ammunition. Indeed, the Negative Mind will absorb the information and use it subjectively against the Actual Mind. "I have been rejected and I have failed—more proof that I am worthless and a burden to my family and society."

Sufferers live in a surreal daze of misery and confusion, sometimes hoping each day will be the last. The devastation to all involved is beyond belief and in its loneliness, inhuman.

The onus of responsibility is being put on our weakest, our most sensitive. As naturally caring children, these individuals take responsibility upon themselves anyway. When they become ill, it is heaped upon them. Does it not occur to us that blame rarely corrects any situation, but makes people feel even more subservient? Is it not likely that not only might this be wrong but that it is highly counterproductive and will just aggravate the problem?

Often what appears to be the obvious answer in the treatment of the eating disorder conundrum—attacking the external behavior of the victim—is actually its antithesis. In the case of eating disorders, seeing is not believing. In the case of eating disorders, people are not their behavior. Anorexia or bulimia is the most visible symptom of a more complicated, complex, and convoluted mindset derived from a misinterpretation of its victim's role in life.

Victims of eating disorders have always felt they must not trouble the world. They are only interested in healing society, not in hindering it. Given that excelling proves almost effortless, how can they now accept the alarming fact that they are suddenly incapable of mastering their own territory—their emotional mind? How can these individuals, who see themselves as subservient to the human race, ask for help or admit defeat in the fight for life? When they fault themselves for their plight, how can they turn to society for help?

Eating disorders offer many expressions. They are all self-negating. They are the epitome of alienation from self and society. Internally, the actual potential person dies a million deaths in shame and contrition for something she apparently has no control over. When placed necessarily in an atmosphere of unconditional forgiveness, the patient is able to begin to allow herself, though slowly and with difficulty, the right to be human—with all its accompanying foibles.

Society has inadvertently created the perfect puzzle—a person so distorted in self-image, so much in the grasp of the Negative Mind, so undeserving of help, that she must suffer psychological purgatory until we—the outsiders—understand her secret language and deliver her from her plight.

Yet, despite the horrifying aspects of CNC, it is amazing to watch the courage of victims of eating disorders. That some are still alive after battling sometimes from twenty to thirty years should be a lesson to humankind. What residue of hope encourages these individuals to get up every day and try again? Their survival would seem, by normal standards, to defy all odds!

As part of their therapy, Peggy asks her patients to illustrate their relationship with anorexia. These are examples of their art.

he victim is in a trance where is forever night, pouring out er life's blood. She is not sure she is fat or thin; part of her body seems fat and other parts look like bones.

This painting is the epitome of the game in the dual mindset. The glazed, trapped gaze of the obvious Actual Mind is managed and directed by the insidious cunning of the behind-the-scenes Negative Mind. The Actual Mind becomes a mere puppet to play out the demands of the Negative Mind.

My daughter Nicole created this
She explains that it represents
the dual mindset of the pessimisti
(no-hope) Negative Mind and the
optimistic yet (faint hope) smaller
Actual Mind. The cross on the rig
figure shows the possibility of belie
The black roses indicate that
most hope has died. The red rose
indicates that the fire of life is
still burning if anyone could fan
its flames.

This victim describes herself in black
worthlessness, primarily bad, ashamed,
yet confused because she feels she has a
good heart. It is significant that the heart is
deep and out of view of the common
perception, therefore not easily available
to be helped.

A very desperate case, this patient is convinced she is in the fires of "hell" being punished for all the bad she has supposedly done. When asked what these bad deeds were, she didn't know. Of course, she is guilty of nothing.

When this artist was anorexic, she was the violin in the background, totally controlled and dominated by the "black figure" who played her at will. In the foreground, the violin herself is now free. She is her own master now that she is "cured."

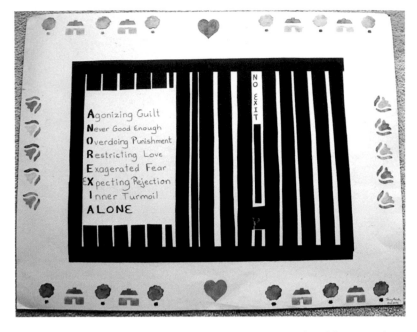

Inside the image:
Agonizing Guilt
Never Good Enough
Overdoing Punishment
Restricting Love
Exagerated Fear
EXpecting Rejection
Inner Turmoil
ALONE

NO EXIT

This artist is now cured of her twenty-year struggle with anorexia. She never thought it possible that she could ever enjoy a home, flowers, and life. She often said that she was hidden in a black jail with no means of seeing life except in other people's pleasure—something she did not deserve for herself.

This artist has had anorexia since she was eight years old. She came to our clinic after years of unsuccessful treatment, in which she was blamed for noncompliance and hurting her family. When we received her, she painted this picture of what was raging in her mind, creating threats and unrelenting fear. She is now completely well and has returned to her wonderful family.

In the upper left corner, the ghost of the patient weeps as she watches her head being manipulated and thrust through with the negativity of the "monster" who comes from a source of such diabolical unkindness.

This thirteen-year-old artist depicted a girl being instructed by an ever-present negative force on how to see herself.

This victim sees herself paralyzed in the living of life—her feet can know no direction; they are locked in place. Her head is a hypodermic needle injecting itself into a black well of negativity—of no return.

The artist sees herself as dejected and in darkness surrounded by flames—an inescapable barrier to the living of life. The artist struggled with eating disorders for over five years.

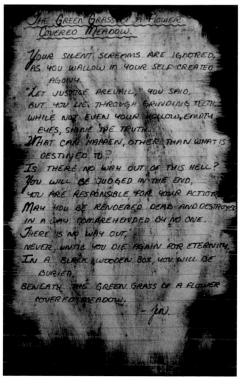

THE VALLEY OF HAPPINESS

As our dreams are shattered,
And our hopes are turned to despair,
You stare into our eyes, stained with
The blood-red tears of torment.

You are full of heartless mirth.
Your laughter is evilly intoxicating.

We cry out in sorrow and in rage,
Yet, we are heeded by no one. —

What have we done to deserve this?
We did not request to live,
Or bring it upon ourselves.

Away from this world,
Out of this life,
We will run to escape this hatred

The never-ending screams will be
washed away by the rivers of peace.
Our anguish will be blown away by
the winds of love.
You will be forgotten, and forever lost
As we live for always, in
the valley of happiness.

THE GREEN GRASS OF A FLOWER
COVERED MEADOW.

Your silent screams are ignored,
As you wallow in your self-created
agony.
"Let justice prevail," you said,
But you lie through grinding teeth,
While not even your hollow, empty
eyes, shine the truth.
What can happen, other than what is
destined to?
Is there no way out of this hell?
You will be judged in the end,
You are responsible for your actions.
May you be rendered dead and destroyed
In a way comprehended by no one.
There is no way out,
Never, until you die again for eternity,
In a black wooden box, you will be
buried,
Beneath the green grass of a flower
covered meadow.
                                    - jen.

A patient has lived eight years in the torment of her
Negative Mind's hatred. She feels her only escape from this
relentless tirade is to dream of a place beyond this life. This earth
appeared to offer her no reprieve. She is well today and safely at
home with her family, riding her horse across meadows with
flowers and unending green.

Typically, this artist focuses on the head as the center of her turmoil. According to this victim, the "voices" are draining the life out of her. She is staring and dismal as she is powerless to stanch the flow of blood from her head.

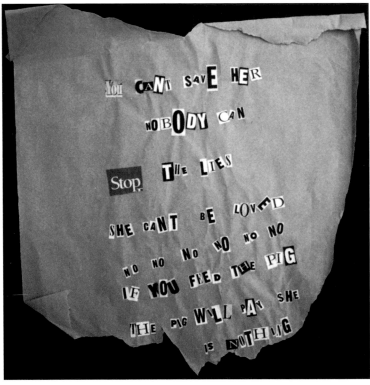

You can save her
nobody can
Stop the lies
she cant be loved
no no no no no
no no no no no
if you feed the pig
the pig will pay she
is nothing

Oftentimes the Negative Mind refers to its subjects as "pigs" if they allow themselves anything or if they allow anyone else to give them the pleasure of food or kindness. When a patient accepts something for herself, the voices shriek at her, deriding her worthlessness. This is usually emotionally exhausting.

3

Myths and Misconceptions

"More are killed by word of mouth than by the sword."
—LEONARDO DA VINCI

"I have always been told I am a controlling perfectionist."

"I can't be cured. I'm too bad. I'm going to have to deal with this the rest of my life. I just have to live with it."

"It's those pictures of supermodels in the magazines that put Jamie on this incessant diet."

"They told me my daughter is going to be released on Sunday. She's only sixteen. Her insurance has run out. They told me to prepare for her death. There is nothing more they can do."

"I don't deserve to get well. I feel so dirty, hopeless, no-good, fat, scared, a failure, insecure. I really don't deserve to live."

"I am disgusted with myself for being the cause of all this."

"My daughter is 5 feet 8 inches and sixty pounds. There's not much left of her. She won't comply with anyone. She's only been out of hospitals for two four-month periods in the last three years. She has ruined the family."

"My husband and I aren't speaking. We don't really have a relationship anymore. My kids hate me for ignoring them because my own problems were more important than they were. I've tried; can you help? It's been almost a dozen years. Our home is a war zone and my therapist refuses to see me anymore because I lost too much weight and didn't stick to the bargains we made."

"They say I am selfish; that all I care about is how I look."

"My doctor told me I don't want to grow up."

"I am the worst case they have ever seen and I'm incurable."

"She refuses to deal with her underlying issues no matter how many psychiatrists she sees."

"I used to be the perfect child with everything going for me, but I have lost it all!"

"I'm not worth saving, but I might prove an interesting experiment."

"I don't want my daughter to die. They say we are a dysfunctional family, but my wife and I are still together. We don't fight and we love our daughter very much. They say they can do no more for my daughter. She is only nineteen. It is not the natural order of things that she should die first. Surely something can be done."

All of these statements are based on myths and misconceptions about anorexia and bulimia. Unfortunately, many of these myths still hold sway today and are often the basis upon which we regard and treat patients with eating disorders.

In this chapter, I hope to offer an alternative to these myths and set in their place what I have perceived is the true nature of eating disorders—CNC and the Negative Mind.

"Anorexia is the by-product of a culture that prizes thinness above everything."

A widely held theory expounds that anorexia is in part caused by a culture that values appearance over substance and prizes women only when they are thin. Much has been said about the cult of thinness, the rise of the supermodel as a public icon, and the belief that victims of eating disorders lose weight to emulate a supposed physical ideal.

Eating disorders are eight times more common in women than in men. Surely one of the external values society offers as a venue of perfection is the female body. Women grow up being complimented more on their looks than on any other quality. We are told that most women are perpetually dieting. Yet we must be careful about assessing blame for eating disorders to this aspect of contemporary society without considering the broader context.

The deification of thinness is dangerous, but where eating disorders are concerned, it can be misleading. Indeed, this is a much more complicated issue than appears at first glance, and if a connection exists between the cult of thinness and anorexia, it is far deeper than mere vanity.

There is a difference between becoming thin for the sake of fitting into society's expectations and becoming thinner and thinner and thinner for the sake of dying. Taken to their extreme, eating disorders are, after all, a slow form of suicide.

If models in their beauteous, supposed perfection are an example to the vulnerable, why do those suffering eating disorders progress so far beyond thinness to emaciation and, ultimately, death? Why are boys and men affected? Why will one model become anorexic and another not? Why do elderly women become anorexics crippled with arthritis? Why do small children?

The distorted perception starts early—I have counseled patients as young as three years old—and I now believe that the "failure to thrive" cited in infants can be in some instances an early manifestation of the Negative Mind. The seeds of anorexia may have been planted at a much earlier age than the one at which individuals become body-conscious.

Society's emphasis on looks clouds the more important issue that children are dying because they are trying to achieve impossible standards of perfection. As we have seen in the previous chapter, this focus on perfection is not so much for personal gratification as it is a misguided attempt to improve the world.

Rather than thinking of the supermodel syndrome as a cause of eating disorders, it is best to think of it as a possible trigger. Modeling is an area in which perfection seems attainable, one of the many venues for perfection (such as sports, academics, dance, and so on) that eating disorder victims will fit themselves into. Most teenage girls try to lose a few pounds for the sake of attracting boys in high school. Many women are constantly on a diet, unhappy with their bodies. But a girl with an eating disorder will use the ideal of the model as a way to hone her sense of perfection; boys are not on her mind. A woman with an eating disorder doesn't want to be a size 6; she wants to be a size o. The difference is knowing how much of what society presents to take seriously.

I do believe that media and advertising images that glorify perfection and beauty contribute to many women's sense of unhappiness about their imperfectly human bodies. I would applaud a movement to curtail the supermodel syndrome. But I am not convinced that the rate of eating disorders would fall as a result; I believe that people with CNC would find another venue of perfection to emulate.

Moreover, anorexics frequently suffer from gross distortion of their body image. They will often claim they are overweight in the face of all physical evidence to the contrary. One young woman planning a third suicide attempt wrote to me that, at five foot four, she weighed 93 pounds. "I feel fat all the time," she said, "but before I kill myself, I must be thin. I cannot let some undertaker see my ugly fat body."

The DSM-IV, the latest diagnostic manual of psychiatric conditions, states, "Individuals with this disorder intensely fear gaining weight or becoming fat. This intense fear of becoming fat is usually not alleviated by the weight loss. In fact, concern about weight gain often increases even as actual weight continues to decrease."

I believe that the Negative Mind will not allow its victims to see themselves as they are because weight is synonymous with life. Given that victims are on an unconscious track to total self-negation (death), if they perceive themselves as fat, this will allow the Negative Mind to demand that they lose even more weight.

Anorexics will lie about whether they have eaten because the Negative Mind, which insists without reason or logic on their

demise, instructs them to. They wear concealing clothes to protect the Negative Mind, to forestall confrontation with the people around them. In the few cases in which anorexics flaunt their
gauntness, they are pointing out that they are more unworthy
than others. They vie to be the best at dying.

Anorexia is about self-loathing and self-hatred for falling
short of perfection. Nora wrote several years after her recovery,
"I didn't look at models and dream of looking like them. I didn't
think that I was becoming beautiful. I thought I was the ugliest,
most selfish, and horrible person."

---

*"Anorexia is more prevalent in females than
in males because females are told that
appearance is important while males are
praised for other qualities."*

I do agree that women are bombarded with images of unattainable female beauty. Women's magazines are filled with
articles and advertisements touting diets, weight loss, exercise
machines, and so on. Beautiful women are featured in television
ads that sell everything from beer to automobiles to detergent.

Though the images of "perfect" women still vastly outnum-
ber those extolling male perfection, I do in fact see a rise in the
number of images of men, although they are perhaps more ob-
scured. *Men's Health* and *GQ* as opposed to *Glamour* and *Vogue*—
the magazine titles may not always be as direct.

Once again, however, I think we are looking at a trigger, not
a direct cause. Eating disorders are not gender-based any more
than CNC is gender-based.

Historically, women have been honed to be the caregivers of
home and therefore of society's needs. For years, they have been
the quiet support person, the one to whom the expressions "The
power behind the throne" and "Behind every great man is a
great woman" applied. So naturally, it would follow that there

would be a higher incidence of eating disorder manifestation among females.

Today, society is evolving. Men can act more sensitively. We are finally a more humanistic culture rather than a culture of warriors.

And eating disorders among men are on the rise—at least one million men number among the eight million people afflicted with them in the United States. I attribute this to the ever-increasing anxiety and attitudes toward perceived stress in society (the macrocosm) and the changing rules within the nuclear family (the microcosm), coupled with the victim's sensitive, caring nature.

Perhaps men are not faced with the anxiety of society's contradictions as often because their stereotypical role is to do rather than to mediate and placate. But given the changing roles in society, men see themselves more often in the position of giving care. One young man who came into my care after years of hospitalization that culminated in institutionalization in a mental facility because of the severity of his suicidality had begun his slide toward CNC and anorexia as a young boy. His mother had suffered stomach problems so intense that she had to run to the hospital for treatment. Jonathan took it upon himself to keep his two younger siblings quiet while his mother recovered from her frequent ailments. She had not asked him to do this, but in his own mind, he saw it as his role.

Each case of anorexia is different. But anorexics all hear the same language and display the same inherent kindness. After their recovery, their Actual Minds will regain control, and these former victims will be objectively, not subjectively, kind.

"Anorexia is caused by physical, emotional, or sexual abuse."

Abuse falls into the category of "Underlying Issues." These issues are real, and they need to be addressed. In this discussion,

I applaud the work being done with people who have such issues. At the same time, however, I question whether these issues are directly related to anorexia. As one victim wrote to me, "I don't know how to change. Any program I've been in was a stop-gap measure—a one- or three-month hospital stay where I'd put on weight that I'd immediately drop as soon as I was released. (Sure, I worked through many important issues—but never unraveled the behavior.)"

I keep reading that eating disorders are skyrocketing because sexual abuse is coming out of the closet. I have had patients come to me and say, "I don't remember being sexually abused, but since I have anorexia, I guess I must have been."

I know of one father who was accused of sexually abusing his daughter because she was anorexic. There was no evidence for believing he had molested his little girl. Even though no one in the family could see how this abuse was possible, the mother divorced him because of the groundless charge. Both child and father denied any abuse took place, and I believe them—it took me two years to put the family back together.

I do not deny that sexual abuse occurs in situations in which child and parent vigorously deny it, nor do I want to minimize the devastating trauma that can occur after sexual abuse. However, most of my patients have not been abused, and I want to set aside the common misconception that every eating disorder is the product of abuse—physical, sexual, or otherwise.

On the other hand, I have worked with several anorexics who have been sexually abused. They felt that they deserved what happened to them, they did not feel traumatized by it, and were primarily relieved that it had not occurred to someone else. Typically, they welcomed what must seem to the rest of us like cruel punishment (the work of the ever-perverse Negative Mind), and still they cared for others first—even their abusers. In truth, they lacked an accurate perception of their reality and responsibility.

Consequently, I believe it may not be the trauma of the abuse per se, but the individual's perception of reality that will cause anorexia. We can change reality only to a certain point (by addressing the trauma and distress that act as triggers), but we can try to change people's attitudes toward and perceptions of reality. In other words, we can objectify abuse, that is, try to help the abused victim understand that she did not deserve or cause the abuse, in order to preserve the sanity of the victim. Perhaps anger toward ignorance only compounds the problem and prolongs the suffering of the victim. Compassion and understanding for the limitations of human awareness would seem more likely to heal the victim than criticizing her for not condemning her abuse or her abuser.

"Anorexia is caused by distant, uncaring, demanding, or otherwise dysfunctional parents."

There is a widespread perception that anorexia is more common in families in which rigid, exacting, uncompromising parents impose their own personalities on compliant little children. The "best little girl in the world" stereotype conveys that nothing the child does is good enough for insatiable, demanding parents, so the child keeps trying harder and harder to please them.

This is blatantly untrue for the vast majority of my cases. In fact, I was alarmed to discover how wrong the stereotype is. It would have made it easier to find that parents were uncaring or demanding or dysfunctional, because then the answer to the eating disorder conundrum would have been much simpler.

Parents are primarily responsible for defining the world in which their children find themselves, but the emergence of an eating disorder is not in itself a response to a specific social structure within the family. Rather, I find that motivation for achievement is far more self-imposed.

I have observed that these children are determined to create the best possible scenario for the ones they love, without having been asked or pushed. Generally, the intense striving to achieve

Myths and Misconceptions

and the insatiable need for validation come from within them, not from external sources such as parents.

One girl wrote in her journal, "I was running track before school, doing homework instead of eating lunch, doing more running after school, studying until one o'clock or two o'clock in the morning and sleeping four or five hours a night, maximum. . . . I contemplated driving my car around a corner and not turning because I had gotten a 97 percent on a project that was worth only a fraction of my final grade. I made *one* stupid mistake on a departmental exam and it haunted me for months! Nothing was ever good enough. And when I did achieve 'perfection,' it meant nothing to me."

Another wrote, "I cannot recognize or appreciate any of my own accomplishments. Others are always better. Even when I achieve excellence it isn't good enough. I recently got 98 percent on my calculus final and was upset with myself for not doing better. My goals are far too high. I lose sight of what is realistic or even excellent, and strive for what is impossible. I never reach it, so I am always a failure in my estimation and that makes me unhappy."

Moreover, young people with eating disorders work at parenting their parents; they insist on caring for the adults. As I explained in Chapter 2, parents are generally struck by the maturity of these children from a very early age and tend to lean on them because they can.

Most of the parents whom I see are incredible—extremely loving and caring. They are also incredibly human—they have flaws and faults like the rest of us. Parents are people—they are human and imperfect. Every family in the world has circumstances that play the scale of that humanness. Motivation and the effort to make things work are all that are available to any of us. Failure requires tolerance and understanding without one being labeled a misfit.

The stress of parents' divorce in particular is blamed for children's eating disorders. However, most of my patients' parents are not divorced, and most of the families I see are not dysfunctional. However, if parents have the slightest squabble, the child with CNC regards it as a crisis of the most major proportions and will try to intervene. This later gets misconstrued by many therapists as evidence of a "dysfunctional family," when in fact it is a reflection of the hypersensitive perspective of the child with CNC.

As I've mentioned, if anything, family traumas such as illness, divorce, or other life crises may act as *triggers* that help shift someone with preexisting CNC into a full-blown eating disorder. If a child is already feeling negative and subjective about what is going on in her life, she is more vulnerable and susceptible to taking these emergencies personally and feeling helpless about them. The more pervasive the pessimistic thought patterns— that is, if they dominate 60 percent of her thoughts rather than 20 percent—the more effective the trigger will be in setting off the eating disorder.

Certainly there are extremes—true dysfunctional families, and that dysfunction can act as a trigger for eating disorders. It is essential that such families come to terms with the dysfunction and seek appropriate therapy to address it. Although I believe that an individual whose CNC has been reversed will not respond to the same trigger—divorce, depression, or other trauma—by relapsing into an eating disorder, the trigger is nonetheless a potent source of stress. For the health of the whole family, it must be dealt with. I'll discuss this further in Chapter 7.

However, not every family that raises its voice once in a while is dysfunctional. Conversely, an eating disorder will be highly distressing to any family system. A cohesive and healthy family unit can be pushed to self-destruction by the very threats and misguided suspicions we have talked about.

I have found that many parents of eating disorder victims, like most parents, are possibly overanxious, but that anxiety is shaped and even inadvertently encouraged by society. Parents may rush to the doctor for every little thing; they may use a pill for every perceived problem. Is this about the child or about the "anxiety of prevention"? Certainly, parents generally come from a place of good intentions.

Because of this, I feel it is imperative to let go of blame. Often parents live with guilt for feeling that they have somehow contributed to and are responsible for the way their children behave. Parents are moved to shame because they have been labeled—rightly or wrongly—dysfunctional and feel they are the objects of a witch-hunt. This serves to create more agitation, stress, and negativity within an already tormented family.

These parents spend untold hours denouncing themselves for their human inadequacies while simultaneously living in the war zone of their sick children's lives. They try to carry on their jobs and lives while entertaining a nightmare within the walls of their homes, a nightmare that they are too often told is their fault and inadvertently their doing. Their most important focus, their child, is at risk of dying. Parents stand helpless in the apparent hopelessness of their situation.

In the long run, placing the blame on parents—even if they are "guilty" of creating triggers for eating disorders—can be detrimental and dangerous to their child. It may prevent them from being available to her when they are most essential as her basic support system. Their energies will be diverted to searching for their error in "causing" their child's condition and possible death. Their guilt will rob them of the strength to stand firm to reverse the Negative Mind, and so they may give in to what they assume are their child's needs when they are actually giving in to the condition's demands.

"Anorexia is the consequence of perfectionistic people failing in their desire to be perfect."

Perfectionism for an individual with an eating disorder is about appeasing society and placating its expectations. One child wrote in her journal, "I don't feel confident with myself as a person, so I feel I have to try to conform to society's pressure to meet the expectations it places on people's acceptance based on their appearance."

Why does a child need to be perfect? Perhaps she does because we, as a society, have told her that she *can* be, and because she feels she therefore *must* be. But there is a great difference between seeking to perfect oneself for self-satisfaction or the accolades of family or society—behavior that we would probably label as "normal"—and the victim's attempt at perfection in order to make society, as a whole, a better place for all. A tall order, indeed!

"Anorexia is caused by low self-esteem."

When Nicole was still ill, an old friend told her that she was conceited because she was always looking in the mirror. "Doesn't she understand? It isn't about that, Mom," she said tearfully. "I was looking to find myself. I was hunting for me."

It makes little sense to talk of self-esteem in the same breath as anorexia. As I have explained in the previous chapter, anorexia is a condition based on the lack of a fully defined self. To recover from anorexia, the victim must first develop a self before she can address her self-esteem.

I become concerned when I hear about people struggling to build an acutely ill patient's self-esteem, because that person has no clear sense of self to which to attribute the esteem. This makes the victim feel more worthless, and the parent and loved one more guilty.

Esteem will naturally begin to develop after the self has begun to emerge.

"Anorexia is the result of trauma from the pain of parents' divorce, adolescence, or other life crises."

In the case of my own divorce, it is natural to wonder whether tensions in the household before the breakup or the stress of the breakup itself were what tipped my daughters toward anorexia. Kirsten, Nicole, and I have discussed this at great length and do not believe these issues were the trigger for their eating disorders. My former husband and I did not have a turbulent relationship; it just gradually became apparent to us that we wanted different things out of the marriage. We did not have an acrimonious split-up; it was a long time coming and the girls knew and were in agreement with it. (It was our friends and neighbors who were surprised.) I've been asked if undercurrents of tension rather than overt drama might have pushed my daughters over the edge. If so, why were they well all during the years when my husband and I were living on parallel tracks yet under the same roof, and only became ill when I moved out on my own? Surely one's parents splitting up—even if my daughters acknowledged that it made everyone happier—must be traumatic; how could a family's dissolution not be a negative? Yet Kirsten and Nikki tell me they didn't see it that way. In retrospect, it is clear to us that the trigger for their illness was not my divorce but their anxiety and hypersensitive reaction to my struggles as a single parent trying to earn a degree and raise two children on her own. In typical CNC fashion, they were worrying not about themselves, but about my well-being. My struggles became their burden, although I wasn't aware of it at the time.

Of course, every divorce is unique because every marriage and family is unique, and I do believe there are children who feel traumatized by their parents' breakup. However, it has been my experience that in these cases, it is not the particulars of the divorce itself, but the manner in which the CNC-disposed child takes the blame and burdens upon herself that triggers the eating disorder. This can happen even in the most civil divorces. A divorce represents a failed marriage, and the person with CNC will inevitably see herself as responsible for the failure—or as a failure for not being able to prevent it.

It is true that the majority of eating disorders begin during adolescence. What is unique about adolescence today? Teenagers live in a more anxious society. The person with an eating disorder takes on the role of caregiver and nurturer. She has to decide many things about her future at a much earlier age. Society's message is anxiety and fear and despair.

Parents are busy trying to accommodate their child's individuality. Given the psychological onus that society places on evaluating the self, parents are perhaps less inclined to make a defined stance on what direction to push their child. Thus the child feels she is sinking in quicksand at the very time she needs direction. She cannot find a platform from which to spring.

I believe that generally today's parents turn the responsibility for decisions—"What would you like, dear?"—over to children too early. Fewer rules, less structure, less black and white. Perhaps parents are loath to appear directive of their child's potential because in contemporary society people are generally less sure of their environment and therefore their role in it. Maybe it is out of a misled "respect" for the child with CNC, given that we are so afraid of harming her integrity as an individual, that we do not create enough structure for her when she needs it early in life.

"Anorexia is a disease of the 'economically advantaged.' "

Eating disorders have often been said to be the province of middle or upper socioeconomic classes. That may generally be true, but it is also understandable. Today there is less physical stress in living in middle- and upper-class households, but in my observation more emotional stress and more anxiety that sensitive children are bound to absorb. Perhaps parents in these circumstances are more rushed and anxious in maintaining their lifestyles. This may result in more perceived stress, which children in turn translate as anxiety.

Perhaps a child's internal interpretation of her parents' achievements creates in her the expectation that she must live up to their "standards," even though this does not come from parental edicts. She has constructed these "standards" herself. The middle- and upper-income child may shoulder more responsibility, not because her parents ask her to, but because she takes it upon herself to fulfill what she perceives as their high aspirations.

I believe that middle- or upper-income children have more choices than their lower-income counterparts. Their parents' lives are not as clearly cut-and-dried as other people's may be, and for sensitive children, the proliferation of choices and expectations, real or perceived, may be overwhelming. Lower-income children seem to intuit their limitations or have them forced upon them—and harbor fewer illusions about their reality. For such a child, the platform to build her identity may not be complicated with the confusion of the parents' search for meaning and society's pressure of expectation. The existence of boundaries, whether desirable or not, at least provides a form of stability. Perhaps, too, children in lower socioeconomic circumstances enjoy the benefits of a larger extended family. Grandparents, uncles, and aunts may share the chore of nurturing, and as I mentioned earlier, the more adults participate in a child's growth, the more likely the child will grasp objective reality.

Nevertheless, in my practice, I see eating disorders in all socioeconomic groups. I think it continues to be more prevalent in the upper and middle classes, but I know there is no clear "class" line anymore.

"Anorexia is a psychosomatic disorder caused by a child's refusal to grow up into an adult."

A common misinterpretation is that anorexics are struggling to remain childlike. As purported victims of the Peter Pan syndrome, they are thought to fear and loathe adulthood. But our case histories show again and again that the fear of growing up may be a consequence of the eating disorder, but it is not a cause.

Before manifesting the condition, these young people had extraordinary capability for self-direction and social responsibility. Depending on their age, they excelled in every area. Far from reneging on adult responsibility, they shouldered too much of it to adhere to society's extended values. They appeared compliant for fear of offending others. Their primary focus was always for the well-being of others rather than themselves.

But by being the "caregiver" and "parent" in their own minds, CNC victims have already tried to grow up before their time. They have taken on mature responsibilities long before they acquired the adult objectivity or reasoning to recognize their own limitations, and naturally they were not up to the task.

The world is large and daunting. CNC-predisposed children have tried to make it all right for everyone and they have failed miserably in their own eyes. It is not that they do not want to grow up, it is that they do not know how. They have had responsibility and failed at it. One young girl wrote to me, as so many others do, "I don't want to die, but I don't know how to want to live."

Saying that a child "refuses to grow up" implies that she is reneging on her obligation. The fact is, she is an altruistic soul, the true caregiver who believes she has already tried to grow up and failed. Her perceived monumental failure overwhelms her with the realization that she has been unable to make the world a better place for everyone else.

In Günter Grass's classic novel *The Tin Drum*, the protagonist, Oskar, gets smaller and smaller and smaller inside himself because he has no sense of self. Just like the anorexic, he gains his sense of self vicariously by being a guardian angel to an adult. When the angel fails, he does not blame the adult for ignoring his instruction; he blames himself as the poor guidance counselor.

Children are also said to become anorexic because they do not want to become sexual beings. Sexuality implies not just maturity but pleasure. Just as the punishing Negative Mind will not allow its victims food, so will it deny them any other form of pleasure as well.

Sexual maturity is also synonymous with graduating to being normal. In their minds, anorexics believe they do not deserve that privilege because they have already "tried" adulthood and failed. Avoiding sexual maturity (or any act of normalcy) is a way of relieving themselves of the guilt they experience for failing to help the world. It is not fear of sex per se, but rather fear of further failure at responsibility and the guilt that new failures would engender. Menstruation, an indication of physiological normalcy, is not a welcome rite of passage for these victims.

The individual in the acute grip of an eating disorder is therefore asexual. I have received many letters from women who have managed to marry and even have children while wrestling with an eating disorder. They are maintaining their condition and their relapses suggest that while they have subdued the inner turmoil temporarily, they are not truly inhabiting their sexual selves.

"Anorexia is an unconscious attention-getting device, a cry for help."

Anorexics are highly embarrassed at being noticed. They typically wear baggy clothing to disguise their weight loss.

There is, however, a contradiction here. Victims of CNC yearn for someone to understand them, but their Negative Mind will not allow them to ask for help, and they do not feel they deserve it anyway. If weight loss is the unconscious cry for attention, why don't victims stop losing weight once parents and other loved ones try to intervene, often with valiant efforts? It is because their unconscious motive is to die, not to get attention. If there were a way to die of anorexia without losing weight—a visible sign—they would do it.

My patients tell me, "I have to die in a way that won't hurt people." It's not that they want to die; it's that they feel they can no longer exist because they are failures in their own minds.

"People with eating disorders are selfish. They just need to get on with their lives and stop ruining everyone else's!"

As I hope I've made abundantly clear, eating disorder victims are the antithesis of selfish. Indeed, they are self*less* to the highest degree. Unfortunately, the Negative Mind constantly accuses them of self-indulgence when they want merely to exist in the world, so any allegation of selfishness from external sources such as family or medical professionals simply reinforces and strengthens the Negative Mind's hand.

The mother of three children in England contacted me about her fifteen-year-old daughter who was dying of anorexia. Gabrielle had had the illness for a year and a half, and during that time had been hospitalized eight times. "The doctors told her she was a spoiled brat," this distraught mother complained to me. "They said, 'All Gabby needs is a good kick in the bottom.'"

This response to an eating disorder reminds me of how people used to regard depression. We once believed that depressed people could just "snap out of it" if they tried hard enough. And somehow we still are of the opinion that if victims of eating disorders cared enough (about their parents' or other loved ones' anguish?), they could will themselves to get better. Nothing could be further from the truth. Indeed, the problems began because these "old souls" cared too much and they need help to find a way out of the miasma that traps them.

"Anorexia is a tool for control."

The misconception is that by denying themselves food in the face of the vigorous encouragement to eat, anorexics are trying to control their world against others. Rather than control others, I believe victims are trying to control the remaining bit of their Actual Mind against the Negative Mind. They are losing power because the Negative Mind bullies the Actual Mind into submission.

If we ignore the existence or misunderstand the role of the Negative Mind, it can only follow that we will misconstrue whom the child is trying to control. The Actual Mind always takes the rap for the Negative Mind, since the latter is so carefully hidden from our view. Consequently, the child will understandably be mislabeled as controlling.

As the Negative Mind gains in strength, it creates internal chaos.

"On the outside, I still look like I am in control and so together, but on the inside I have nothing."

"I have been in turmoil. I'm so completely without direction."

"I feel myself completely shattered and I'm so afraid."

"Emotions control my food. The life that I can't control, controls my food."

"There is always that fear of criticism, ridicule, being scolded, losing a job, losing a friend, or failing. I'm always afraid when asked to do a job, or left with the decision of what to make for dinner that I'll do it wrong and thus be rejected."

Controlling behaviors can be seen as a child's attempt to create a structure for herself. Indeed, at the clinic I give a mug and plate with an individual design to each patient who comes to us. This seems like a small gesture, but it's an important one. The unique mug and plate are hers alone—part of the interim structure she so desperately needs. Until that point, she is searching for any level of structure in her habits, food, and being.

The anorexic's habit of preparing food for others while refusing to eat it herself is commonly misinterpreted as a need to control her environment. Again, understanding the motivation behind the actions is useful.

This behavior demonstrates the Negative Mind's domination of the Actual Mind. Victims stand near food; they spend time focusing on it because they are desperate to be allowed it. They consciously deny themselves but subconsciously desire food because they are physiologically starving. So as they eat vicariously by preparing food for others, they also demonstrate their own unworthiness to be normal human beings. In fact, many children will adulterate their food with hot sauce, vinegar, or even chlorine cleanser to make it unfit for human consumption and only worthy of them, the unworthy.

According to DSM-IV, in the anorexic, "weight loss is viewed as an impressive achievement and a sign of extraordinary self-discipline, whereas weight gain is perceived as an unacceptable failure of self-control."

For normal dieters, weight loss may be considered a bona fide achievement, but for those with eating disorders, weight loss is the antithesis of achievement, despite what the victims consciously believe. Weight loss is an unconscious acceptance of failure, an acknowledgment or resignation that the anorexic is giving up the right to live. The only "impressive achievement" is that she has proven to herself that she is indeed unworthy of life. She is controlling herself to death.

The stereotype is that these children want to control everything, but in fact they want to serve everyone and ensure the well-being of the planet. They see themselves as "troubleshooters" and are ever on the alert for problems to solve.

It is contradictory to be both pliable, as a common stereotype goes, and also controlling, as another common stereotype goes. It is contradictory to be both a good caregiver and listener —which implies an adult sensibility—AND someone who does not want to take responsibility for her controlling actions.

"Anorexics are to blame for their situation. They're doing it to get back at others."

Given that the dynamics of an eating disorder occur at an unconscious level and are as perplexing and complicating for its victims as they are for their families, the view that anorexics are intentionally guilty of hurting their beloved parents just adds to the nightmare of their existence.

When unwitting practitioners blame parents for their children's anorexia by insisting that anorexia results from favoritism, abuse, or some other symptom of family dysfunction, they often create animosity among parents toward their children, and the victims end up the losers. After such finger-pointing, parents often ask victims, "Why have you done this to us? How could you continue to be so cruel?"

The victim will cope more easily if a therapist tries to teach her with compassion and intelligence that everyone is imperfect. And so it is healthier for all involved to translate "blame" into "limitations." The individual stops hunting for wrongdoers.

The very word "victim" implies helplessness at the hands of another. In this case, the victimization is neither by the inadvertent ignorance and unawareness of society nor of any given individual. Eating disorders are an exceedingly negative response to a misinterpretation of one's role in the world. The victimization occurs in the negative construct the patient has unwittingly built against herself. She becomes helpless against the onslaught of the Negative Mind within her.

"Sufferers need to hold on to their condition as a crutch."

I have often heard it described that victims of eating disorders are in some perverse way clinging to the crutch of their ill-

ness. It is more accurate to say that they are dominated and enslaved by it. They want to let go of it, but they have nothing to
replace it with. As Carrie wrote in her journal, "One reason I've
held on to anorexia for so long is probably because every time I
feel a bit stronger or happier, I worry and immediately retreat.
It's because I feel guilty for feeling good. . . ."

Ultimately, victims are terrified to relinquish the condition
because they know no other way of being. For example, Sharon
wrote to me, "I basically have resolved to accept my life as an
eating disorder. It's the only thing I've ever been able to capture
and call my own and the only thing no one has ever been able to
take away from me."

Therefore to give up the condition is to cease to exist—even
worse than death. Anorexia becomes a negative structure—
"Who am I if not my illness?"—and an all-pervasive way of
being.

"The longer you have anorexia, the harder it is to cure."

On occasion, this may be true because the condition has
been confirmed repeatedly, possibly due to so many futile hospi-
talizations. With each failed program, the Negative Mind recon-
firms itself and becomes more pernicious. Similarly, the longer
the Actual Mind has learned to exist marginally and the longer
it feels the negative comfort of that existence, the more difficult
an eating disorder is to cure.

However, I have also found that it is just as difficult to cure
anorexia in people who have had it for a short time as it is to cure
those who have been ill for years. Once the Negative Mind has
enough control to manifest an eating disorder, healing appears
to depend more on the basic personality of the individual than
on the duration of the eating disorder manifestation.

"Anorexia can't be cured; it can only be managed. You'll live with it and die from it."

Eating disorders are a silent epidemic. Anorexics have no constituency. They cannot rise up en masse to say, "We need help." You do not see them banding together to form research societies and associations, although others have formed these organizations on their behalf. Nevertheless, these conditions are completely reversible, though the cure requires a total re-nurturing of the afflicted individual.

However, to "manage anorexia" is merely to maintain the condition's status. To maintain it is to invite recidivism. In order to correct the eating disorder symptom, the CNC must be addressed and reversed. This reversal requires patience, complete understanding, and as much time as each individual needs.

How can we integrate this concept into society as it exists today? How, given the vast tragedy we see before us, can we not?

4

∞

The Acute Patient:
Held Hostage by the
"Forever" Intruder

Confirmed Negativity Condition is not cyclical; it progresses along an intensifying continuum. However, in its early stages, it can be reversed with relatively less difficulty than when it becomes more deeply entrenched. An individual whose thoughts are dominated by subjectivity and negativity 25 percent of the time, for instance, is capable of springing back to normal thinking if she encounters a positive intervention, even if that intervention is fortuitous. If this occurs again and again, she can regain a normal course in life.

At fourteen, Danielle was well on her way toward anorexia. Measuring five foot eight, she weighed one hundred pounds, and had remained in that condition for a year. But in high school, she encountered a group of new friends who were so supportive of her and so accepting that they seemed to erase the negativity that was plaguing her. "I truly believed they were my family when I wasn't anchored by family," she told me as she described her brush with eating disorders so many years ago.

Outpatient psychotherapeutic intervention can also be helpful during the early stages, as long as those at home are able to participate in a loving situation. (See Chapters 7 and 8.)

When accidental interventions do not occur, or if loved ones have not recognized the signs of the encroaching CNC and did not involve professional caregivers, the Negative Mind becomes more pronounced and reinforced. It fills its victim's mind with anxiety, and thoughts of unworthiness, self-deprecation, and doom. Subjectivity begins to reign, particularly if set off by triggers, which feel the negativity. Inwardly, life turns dark as the victim slides toward the confusion of emotional childhood and then the helplessness of infancy, while outwardly she frets about food and weight and exercise. She appears indecisive and withdrawing. Eventually she stops eating. Soon the condition worsens to the point of acuteness.

THE PHYSIOLOGY OF THE ACUTE PATIENT

One might think that someone with an acute eating disorder will always resemble a famine victim—skeletal body, ribs, pelvis, and spine nearly protruding through translucent skin; abdomen bloated; eyes sunken; hair sparse; spirit broken.

While this may describe many acute patients, it certainly does not portray all of them. Bulimic patients and even some anorexics may pass for low "normal" in weight and therefore not be so easily recognized as having a problem (see Chapter 7 for more warning signs). Nevertheless, they may be as seriously ill as those patients who weigh forty-seven pounds and appear at the brink of death.

"I was hospitalized with atrial fibrillation and severe electrolyte imbalance plus internal bleeding," wrote one woman. "My daughter is severely osteoporotic and she hasn't even gone into puberty yet," wrote another. These are only a few of the physiological effects of acute eating disorders.

Indeed, an acute patient may experience the breakdown of body organs. She is at high risk for heart attack from electrolyte imbalance, for instance. And though low potassium levels are not always necessarily a marker, frequently they can indicate that a patient is in danger of dying.

Other physical indicators of acute eating disorders can include:

- bradycardia (low heart rate) and irregular heartbeat
- edema (tissue swelling from water retention) due to electrolyte imbalances
- potential kidney failure
- potential liver failure
- osteoporosis
- extreme fluctuations in blood pressure
- in bulimic patients, esophageal scarring and dental decay from excessive vomiting
- intestinal rupture from excessive use of laxatives
- insomnia

In its desperation for nutrition, the body begins to cannibalize itself. First the protective fat cushions around the heart and kidneys disappear, resulting in more potential for damage. Then, the protein structure of the muscles and internal organs is mobilized for nutrition (just as the calcium is taken from the bones). The body eventually deteriorates and wastes away.

Edema gives the victim the false impression that she is gaining weight. Upon noticing the swelling, a victim often becomes frightened that she is gaining weight and further restricts her intake of food, thereby exacerbating the bloating and starvation in a vicious cycle.

Skin becomes dry and raw because the body lacks necessary oils. Feet can become bloodied from hours of intense exercise. Hair thins, breaks, and falls out. Nails split. In extreme cases, a soft downy growth of hair called lanugo appears all over the skin, including the face, in the body's desperate attempt to maintain warmth in the absence of protective layers of fat.

One of the first physiological markers of illness in adolescent and adult females is amenorrhea. The body stops menstruation as a way to conserve vital resources such as iron and protein. When menstruation returns, this is a valuable indication of the body's healing.

In the acute stage of anorexia, victims cannot concentrate; their eyes dart furtively, and they are usually incapable of any sustained eye contact. They are afraid of being "read" and recognized. Nevertheless, the intellect is the last to go. Victims will often accomplish extraordinary academic feats while on the verge of physical collapse.

Parents and professionals should take care not to use this information to threaten or scare their children or patients. Telling someone she "looks like a concentration camp victim" or that he "could drop dead if he doesn't stop" is counterproductive. The victim already feels like a "walking freak" and further blame-inducing language will only exacerbate her already overwhelming sense of guilt or unworthiness.

Any of these signs and symptoms require professional medical evaluation and treatment. It is essential to realize that physical appearance is not a valid indicator of the severity of an eating disorder. If you suspect a loved one has an eating disorder, make sure that person sees a medical doctor immediately.

THE PSYCHOLOGY OF THE ACUTE PATIENT

How can anyone allow herself to fall into such a dreadful medical condition? It has been my experience that the origin of this physiological deterioration is the CNC victim succumbing to the Negative Mind. Edna, one of my correspondents, described the power of the Negative Mind in a poem she sent me:

My Mind Is a Cannibal
My mind is a cannibal,
reveling in vicious pleasure,
watching my body devour itself.
The always truthful looking-glass
has agreed to a bribe, offered by the inner-eye,
and distortion assures me that my skeleton-like state
is ravishing . . . that I am the envy of all.
Pernicious pain makes a sculpture out of me,
a ghastly creation,

which no audience would ever pay to see,
except for me.
Almost consciously,
I permit coercion to comfort me
with an insidiously vile routine . . .
leaving my emotions famished.
My bones have dried like winter's twigs.
My concave curves have draped themselves loosely in skin.
Like a star burning bright on the threshold of death,
I collapse into myself.
All day is night, and night . . . eternal blackness.
I die. I swallow death.
I consume it with my voracious appetite.
It eats me. It digests every part of me
(or at least all that is left).
I must be happy with death.
It loves me . . . passionately. It sings to me. Lullabies.
I will sleep soundly, safely in the moist darkness of its
    stomach. . . .

The Negative Mind is an intruder whom the acute eating disorder patient feels she has inadvertently invited upon herself. As one patient wrote to me, "I don't think there was an exact date. It felt like anorexia had sneaked up behind me and inserted itself slowly inside me without me really noticing it."

It is as if she is being held hostage with a gun to her head. Though (and perhaps because) the threats are internal, they inspire more fear than if they existed in the "real" world. Thus, society is generally unable to recognize and identify the enemy in the same way that the victim does.

Science fiction has no edge over what the Negative Mind has created to frighten its acute victim to death. Its hold on her psyche becomes all-enveloping and all-involving. When family or friends in all innocence attempt to extend help, the Negative Mind necessarily instructs the weaker Actual Mind to reject it since the sufferer does not deserve it. To her, the mind game is very real and terrifying. Often what seems to the victim to be a real voice mocks, leers, threatens, and instructs her to self-destruct.

One of my patients, Mariah, recorded the civil war inside her head as she battled anorexia and bulimia. She neither censored the voice nor could explain her actions, but felt absolutely compelled to obey the Negative Mind:

6:00 A.M. Get up you fuckhead, get up. You'll be late if you don't and you know you're not leaving till it's done [exercising]

6:45 A.M. Fifteen more minutes. Come on you fat pig. You're **tired???** You can't be, I won't let you. If you don't go the full hour you're not eating anything today.

8:00 A.M. Get off the bus now, you have time to walk the extra five blocks and not be late. You'll burn off the milk you had in your coffee this morning.

12:00 P.M. ["Mariah, do you want to have lunch with us?"] Fuck, now what? Think bitch **think!** Just say no ("I can't, I've already said no too many times"). Go, then, but you better get rid of everything you eat.

12:30 P.M. ("Tuna sandwich, please.") Tuna! Tuna!!! **You fucking fat bitch.** Don't you know they use tons of real mayo? You can't bring up every last bit of sauce. I keep saying only solid foods. No sauce. No combination of foods or shit like that. That way you know exactly what to look for when you throw up.

Laxatives! You have to get them before you go back to work. Three big boxes. ("I have to go out tonight and they'll be working by then.") Listen, bitch, you fucked up by asking for tuna. Besides, no one cares if you show up or not.

4:00 P.M. The laxatives won't be working for another hour or so, the shit is probably stored quite nicely on your ass already. You'll have to stay a half hour extra at the gym.

6:00 P.M. ("Oh shit. I'm coming home late again—she'll kill me—damn, she's going to be furious.") You deserve it though, you selfish bitch—going to the gym behind her back.

7:30 P.M. You promised yesterday was going to be the last time. You fucking bitch—you are shit and you always will be shit. They're all right about you. How can you live with your-self? You're dishonest and selfish. You never do anything right and you are a **fat! fat! fat!!!!** useless poor excuse for a human being Bitch. I hate you bitch I **hate** you. Look at your-self in the mirror and tell me I'm lying. You can't because you see what I do. You lost only 2 pounds today and it's not good enough!

Now hurry up and get rid of it. I don't care if you have to stick your whole fucking arm down your throat—you're going to get rid of it. I don't give a shit if you're bleeding. Your whole insides can come up and **you still won't stop.**

The Negative Mind speaks to its victim in a vile, degrading way while the victim herself is generally possessed of a great dig-nity and would not express herself in such a manner.

By the time people have become acutely ill, the Negative Mind is so real that most can actually conjure up a physical description of "it." My daughter Kirsten described "it" as a "beast" in one of her poems:

Glancing Toward Defeat
External beauty defies itself with the markings of the beast,
Smiles like the quick drop of sharpened knives
Scathing saws glistening upon other sorrows

Tearing apart lips
Wrenching out eyes
—leave them in bits

Internal beauty mistakeningly
Collapses when shadowed by the beast
An onlooker watching through mirrors,
The slow death of the dying
—their final feast

A marching hand in hand,

Beating tears
—label them "pathetic"
I know, I know
let them go quietly, one slip gains a remark
to encourage further crying, if only it didn't
hurt while crying inside.

Another way the victim can reveal the torment in her mind is through pictorial representations. We encourage the patients at the clinic to make paintings of their tormentors. Often many have done so even before coming into care.

The artwork is a nonverbal way of soliciting the alliance of the outside world in the victim's struggle. One eight-year-old, for instance, would slip her drawings into her father's briefcase as a way to communicate her anguish to him. Although horrified by them, unfortunately he did not know what to make of them.

Though there are many variations on the theme, the acute patient's artwork often shows the sufferer's lack of power. Victims are being controlled by a dark, "evil" demon or monster who is intent on torturing its victim internally, slowly.

Often these artworks show red, fanning flames of what one would suppose is a "Hell," and some shadowy form in black. Though I treat my patients with therapy based on a humanistic psychological premise, I am scarcely surprised that some parents might think that their children are "possessed." They are not. This mindset and its resultant behavior become more understandable in the context of recovery. Other depictions show the eating disorder sufferer:

in cages or jails surrounded by words of negativity such as
    "loser," "failure," "fat pig," "guilt," "responsible."
swimming in an ocean with no hope of shore; treading
    water to an inevitable end.
down a deep well with sides of slippery moss that renders
    scaling it impossible, yet the victim can see the light at
    the top.

standing against a brick wall that covers the page with no
means of climbing it. (The victim appears minuscule.)
as a child standing on a scale with the world held on his or
her shoulders.

One of my daughter Nicole's drawings, created before I was
able to recognize its meaning, was of twins. One held her eyes to
the future and had a red rose of life's blood at her feet (where it
was elusively available) and a cross on her neck representing
hope. The other looked slightly downward and dejected; she was
thinner than her counterpart and held the black rose of hopelessness and despair. (This illustration appears in the inset.)

Three-year-old Zev always refers to the Negative Mind as
"the man under his hair." That was his usual answer to his
mother and me when we asked him why he would not eat. "The
man won't let me. He will be angry," he would explain.

"Darling, you are safe now," I would assure him. "The man
under your hair can't hurt you anymore. I'm holding you very
tightly."

"Yes, Peggy, you are holding me, but he is still hurting me."

"How can he hurt you, darling? See, you are in my arms."

"Peggy, he is angry that you are holding me, so he is playing
drums loudly in my head so I can't hear the nice things you are
saying to me."

When anorexia is in its acute stage, the Negative Mind allows the victim no pleasure. When I first met Zev, he was forbid-
den by it from accepting or opening presents. Everyone else
deserved them, but not him. He would put his hands behind his
back if anyone would extend something in his direction. His eyes
became very dark, intense, and fearful.

If he agreed to eat anything, it could not be called "food"
and it could not make him grow because he was not permitted to
grow. Growing would mean extension of life.

Once when asked what he wanted to be when he grew up,
this three-year-old answered very quietly and thoughtfully, "I am
not going to grow up. I am going to be dead before these pants

are too short." Incredulous, we assured him he would grow when he was supposed to. He started to cry and said, "No, I'm not. The man told me I wouldn't be allowed to, and I'm scared of the man. He is always mean to me."

This child never played with other children. He always stood aside and observed. His development, however, was extraordinary. He would memorize pages of the telephone book for amusement. He loved sports and could act out an entire baseball game, playing each position in turn as the ball went around the "field." He had spent a year and a half undergoing medical testing (before we had been contacted) which failed to turn up any organic reason to explain his refusal to eat.

In the acute phase of an eating disorder, victims have no road map for direction. They feel as if they are in a complex maze running against time, as surely they are. Sometimes their mental pain is so intense and so powerful that they will wound themselves to distract themselves from it.

Some sufferers mutilate themselves, scraping, scratching, or cutting their skin. This is an attempt to escape from the relentless hounding of the negative; the physical pain of the mutilation temporarily blots out the internal voices.

When Mariah was acute, she would scald herself in the shower because her Negative Mind told her she was not allowed to temper the hot water with cold. She was told to harm herself constantly and in the early stage of recovery, when she had around-the-clock care, she held on to people all through the night with the TV and radio on in order to tune out the Negative Mind urging her toward destruction.

Another victim wrote in her journal, "I cut my arms and punched my legs up too. I don't regret doing it. I deserved every bit of it. I am a bad person and deserve to die."

Victims have said that on occasion, their wounds are mistaken for suicide attempts. Though on many occasions victims found it difficult to conceive of living under the merciless regime of the Negative Mind and might have attempted suicide, at other times marking or cutting was an added form of self-punishment.

The reign of terror effected by the Negative Mind creates a conspiracy of silence in the victim which in fact unites all victims of CNC. One sufferer wrote and asked me, "How is it that *you* know the *secret* that we are not allowed to tell?"

Eating disorder victims are desperate for help and at the same time afraid and guilty for asking for it. Carissa wrote to me, "Please let me come to you, even if I sleep in a doorway. I won't take up much room. I'm afraid HE will make me kill myself if you don't let me come soon. I know you understand."

Others have written, "I feel overcome by guilt for having received your attention," and "How can you choose me? I am so unworthy. Should not some more deserving soul have my bed?" Even in their misery and minuscule hope for a life worth living, they are more caring of another in the same plight.

BIZARRE BEHAVIOR

As the victim becomes more entrenched in her condition, she becomes increasingly oblivious to the effect of her behavior on society. Bizarre behavior serves to isolate her both in its commanding focus of the Negative Mind and its power to alienate family and friends.

Victims experience agitated sleep both because of their physical imbalances and their constant need to forage for food, whether or not they actually eat it. For six months, my daughter Nikki slept no more than an hour and a half each night. The intense drive to find and then deny food will send the person back and forth from the refrigerator endlessly at the expense of rest.

Patients have hurled verbal abuse at me. They tell me repeatedly how much they hate me. They have spit food in my face, flung dishes at me, hit me, refused to get out of bed, and rebuffed interactions with others.

In public, it is not unusual for my patients to try to embarrass those around them. They may scream at the top of their lungs, sit down in puddles, or smear cold cream on their faces before going out in public. Patients often dress in bizarre ways, trying identities on for size. Boys might dress up in women's clothing.

In private, I have witnessed and parents have oftentimes reported to me exceedingly disturbing behavior: patients smearing themselves with excrement, eating garbage out of garbage cans, eating their own vomit. One patient consumed pounds of raw sausage. Another, a bulimic, wrote to me that she eats and then vomits two hundred pounds of food a day. The self-mutilation mentioned earlier is perhaps the most distressing to others.

It is important to understand that this antisocial behavior is intended to prove to the victims and others that they are worthy of alienation. They seek rejection at all costs in order to reconfirm their own sense of worthlessness. Simultaneously, they are terribly frightened by this Negative Mind they do not understand, and embarrassed and ashamed by the negative behavior they can neither explain nor discontinue.

TRANCES

About 25 percent of people with eating disorders will go into trances when in the acute stage. A trance indicates that the victim is in the most extreme psychological state of the illness. The Negative Mind virtually overwhelms the Actual Mind. The victim has tuned out external reality and assumes a dissociative state—she is temporarily oblivious to reality.

The warning signs of an impending trance can include:

- the voice of the patient diminishing to a whisper.
- fear entering the voice or showing evidence of "flat affect" with no modulation.
- the body beginning to immobilize. The victim may curl

up in bed in a fetal position out of fear, or freeze seated in a chair.

• the person making no eye contact and being obviously preoccupied with what is happening in her mind.

• the person not answering directly and/or being slow to answer.

Trances are a consequence of the Negative Mind shutting out any possible optimism or positivity from the Actual Mind or from the external voice of loved ones. When in a trance, the anorexic person is almost completely focused on and at the mercy of the Negative Mind.

A person in a trance stares straight ahead, not even blinking or moving her eyelashes; she is open-eyed but unseeing. The bridge of the nose often becomes pinched and slightly protruded, perhaps indicating overwhelming concentration. The teeth may become clenched, and breathing turns short and rapid. It appears that the victim is listening intently to something internal; she is hearing the negative voices in her head which can take the form of loud commands against her.

Most often, at the clinic, patients go into trances during the first three months of treatment when the Negative Mind feels trapped, cornered with no back door. He (for most of my patients call it a "he") can no longer order an external manifestation such as making the victim overexercise or vomit. He therefore doubles his efforts internally. The Negative Mind at this stage will make statements such as:

"Don't listen to them; they're lying to you."

"They're trying to make you fat."

"You're a selfish, ugly pig who is taking up a clinic bed that somebody else deserves more."

"You're not sick."

"I'm going to make you pay by making your family suffer. Your father is going to die in a plane crash because you told them you needed help."

"Your mother is going to have a heart attack because you
    told them you liked that sandwich."
"Nobody loves you. Who could?"

The patient might also hear loud clanging, music, pounding
drumbeats, anything to drown out the positivity coming from the
caregiver.

The victim in a trance is terrified. At this stage, she thinks
that anorexia is stronger than her caregivers because that is what
the Negative Mind repeatedly tells her. (For more on trances, see
Chapter 5.)

TRICKS

In the person with an acute eating disorder, the Negative Mind
is skilled at maintaining its status. The Negative Mind tries to
make the victim's behavior seem reasonable to cloak its real intention and convince the external world that the victim is behaving as any normal person would.

At our clinic, acute patients present our caregivers with a
great variety of "tricks." A patient may say, for instance:

"I can't eat this kind of bread because it bothers my gums."
"I'm diabetic, so I can't have sugar."
"I'm lactose-intolerant, so I can't have milk."
"I'm hypoglycemic, so I can't have fat."

Some patients might claim to be vegetarian or vegan, hiding
behind humanitarianism. Yet often these individuals tuck into
steaks and hamburgers once they get better.

Patients feign a love for plain food because they are afraid
that salt will make them retain fluid or that spices will have calories in them. Others deliberately overcook their food not only to
make it less enjoyable but also to boil the nutrition right out of it.
Some hide food in dishes, clothing, paper towels or napkins, or

coat the sides of the bowl with it so it will appear to have been eaten. Others dilute juice with water.

Even when the scales are taken away, many sufferers will find ways of charting their progress toward nothingness, using measuring tapes, shoelaces, belts, or clothing. If mirrors are removed so that the victim cannot be obsessive about her appearance, she might use windows, the blank television screen, or the oven door to study her reflection.

Weigh-ins at the doctor's office can also pose challenges. Some victims drink great quantities of water or refuse to go to the bathroom before weighing sessions. Others might weigh down their clothes with coins or rocks, or wear many layers of heavy clothing to foil the scale.

Some acutely ill victims pretend to be constipated in order to trick the physician into prescribing laxatives.

I have also seen patients go to great lengths to burn off extra calories. They may fidget endlessly. Some victims invent an incessant stream of errands that require constant motion. Others stand for long periods of time because they suppose this will burn more calories than sitting. An acute patient may refuse to wear an overcoat in winter, believing she will burn off more calories trying to stay warm. Others exercise while showering or bathing. One patient said she needed privacy; in reality, she was exercising inside her closet.

Some patients will tell me, "I can't sleep with the light on." They want to exercise under the sheets undetected. Or they will say on a warm summer's day, "Turn off the fans, I'm too cold." They believe that they can sweat the calories away.

Offers to do housework, once a sign of the person's caringness and willingness to help, can now be construed as an effort to burn off calories.

After having fallen victim to one of these ruses, we might abashedly declare, "Hey, I just got snowed." Nevertheless, we cannot accuse the victim of lying or manipulating us when perpetrating these self-defeating behaviors. Beyond lying to herself, she is dancing to the tune of the Negative Mind.

SMALL WRITING

People in the throes of an eating disorder might leave other clues, awaiting translation by those aware enough to detect them. Some, but not all, sufferers will change their style of handwriting; as CNC is confirmed and the eating disorder progresses, their words become smaller and smaller, almost as though they were trying to disappear altogether.

Every day at the clinic we receive dozens of letters crammed with handwriting so tiny it can require a magnifying glass to decipher. These letters might even include an apology along the lines of, "Please forgive the size of my writing; I didn't want it to take up space." What more eloquent statement of a sufferer's sense of non-self, of subservience to others?

As patients at our clinic work through the first two stages of therapy and move into the third (see Chapter 6), their identity, their evolving sense of self, begins to manifest even in the size of their writing, which expands and opens. This coincides with their availability to others, their openness and clarity of thought. As they grow in allowing themselves into the real world, their writing quite noticeably changes from dots of illegibility to normal-size words. They are beginning to free themselves of the warped perspective that has hounded them into subhumanism.

If we can appreciate the handwriting as an analogy of smallness—infancy—it will help us understand why the victim feels unable to cope with any responsibility, even, ultimately, the caring for herself.

SUICIDE RISK

The risk of suicide is twofold in the acute patient. On the one hand, the Negative Mind may have given the victim constant instructions to hurt and destroy herself because of her unworthiness. Julie wrote in her letters to me, for instance, "It makes me want to cut myself all the more, every disgraceful, despicable, hideous second I live, every unforgivable, shameful, evil time I eat." And later, "No pure, kind mind can comprehend one as evil as I. And so, is it not my responsibility, my most important obligation, the only thing I have to offer, to so rightly die, to finally spare you?" The strength of the Actual Mind will determine how well a victim can fight off these directives.

Usually when a patient comes to the acute stage she is also exhausted with the efforts of holding at bay the Negative Mind. Think of a deer separated from the herd, chased by a pack of wolves. Eventually he loses hope of a way out and gives up. Risk of suicide is high with acute patients because they are so weary of fighting.

As one young woman wrote to me, "I'm 24 years old and have had an eating disorder for 8 years. I've been in and out of the hospital for this a dozen times. . . . It's not that I don't want to get better, I do. It's just that I have tried so many things and it just seems hopeless. . . . Suicide is looking better and better every day. I'm not sure what else to do."

And another one wrote, "Lately I've decided not to fight it anymore. I've dropped 13 pounds in as many days. . . . I'm writing my will and am readying my personal affairs. I just can't fight it anymore. This isn't a cry for help because it's too late for me."

We can also look at the condition itself as an unconscious form of slow suicide. An eating disorder is a relinquishing of the right to live cloaked by the Negative Mind in an irrational logic.

SOCIAL WITHDRAWAL

Social interaction depends on communicating on many levels. Some victims seem to communicate quite well, but in reality, they have become wonderful actors. They pretend that they are happy and present a front of normalcy when they are hiding "terrible secrets" inside. "I play-act my entire day until I am home and can lapse back into the behavior that I've known for so long as me," one woman wrote to me.

"I have been able to keep my behavior hidden from my family, which, in the end, only makes the situation that much more agonizing," another one wrote. "My guilt is intolerable. . . . I do my best to appear well. I have become too good an actress, but I know it cannot last."

For the most part, acute patients can no longer hide the intensity of their preoccupation with food or their lack of self-image. Most often, they isolate themselves from anyone who does not understand their predicament including friends, family members, and society in general. "For the longest time, I didn't care if anyone knew about my problem," one woman wrote. "In fact, I was even able to help a few people because of my openness and knowledge about it. But recently, I've lapsed back into hiding."

Patients with eating disorders know they cannot be normal, and as their condition progresses, they become more lonely and separated from their support systems. One young woman wrote, "I feel as though I am not a very pleasant person to be around. I am ashamed of who I am and what I have become! Ugly, fat, selfish, guilty, and an unfriendly personality. *Unlovable*. An overall *misfit*."

A thirty-eight-year-old woman battling anorexia for twenty-six years wrote, "The past 13 years have been my worst. I have no friends. (I have never experienced a close personal relationship with another human being outside my family.) I reside with my parents in their home, and essentially exist in a surreal state of apathetic anonymity."

Their habits become abnormal including the excessive hours devoted to exercise and food preparation, the odd mealtimes, and the frequent trips to stores for laxatives and/or diuretics. The whole focus of their lives becomes the illness.

Moreover, the more friends and supporters victims have, the more likely they are to be detected. The Negative Mind will not allow that. Detection goes against its instruction. It demands isolation to protect its secret. A recovered young boy wrote, "I was withdrawn and isolated from my family and society; I couldn't trust people and was terrified of life and people. I felt completely unworthy of love and friendship because I was a failure as a person and could never be good enough or live up to the unrealistically high expectations I placed on myself and that I perceived were placed on me by others."

"This whole thing has been so hard for my friends to observe that I have pushed them all away," another young person wrote. "My family does not understand what is happening to me and they do not know how or what to do to help me. I have alienated everyone around me. Therefore, I am all alone and going crazy."

And an acute patient in the early stages of recovery at our clinic wrote in her journal, "My family came up to see me a few times over the weekend. I don't like seeing them at all. I wish everybody, my family, friends, and everybody else that knows me would just leave me alone. Let me live the way the ANOREXIA has driven me, towards HELL!"

A distraught father wrote, "Caroline is dying now as she said she had planned to do all along. I live in Miami and Caroline lives somewhere in Colorado. I don't have her address or phone number. She had been living with a man but she got so bad she had to move out. . . . Her boyfriend doesn't even know where she lives now."

If acutely ill victims do find "friends," they often come from therapy groups. Misery loves company. These friends often compare notes with one another. Commiseration is an important concept. This is not a situation in which girlfriends get together to talk about boyfriends or compare prom dresses.

Alexandra had been in eating disorder programs and in hospitals for five years and had amassed seventeen like-minded friends. Immediately before her arrival at our clinic, the entire group had conspired to conceal themselves in the attic of one of their homes so they could all waste away together. Fortunately, Alexandra dropped clues that enabled her parents to intervene.

In the acute stage, victims become asexual beings for biological and psychological reasons. The same biochemical imbalance that halts menstruation also impacts sex drive. By the same token, the Negative Mind shuns any close relationship because it might provide a helpmate. Intimacy with parents and loved ones is the first to go. Moreover, victims feel disgusted by their bodies and are not allowed to give themselves the pleasure of an intimate relationship.

Victims stay in school until they collapse, but they do not participate in social life there. They use studying as an isolating strategy. Recall the young girl whose journal I quoted in Chapter 3. She ran track before and after school and did homework during her lunch break and studied until 2 A.M. In her quest for "perfection," what time did she leave herself for socializing with such a relentless schedule?

Finally, unlike cancer or AIDS patients, acute victims do not have a constituency of support precisely due to the social isolation their condition engenders.

FEEDING THE BODY BUT NOT THE SOUL

The feeding phases of existing traditional intervention methods can provide relief for the moment. Patients are temporarily *physically* healthier. Their weight gain has assuaged their parents' anxiety, as well as their body's physical pains. But the internal mental pain never ceases and with feeding, it can become intensified because the Negative Mind insists on weight loss.

One young man wrote to me about his dilemma. "I have been struggling with anorexia for 4 years. I am 16 years old. I have been hospitalized 8 times in the last twenty months. It is just so hard because I have gained 43 pounds in one year, but the program that I'm in is doing nothing for all the terrible things that go on inside of me—what I call 'The Angels and The Devils' inside. . . . I just can't talk to my doctor. I feel he doesn't have a clue what I'm going through. Everything is centered around weight gain and I never get a chance to talk about what's really wrong with me."

When the origin of the condition, the CNC, is not corrected, feeding programs will fail and the disorder will persist. In Part II, we will look at how one can effectively address CNC and the Negative Mind so that these sensitive and giving, yet afflicted, individuals are no longer held hostage to this insidious condition.

PART II

Addressing the Negative Mind

5

Reversing
the Negative Mind

The Negative Mind is nasty and uncouth and is the antithesis of the gentle nature of the Actual Mind. Alarming in
the shocking, base language it uses, it holds the patient in helpless horror at its effectiveness in alienating others.

Imagine that we are engaged in the highest level chess game
with this parasitic mindset. The Negative Mind will use every
trick, every gambit to gain the advantage and destroy its victim,
prompting her to starve or otherwise harm herself, to undermine
treatment, to shun all help and affection, to hurt and drive away
loved ones with offensive and bizarre behavior. It serves to be
two moves ahead of the Negative Mind, aware of all of its possible countermoves.

Very rarely does the acute patient speak for herself. Her Negative Mind is always conniving methods for mayhem and will do
almost anything to achieve the demise of the Actual Mind unless
we prevent it from doing so. Thus, as the Negative Mind pro-
ceeds with deceit and deception, so must we find ways to fool it
into loosening its grasp on its victim.

Clearly, there is no shortcut to reversing this condition. This
is truly a challenge for the patient, her loved ones, and those
charged with her psychological and medical care. Yet there are
some principles and strategies that we have found not only helpful but highly effective in subduing the Negative Mind and

bringing about the reinterpretation of the patient's identity and healing. I would like to share these with you in this chapter.

As you read, remember that though this condition is painstaking to work through, it is reversible. The difficulty notwithstanding, if the patient has the courage to undergo the process, how can we deny her our support?

RECOGNIZE THAT THE
PATIENT IS DESPERATE FOR HELP

Since the eating disorder neither knows logic nor entertains reason, it would seem remarkable that any person afflicted with it would be unable to outsmart it. The victim's Actual Mind wants help, or she would not search for it relentlessly.

It is easy to detect the split between despondence and hope in the letters we receive: "I want to go back to work, get my own apartment, and be a responsible human being that works hard and doesn't rely or need other people to take care of me. I'm doing nothing except sitting around getting in everyone's way and getting fatter and fatter. Suicide is looking better and better. . . . I am desperate for help and would appreciate any suggestions."

Another victim wrote, "I am now convinced that nothing will help. It seems there is no 'cure' for someone as damaged/ broken as I am. Try as I might, I cannot stop this horrible binge-purge cycle. It controls my life. I find it difficult, if not impossible, to hold a job, go to school, or commit to a meaningful relationship. My life has been on hold for the last 14 years! I am desperate. If I don't get some help, I will die. Please help me."

In the same breath—my case is hopeless; please help me. I want to kill myself; I want to be independent and productive like everyone else.

Sadly, victims find it difficult to reach out; they gather more courage to do so when they know that others are speaking their secret language. Therefore, we must be attuned to their muted cries for help if they are to be rescued.

SEPARATE THE CONDITION
FROM THE PATIENT

In dealing with a person who has an eating disorder, we must be constantly aware of the dual mindset. It is essential to separate a victim from her condition, placing anorexia or bulimia on one side and the individual's uniqueness on the other. We do this so the person understands that the illness is not who she is, but merely an imposition, a parasite she is hosting.

The victim is not anorexia or bulimia, but because of the relentlessness of the Negative Mind, she may believe that she is. She may abuse, degrade, or mutilate herself, or alienate others because the Negative Mind orders her to do so.

To help the acute anorexic, we must recognize the negative mindset and create an alliance with the victim against it. At the clinic we use several techniques to separate the condition from the patient. If her behavior seems abusive or bizarre, we might say, "Honey, I know you didn't mean that; it was your head talking" or "I know your head is giving you a rough time. It is making you do this."

Patients may respond, "But it is so hard. The voices are so mean. I am so embarrassed" or, through tears, "I don't know why that happened. I would never hurt anybody's feelings." We also ask patients to paint pictures of their condition (see Chapter 4) and to write down what the Negative Mind says. Here is one young woman's Negative Mind in action: "No one can help you because you're psycho, and no one can deal with you. You're not worth it anyway. Everyone HATES you; you only cause trouble. There's nothing you can do right. Things will never work out for you. You'll ALWAYS be miserable. Everyone knows you're shallow and two-faced. Even strangers HATE you. You make the world miserable. You should burn in hell. You're not the victim, you're the evil one."

Another acute patient begged her Negative Mind to leave her alone: "I need to be loved by my own being. Please do not punish me for the years that I was so destructive. Please! Let me live and be happy with myself and my body. Don't hurt me any-more!!!!" And then she wrote, "I hate you to the ends of the earth. Anorexia leave me alone, surrender. You are the enemy and there is no place for you in my life."

As a part of their treatment, we also ask the patients to write what the Negative Mind ("Condition") tells them in one column of a steno pad and the response of the Actual Mind ("Me") in the second column. This is so they can identify the negativity more clearly and therefore fight against it. It follows then that given that the Actual Mind is logic, they use it to question nega-tive comments and reason themselves away from them. This strengthens the Actual Mind.

Here is an example of Mindy's dialogue with her Negative Mind. Since she was still in the very early stages of recovery, her Negative Mind had much more to say to her than did her Actual Mind:

CONDITION	ME
• Don't buy it! She is only trying to get you fatter. What makes you think she is any different than anyone else? Why would she? What do you have to offer anyone—only ugliness and boredom. Look at you—disgusting, selfish pig. You eat all day every day—Such a loser.	• I have to trust someone. Why would she want me fat? What is it to her? How can she benefit? I want to believe she cares.
• I don't deserve to be helped. I can never do anything right. Nobody could possibly care	• I'm not going to listen to you. You are nothing but cruel all day long, every day.

CONDITION	ME
about me. I am demanding and selfish and mean.	
• I shouldn't be here. I shouldn't eat.	
• I don't choose to be here. I am alone and should isolate myself from people around me. I am too fat.	• I have no control over that. Peggy promised me she wouldn't make me fat. He will be with me forever and no one can make him go away. I should live like this forever. Why won't he fuck off and leave me alone? Peggy said it would. In time it will.
• I am a bad person because I can't fight him myself. I can't believe in people here and shouldn't trust them. Why can other people believe and I can't? I wish I could believe. I ruined my family's life. I have to do everything he says or he will punish me. Peggy and the other people here say he can't do those things that he says. Why won't people give up on me?	

Mark's journal in the acute phase of his illness is a typical expression of the relentless negativism of the condition badgering the victim.

CONDITION	ME
• Embarrassing—she must really be grossed out looking at you work out. Feel like such a nerd. Wish you looked normal— Eyes down, don't look around. Hate rooms—so embarrassing and feel so sick. So inept at sports. He must really laugh at	

CONDITION	ME
you. Wish you could play like him, and be so in proportion. You're awful. That cloud is shaped just like you; totally out of proportion. The careworker is lying. He's just trying to be nice. Fat. Ugly. So disgusting; look almost pregnant.	
• You're such a pain, such a freeloader. You're a burden. Everyone hates you. You're useless. They are pushing you too much; won't let up. They want too much; you weigh enough. Don't let them make you do it. Too many choices, too many types. Too much in the basket—return some—return it all. Leave. Go home. You don't belong here. Those people are staring; your shirt is too damn tight and you're grossing them out. Hurry and get this over with and leave. The careworker must think you're a real idiot—a real nerd. Sweating like crazy. Even getting dizzy, you idiot—stop breathing. Put the basket down and leave. Do it tomorrow.	• It's just his job. He needs to keep you safe.
• You're bothering all the other exercisers. You're never thinking of others. You're a jerk. You're so unsociable, so boring and self-centered. They must all laugh at you when you	• Don't think about it—close it all out. Don't panic. Calm down. Peggy won't lie to you and you need all this stuff. Just keep going and leave. Trust.

CONDITION	ME
leave. They must think you're such a nerd. Why can't you be normal?	
• You were really stupid talking to that lady/mother on the phone. You should have been more professional and less excited. She likely thought you were a salesman of all things. You likely scared her off. Peggy will have to do damage control, thanks to you.	• Calm down. Ignore all that.
• That earring lady looks at you as if you're nuts. What's she thinking? Must really be disgusted. Why doesn't she look at the careworker like that? Stop. Do it here. Don't drag him back to the first store. They won't hurt you. You shouldn't have put in that earring. You're so vain. It was a dumb idea. Rip it out. It makes you look even worse. You're so ugly, such an idiot. Why did you do it? So huge. So bloated and out of proportion. Must be the food. Three hot dogs. Good grief. You've said something wrong. You never think before opening your mouth. Better shut up or you'll screw up again. Wish you'd watch your big fat mouth.	• Mom and Dad might freak, but it's done!
• Nothing fits. Nothing covers you enough. You must be	• Apologize; say sorry. It might help.

CONDITION	ME

gaining. You must be. Should be being useful, should be doing more. You don't fit in here. Everyone knows what a bore you are. What a jerk. You shouldn't have had so much protein; you did nothing all day and remember what you looked like this morning. This will just make it worse. Ask to go to the end of the beach; this isn't far enough. Go up the road and back; don't stop walking; it's not long enough. Too much food the rest of the day still. What if it rains and you can't get out? You're boring the careworker. If you weren't such a pain he could be with someone else, having fun instead. So ashamed and embarrassed. You are so ugly. Pray he isn't grossed out.

- Too much food, so many people. So busy. Leave. Get out of here. Must get out of here. Too many people running around, too many types of yogurt and tofu. You idiot. You're such a pig. Such a fat, ugly, boring pig. They must be shocked that you eat so much. How could you? Damn you. So ull, so afraid. Imagine how the fat will pile up. No one eats three hot dogs. Crazy. You fat pig.

- Don't worry. You don't want to lose weight. Have to try harder. Trust and eat more. It's okay. Be patient.

CONDITION	ME
• You are such a jerk. Why didn't you phone him? Now the careworker called you—exactly opposite. Can't believe you—you should have phoned and left a message—he must think you're an inconsiderate, uncaring idiot. You are. Why'd you wait? Even a message. Damn you. Could have eaten later—no rush. Too much food. Won't go away, won't leave. You never see the other careworkers anymore. Should keep your mouth shut, as if you should be talking. Look at you.	• He wanted to call you. It's OK. He really does want to talk to you.
• Imagine how everyone feels about you. They are stuck with you. They have no say. And neither should you. You're a jerk. No one wants to be with you. They're so uncomfortable and uneasy. You never say anything right—you just upset people. And here you are, ruining everyone else's prospects and future—who are you to talk? Hypocrite. You're complaining of others when you are no better. He's trying so hard. It's impossible for anyone to like you. You shouldn't criticize him. You've ruined everything. At least he was friendly, and happy and interesting and caring. Look	• Wow! They said "I hope you're not planning on leaving soon!!" Wow—they even meant it! Right on!!!

CONDITION	ME
what he must think of you. He's stuck with you. He has no choice. You are no-good, useless, inept.	
• That clerk is staring. Better not get the pants. He knows you'd look ridiculous in them. Besides, you don't deserve them. And they don't fit you. You can't wear them. Why can't you be normal? Damn you.	• No one notices. You're too self-conscious.
• Forgot to thank Peggy for the chest, you jerk. She must really think you're an inconsiderate, unthankful idiot. Why can't you remember simple things. Where's your brain?	
• Those people are wondering why you're in McDonald's and not having anything. As if you should. That burger is huge; imagine the calories in that. And he's in charge of telling you what's appropriate sizes? Look how huge that is; it's enormous. Afraid you'll gain weight like crazy if you listen to his ideas of food amounts. You are such a pig, such a fat ugly pig. Why did you eat that hot dog—that was so stupid. You totally overate. The care-worker must be the one that's wrong. He's the one who ate at McDonald's without any guilt.	• This burger is not going to make you fat. It will be okay. Trust. No one will let you get fat. Hey—maybe you really are getting somewhere.

CONDITION	ME
• The careworker must think you're a real idiot. You should act your age for once. People will discover what you're truly like and you will lose everything. It will all disappear and you will be lonely again. You'll lose everything.	
• I wish I was normal. Wish I was less boring and looked better. You're such a nerd. You act so stupid.	• Trust Peggy. She doesn't lie.
• You idiot—you jerk. The careworker's going to kill you. How could you say such a stupid, insensitive thing. Why don't you think before you open you mouth. So embarrassing. He's going to think you're a real jerk. He's going to be upset when he hears your message. Explain what you really meant. You should never have called him. That was stupid. Your mouth is always spewing off and insulting and hurting. He'll be really shocked. How could you have said it that way? You're forever getting flustered on the phone and when you talk to people— damn you. I hate you I hate you. I hate you so much—go to hell. You never think of anyone but yourself. He'll wonder how you could have	• Call him back and leave a message to clarify what you said. Simple as that.

CONDITION	ME
said it. He'll know what a jerk you are. He'll stop wanting to work with you and be quiet and more curt when you're around.	
• Go to bed. Go straight to bed. Forget it. Ate too much today and you're fat enough as it is. No more food. Just sleep and start a new day tomorrow. Don't eat any more today. Keep eating so much and it will get worse. Just call it a night.	• No, don't use this as an excuse. Just one hour. Stay up and try to finish. Ignore how you look; it's all in your head. Eat one more thing. It's okay—you can handle it. Trust Peggy and try hard.
• You're not important enough to have so many sessions. She's bored with you. You're wearing her out like all the other doctors. You aren't working hard enough. She doesn't really like you—she's pawning you off on someone else. You're not worth her time. She isn't so eager to be with you; you're boring.	• Give it a break. She's very busy. The other counselor is excellent and you are so much better. She knows what she's doing. It's really only one less session per week. She likely feels you can handle things on your own more.
• Look at you. You're huge. Peggy's lying to you. You're the ugliest, most revolting thing. You're eating too much.	• Trust Peggy. You've got to. It's your eyes.
• Oh hell, way to go, you idiot. You forgot about the meeting. You never even thought. They must have been upset. Where was your brain? Only thinking of yourself.	• Okay, so you forgot. Apologize tomorrow—it wasn't on purpose.

CONDITION	ME
• You look so disgusting, so revolting. Find something else to wear. Don't wear that shirt. Cover up more. Gross. Peggy must be wrong. There's no way you can look like this.	

As the patient moves further along toward her recovery, the Actual Mind becomes stronger and more adept in its arguments against the Negative Mind. The following is Darlene's journal:

CONDITION	ME
• No one cares about you. • Dying is a welcome prospect. • You will always fail. • You don't deserve good things.	• People love you. • Life in its true form is worth living, • Life has ups and downs. • You deserve goodness.

Faith's journal shows the progress she has made. As her Actual Mind engages in logical discussion, it is clear that she now has vision toward her eventual recovery:

CONDITION	ME
• My body is too big. A lot of it is probably fat. The more I look at it, the more disgusted I get.	• I have been told time and time again that my eyes aren't seeing things the way they really are. I am looking at my body through the eyes of anorexia so therefore I cannot rely on my own perception. Instead, I have to trust in what Treena has told me which is: My weight is at low normal.

CONDITION	ME
	I am not "too big." I more or less look like a teenager rather than a 21-year-old woman.
• I am bigger than all the other girls at the house. Most of them are allowed to maintain an anorexic weight and they don't have, as I do, to accept their body at such a high level.	• Once again, my perception of the others I'm comparing with isn't very accurate. I always look for things and, of course, I'm going to find them one way or the other. It's a very twisted game in which I can never "win." But mostly, it doesn't matter what weight anybody else is at because I'm me and they're them. That's the bottom line. I can strive all my life to be like this person or that person. All that's going to do is take away from my own self. It doesn't accomplish anything! I want to do something with my life, not let it go by, wasting my time envying everybody else.
• I have gained a lot of weight since I've been put back on a food plan. It's also been a very, very fast process. Probably only 2 weeks to dump at least 10 pounds on me. . . .	• I really have no way of knowing numbers as facts. I may feel as though I've just been fattened up big time but I have to remember that my feelings are strongly influenced by the condition at times. Trust is really the key. . . . I've been promised that I will be comfortable with my body in the end. . . .

Paula's journal indicates that as she progresses through treatment, her negative thoughts become less specific, more diffuse and ineffectual. She also gains enough objectivity to notice the changes, strengthening her resolve to move ahead.

CONDITION	ME
• obese	• probably not
• something is wrong with my body	• trust counselor
• i am gaining too much weight too fast	• trust counselor
• i am a bother	
• i am a mean nuisance	• anorexia is mean
• i am being punished and i deserve it	• no one deserves anorexia
• i look pregnant	
• i am so swollen my legs are going to explode	
• i am a failure	
• There is nothing good about me	
• i have no talent	
• i have no worth	
• i am an embarrassment to my family	• they love me unconditionally
———	———
• no worth	
• no talent	
• i am crazy	
• i hate me	
• i am ugly	
• i can't do it	• i don't have to; Montreux can do it.
• i am too disgusting to be hugged	
• i am an evil sinner	• anorexia is evil

CONDITION	ME
• i am doing better than i deserve	
• i am too fat to be here	• it doesn't matter if i think that i am too fat to be here because i am committed to be here until i get better
• i am a bother	• i am supposed to ask for help. It is part of complying with the program
• i can't do it	• i do not have to do it. i just have to trust Montreux and let them do it.
• intake is my choice	• intake is not my option. i am being good by trusting and complying.
• i am bad	
• i feel guilty for asking for help and bothering my workers	• it is my job to ask for help; it is part of the program.

The voice has shifted. It used to torment me with very negative, specific thoughts, but now it is just a mass of negative confusion in my head. Instead of a voice it is more like a resounding gong or a clanging cymbal. Before, I could combat a negative thought with a positive one by telling my careworker what it was saying and having them respond. Now, however, there is nothing specific to combat.

CONDITION	ME
• i can't do it; it is too hard	• i am supposed to be here. It is part of a bigger plan. i will stay as long as it takes. This pain is nothing compared to what the past few years have been. I will have my life again.
• i am scared	• anorexia is scared

CONDITION	ME
• i do not deserve a happy life	• i hate anorexia and want to have a happy life. i want to be able to go out to eat and enjoy life.
• i will always hate myself	• i cannot finish the program and still hate myself. When I get through the program I will like myself. Liking myself is part of the program
• Something is horribly wrong	• Trust counselors
• i am miserable	• this bad feeling will go away. Everyone goes through it. The others made it.

THE NUMBERS GAME

Given that the Negative Mind uses all it can against the victim, we must be aware of the material that we present it. One of the best ways of offsetting the Negative Mind is to refuse to play the numbers game in order to weaken its effect.

For instance, hospitalized anorexia patients have often been told their weight and threatened with having to maintain a target weight. To the Negative Mind, this will translate as a weight to reach, albeit reluctantly, in order to effect release from the hospital. Once on its own, the Negative Mind will have free rein once more and will command its victim to stop eating. I believe this is one of the reasons why recidivism is so high among anorexic patients soon after hospital release!

Many patients hospitalized in traditional programs refer to gaining weight temporarily to appease their doctors and therapists as "playing the game." One of my patients called her hospital weight-gain program "Anorexia University."

Scales can also give the Negative Mind a number to use

against its victim. Usually, it commands her to weigh less than the weight recorded each day. However, denied that number, the Negative Mind has less clout and nothing to go on. Its threats become, of necessity, more scattered and obscure—and less effective. Faith's response, for instance, that she has no way of "knowing any numbers as facts" when her Negative Mind asserted that she had gained ten pounds, underscores how this can be helpful. Unawareness of her weight gives the victim some protection from the Negative Mind's hectoring.

It is for this reason that at the clinic, we weigh our patients backward. They are never told how much they weigh (the number is simply noted silently on their charts), nor are they given a "target weight" to achieve to obtain release.

FOOD STRATEGIES

Another way of circumventing the Negative Mind is to present food in a way that is not as fear-inducing to the patients. Small nutritious meals or snacks presented six times a day serve the mind and body well without grievously offending the patient.

Smaller portions at one sitting are less threatening than three large meals a day. If the patient finishes a meal and stops eating before she feels full, she is less inclined to feel the need to purge or exercise. We are aiming for a slow, steady process that encourages gradual weight gain for physical safety and physiological balance. Force-feeding huge quantities of calories to a patient with an eating disorder is extremely unkind. Ultimately such a strategy is counterproductive and physiologically dangerous. It is gentler to body and soul to encourage slow, safe weight gain that allows the patient dignity and time to adjust emotionally.

Giving the patient her own individual plates and dishes, provided for her on coming into care, makes her realize she is not a number and gives her confidence and structure. Indeed, even the style and color of dishes are important in that they indicate respect of individuality and consistency—cardinal principles of the Montreux program. Every day she will eat from the same dishes until she no longer feels the need to focus on any of the utensils she uses. This is another marker of her recovery for at that point, food will no longer be the center of her life.

In the acute patient, feeding has to be justified often mineral by mineral, vitamin by vitamin until the Actual Mind subsumes the Negative Mind. Sometimes for the satisfaction of the patient we have to analyze and explain the reason for eating almost every bite.

"Why am I eating a banana, Peggy?" I am asked. "Why should I eat papaya? Why are they giving me yogurt?"

"Bananas have potassium to keep your heart strong," I reply. "Yogurt has the calcium to keep your bones from deteriorating, and papaya has enzymes to help your digestive system." Everything must be justified.

COUNTERACTING THE NEGATIVE CHATTER
WITH UNCONDITIONAL LOVE

Through the whole term of recovery, eating disorder patients will spew negative chatter. Their heads are full of it. It is a decided challenge, therefore, for anyone to contend with. Nevertheless, we answer every negative thought with a positive one. It is essential to respond to every self-defeating outburst with unconditional gentleness and kindness. We offset every subjective comment with an objective one.

If the patient says, "I'm worthless; don't bother with me. How could you even want me here anyway? I should give my bed to someone more deserving," we will respond, "You're very valuable to us and the world. There is a wonderful person inside you who is going to come out when the negativity is gone. You are deserving of all the care you get."

Or if a patient says, "I've just eaten. My mother is going to die," she receives the response: "Honey, that's just your head talking to you. Your fear has no basis in reality. No one is going to die. What has your eating to do with your mother except to make her happy?"

At the clinic we are firm believers in the benefits of unconditional love, and so we build an environment of unqualified support, responding to each patient with terms of endearment. Given that the patient is at the mercy of an onslaught of unrelenting negativity, showering the patient with unconditional love is necessary to create balance. Unconditional love counteracts the harsh voice of the Negative Mind as it teases out the possibility of reconnecting with the Actual Mind. It lures the Actual Mind into a place of comparison of stark opposites: the punishment of the Negative Mind and the caringness of unconditional love. The victim eventually allows the unconditional love because it feels so much better and is certainly more conducive to healthy living.

If a patient can goad a careworker to frustration, the Negative Mind has won. The careworker has "proven" to his subjective patient that his caring is conditional. The patient in the acute stage will brood and pout and the careworker will have a difficult time proving himself truly caring. The careworker must then be removed from the case since the trust so critical to the healing process will have been destroyed. Remember, the Negative Mind hunts to confirm that the Actual Mind is useless.

Moreover, given that the CNC victim has highly developed receptors for everyone else's problems, we at the clinic must always appear calm and unruffled to the patient. Caregivers studiously avoid involving the patient in their own personal dramas. Of course, this can be very taxing to caregivers; they aren't permitted the usual ups and downs, hardly a normal existence. But we are dealing with an unrealistic mindset here which is so extreme that we must be as extreme in the opposite direction. Remember, as well, that the Negative Mind dominates only in the first two stages of therapy before the patient begins to achieve mental balance.

KEEPING SAFE BOUNDARIES

The CNC victim may continually test her boundaries to ensure her own safety. We find it mandatory, therefore, to stay close to the acute patient at all times. This is one of the reasons that we have such a high ratio of careworkers per patient (one to one or higher around the clock), especially during the early phases of treatment. The careworker's responsibility is to "shadow" the patient from the time she comes into twenty-four-hour residential care to the time she leaves it and moves into partial care.

The carefully trained careworker provides unconditional support, caring, and a normal perspective to enable the patient to feel secure. Until she indicates a true belief in herself and begins to wish some independence, the patient will use this positive shadow as a reference point. Should she need to talk about her feelings, to have an explanation and interpretation of her internal dialogue, the careworker will be ever-present.

Careworkers prevent the Negative Mind from manifesting by gentle talking, being with the patients, and impeding them from exercise or any other destructive behaviors. They accompany patients on walks and keep a constant vigil beside their beds through the night. Such faithful attention is necessary because if a patient is able to fool a caregiver and manage to hide food or do anything counterindicative of care such as exercising, vomiting, using or securing laxatives, or even cutting herself, she will see the care as inadequate, feel unsafe, and become increasingly anxious.

Also anorexics are poor sleepers, and it is often comforting for them to find someone at their side with whom they can converse in the middle of the night.

Safe boundaries are imperative for healing. One patient came to us after hospital authorities had allowed him to vomit for one hour each day and to exercise for one and a half hours. As a consequence, his condition did not improve and the victim realized more markedly his aloneness. How could he put his faith in therapists who brokered compromises with his Negative Mind?

When caregivers bargain with the Negative Mind, the victim is always the loser. She feels misunderstood and helpless. In fact, any compromise strengthens the Negative Mind's position and weakens the victim. Even in an ideal situation, the battle to support the victim is a constant struggle. Given that in acute anorexia, the victim always believes she is wrong in her own mind, surrendering to the Negative Mind only reinforces those beliefs.

As other safety precautions, at the clinic, we also keep kitchen knives locked away; no razors are allowed in the bathroom. We keep vitamins and medicine locked up so they cannot be abused.

As I'll explain more fully in the next chapter, when a patient has enough focus and concentration to be able to sit through a session, usually in the middle of the initial stage, she will begin receiving counseling three or four times a week from one of three levels of counselors.

DISTRACTION

The goal of distraction is to keep a victim's attention external, to prevent her from disappearing inside her Negative Mind. Eating is such a frightening time for anorexics, because the Negative Mind will come out in force. Immediately after meals, victims will often feel extremely anxious. This is when distraction is most essential.

At the clinic we have found anything that encourages external focus and concentration, that keeps the person in the present, can be helpful. We use lively conversation, board games, pool, Ping-Pong, humor, art, writing, studying foreign languages, and other educational outlets. However, watching TV can allow a person to "zone out" and give the Negative Mind an opening for silent abuse.

The first twenty minutes after feeding is generally the most difficult for the patient and she may become agitated. A skilled careworker takes it upon herself to go to extremes to entertain the patient because diversion through laughter really proves to be the best medicine.

Distracting questions give the Actual Mind another focus to reclaim the patient's attention. The Negative Mind has no way to process information that cannot be used to demean the victim. This can give the careworker the advantage for the moment.

ROCKING AND TOUCHING

Sometimes words are inadequate to express the depth of our caring. When we see a crying baby, our first instinct is to pick him up and cuddle him. When we see a wounded animal, we want to cradle it.

Children with eating disorders are wounded and extremely frightened. I think there is great therapeutic value in giving in to our natural impulse to soothe them with healing words and touch.

On several occasions, I have spoken to nurses in wards for children with eating disorders. The first thing I ask them is whether they have a rocking chair. Then I will say, "Is it possible for you to hold that child in your lap and rock her?" The sufferers need the comfort and security to offset the terror of their mental state.

At the clinic, we try to find the connection that works for each patient. If it is not rocking, it can be sitting by the bedside, talking in a gentle tone. The words themselves may not even be that important, but the attitude is. We also take patients to massage therapists. One mother told me she would rub her daughter's back. The child obviously enjoyed it but told her, "Please stop doing that because I like it."

Remember that though the victim is an intellectual prize, her emotional maturity has been arrested at an earlier stage. She is in constant need of the reassurance and comfort we would naturally offer a young child.

WORKING WITH TRANCES

At the clinic, careworkers recognize the signs of a patient beginning to go into a trance and will call a counselor to attempt to prevent it. Anyone attending a victim in a trance must display absolute confidence in his or her ability to retrieve the Actual Mind from the clutches of the Negative Mind. The Negative Mind will seize upon any hesitancy or doubt betrayed by caregivers and use it to prolong its absolute hold over the patient.

As soon as we realize that a patient is in a trance, we sit on the floor or a chair, and gathering her into our arms, we rock her while holding her tightly. We speak soothingly, encouragingly, saying, "We can do this. Anorexia is very frightened of us. He is nothing but a bully in the schoolyard. Even though he feels real, he is not. He is just a construct in your mind. We are much stronger than he is. You can come out now; it is safe. He will never win with us here."

If we ask a patient, "How much of you is here with us?" the initial response will be muffled and barely audible. Persistence on the part of caregivers, albeit extremely gentle persistence, will most often strengthen the Actual Mind and bring the patient back. Indeed, the level of preoccupation and the length of time it takes the acute patient to answer can indicate the degree of control the Negative Mind exerts.

We have also found that distraction is quite helpful when a patient is in a trance. If we ask her distracting and diversionary questions such as, "How is your dog doing today?" or "What is the weather like?" we can often bring her back quickly. We are giving her Actual Mind tools to circumvent the power of the Negative Mind because she feels she cannot tackle it directly. A question about one's dog, for instance, is neutral territory. The Negative Mind is not anticipating us to come back with such a question. Usually it would expect a query about well-being or food. The caregiver may need to repeat a question gently three times or more because the patient is so internally preoccupied.

Usually there are a few other people nearby, gently stroking the patient's forehead with a cool cloth, comforting her with terms of endearment and encouragement. How long it takes to bring a patient out of a trance depends on her sense of trust in her careworkers' words. It is unwise to let her stay in the trance, because the Negative Mind is given more time and jurisdiction.

Gradually the patient's eyelashes will begin to flutter, indicating that she is beginning to come back to consciousness. We make statements such as, "See, your eyes are starting to flutter. We see you are coming back. You are starting to see us right now. It's all right." As the patient comes out of the trance, she usually breaks down, sobbing uncontrollably, holding on to her careworker tightly, repeating any number of things that she has been instructed by the messages holding her hostage.

Usually extra staff members stay with a patient for a good half hour after she has "come back." Following much more reassurance and soothing talk, we put the moment into perspective for the patient. We tell her, "You were in a trance. You're safe and it's over."

Apparently patients are usually aware of the fact that they have been in a trance. They felt themselves slipping into it. They will then tell us what the voices told them to do: "I'm supposed to run outside in front of a truck. I don't want to be killed." We always then attempt to distract them. Only after we are certain that they are completely stabilized will we give them a change of scenery, usually by having them go arm in arm with two careworkers outside to the garden or to some other pleasing, distracting place. They are in a fragile state at this point; it is never wise to allow such a patient to go anywhere unaccompanied because she needs to feel protected and secure.

STAYING TWO MOVES AHEAD

In this dangerous chess game, caregivers must always be two moves ahead of the Negative Mind because the Negative Mind is always two moves ahead of the patient's Actual Mind.

One of our most useful tools is to hunt for ulterior motives in our patient's behavior. If a victim says, "It's a beautiful evening. I love walking in the rain. Would it be all right to go out for an hour or so?" we must question her motives.

And so we would ask, "Who wants to go for a walk, you or anorexia?"

Frequently the child replies, "Actually, anorexia does. I don't like the rain at all. It's wet and dreary."

In understanding the child's motivation, we are creating an alliance with the Actual Mind. She then realizes that the battle is not hers alone to fight.

But immediately thereafter, we must create a distraction so the Negative Mind does not "beat up" the patient. In that distraction, we are confirming the patient's security with us. She knows we can see past the outward behavior. That strengthens her trust and moves her ahead. She does not have to take the responsibility for making the decision.

If we had allowed her to go on that walk without questioning her motivation, on the other hand, she would have felt despondent that nobody had recognized she did not want to walk in the first place. Her Negative Mind was ordering her to exercise.

By staying two steps ahead of the Negative Mind we create a sense of security and deep trust on the part of the patient.

CHALLENGING THE SUBJECTIVITY

At the clinic, once a patient is no longer acutely ill and has a better grasp of reality (see Chapter 6), counseling that focuses on reversing the subjectivity of the Negative Mind helps her begin to put her life into a more tenable perspective. We are constantly challenging the subjective in order to do what we call Objectivity Training.

For instance, if patient Patty's mother seems highly emotional, Patty's subjective response would have been to take responsibility for her mother's moods. In counseling sessions, we might point out, "Your mother says she's very unhappy and you believed you caused that, but it's your mom's issue. You didn't cause her unhappiness." We explain that perception is not always reality and gently guide the patient to step outside the situation and see it as an objective observer.

In response, Patty might respond, "I always thought the divorce was my fault, but now I understand that my mom has her own problems."

Because the patient is subjective in so many areas of her life, this Objectivity Training becomes an ongoing part of treatment.

We also use role-playing situations to reinforce objectivity. We break down situations for the patient to analyze and carry out mini-dramas. One patient will voice the perspective of the subjective mind while another will speak for objectivity:

> THE FACTS: Your brother is ill with cancer.
> THE SUBJECTIVE RESPONSE: "It's all my fault. If only I had done more for him, if only I were a better person, I would have spared him this pain and suffering."
> THE OBJECTIVE RESPONSE: "Cancer is a terrible illness. No one is sure why some people get it and others don't. Heredity and environment are most likely to blame. I love my brother and will do everything in my power to help him, but I didn't cause this disease and I am not responsible for curing it. I'm only responsible for loving him and being there for him as much as I can."

> THE FACTS: Your mother has depression.
> THE SUBJECTIVE RESPONSE: "She's depressed be-

cause I've disappointed her. I've got to pull her out of it. I'm to blame."

THE OBJECTIVE RESPONSE: "Depression is a clinical diagnosis and requires professional help. Mom, Dad, and other adults have to get her the help she needs. Mom's depression has made her respond inappropriately to me. That's not my fault. If Mom can't get her depression under control, we'll have to adapt, but it's not my responsibility."

We often do role playing with situations drawn from typical family or school interactions.

THE FACTS: Father comes home tired and agitated from work. Hannah asks him if he would go over some homework and he snaps, "I've got too much on my mind now."

THE SUBJECTIVE RESPONSE: "My father doesn't like me. I knew I shouldn't have asked him for help. I never will again."

THE OBJECTIVE RESPONSE: "Poor Dad. He's had a hard day and he's tired. I should have waited till later. Now I'll get him a cup of tea and maybe I can ask him again later when he's more relaxed."

We act out many situations such as these to help patients understand the difference between their subjective reality and objective reality.

THE PARENTS' ROLE

Often, in our modern psychological world, patients are taught to blame or find reason for their disorder in other people's failures. This can prove counterproductive to the person with an eating disorder in the long run. It may teach her to not see herself objectively and this may prevent her from forming a too compassionate perspective on life.

As I've said, blaming parents for the condition might also cut off the sufferer's essential support. A parent will always be a parent and ideally will always be there for the child. It is better to strengthen the existing structure of a family than to weaken it by criticism. Since the anorexic's first interest is in the well-being of her family, the lesson she must learn is that the world hosts many differences and variables, and her family is no different.

That having been said, at the clinic we provide residential care for patients without their parents. This is not meant as a criticism—far from it. The patient realizes that to get through the condition, she needs to concentrate all her efforts with the group supporting her. She knows that her parents are not the best people to do that at this point. Putting distance between the patient and her parents is often misconstrued by the well-meaning public and can be terribly distressing to parents if not properly understood.

Nevertheless, some innate sense seems to direct the victim to perceive that the staff understands her needs better than her family does. The analogy that comes most easily to mind is that of a woman in labor whose need is temporarily more for a doctor or midwife than for her parents or husband. In no way does that belittle her love for her parents or spouse. It makes sense that a person whose job involves itself in obstetrics may be more objective than anxious loved ones.

Many parents are concerned that their caring of their child was inadequate. Nothing generally is further from the truth. But in order for the victim to fight her battle to wellness, she cannot also have the responsibility of her parents' worry about her. She must be temporarily relieved of this and other responsibilities until she can put things in the proper perspective. The child's need is so great, she must for the interim not perceive that her loved ones have any needs, lest she divert her energies toward helping them rather than healing herself. Obviously, that is all but impossible in most settings in which parents come into contact with their children. Parents, siblings, and other loved ones are so emotionally involved that they may be incapable of delivering unconditional love unemotionally and without fear, or masking their understandable anxiety.

When families and loved ones try for months and sometimes years to accommodate the unrealistic situation they are facing, they can be nearly destroyed. But as victims in care become confident that their structure will be intact until it is no longer needed, they are more and more capable of responding to their loved ones. We also counsel family and friends to help them understand the youngster's condition and how triggers in the home may contribute to her CNC.

The patient's progress toward wellness will define how parental visits are structured. In the early stages of recovery, the careworker will accompany parents on outings during the time of their visits. This comforts both parents, who are unsure about how to be with their child at this point, and the victim, as she is beginning to find herself but does not yet always know how to interpret comments without being subjective.

The victim will venture slowly back into the world when she decides it is safe to do so. And she will do so when she is armed with the objective perspective that people do the best they can within the limitations of their own humanity at that moment, that whatever they do depends on myriad variables, many of which they never had any control over and never need to feel any guilt or responsibility about.

6

The Five Stages of Recovery

We have found that most patients with eating disorders experience recovery in distinct, defined stages. As you will see, each stage of recovery presents its own problems, possibilities for backsliding, and triumphs. Each stage demands its own breed of security, gentle prodding, and persuasion for the patient. Each demands a solid platform from which the patient will spring. Each demands the hope of eternal possibility.

Interestingly, the stages of recovery can be compared to a crash course in the normal development of a human being, from the utter helplessness of infancy to the self-confidence and autonomy of adulthood.

THE MONTREUX LIFE WELLNESS SCALE

The Montreux Life Wellness Scale is our way of clarifying a patient's progress. It encompasses the five stages that eating disorder patients experience as they work their way toward wellness.

This is a percentile scale as well as a human developmental stage scale. The percentages refer to the degree to which the Actual Mind is in control. The lower the percentage, the more dominion the Negative Mind holds over its victim's life. After working with many patients, I have arrived at these numbers intuitively, and they explain perfectly what goes on during recovery.

The Montreux Life Wellness Scale

THE ACUTE STAGE: Infancy. This is the stage of total dependency. 1 percent to 30 percent.

THE EMERGENT STAGE: This stage is equivalent to the development of a young child. It is one of investigativeness and limit testing. 30 percent to 50 percent.

THE REALITY STAGE: This is the adolescent phase of treatment. It is a time when the pendulum swings from dependency to a false courage and the new identity begins to coalesce. During this stage, the patient moves into partial care. 50 percent to 68 percent.

INTERACTIVE STAGE: This is equivalent to young adulthood—the beginning of maturity and objectivity. It is a time of moderation. She becomes an outpatient. 68 percent to 80 percent.

ENVIRONMENTAL INTEGRATION STAGE: This is the final stage of recovery. The patient returns to her home environment but makes three to four assessment return trips within twelve months and has a five-year follow-up. These assessments determine the patient's ability to reintegrate and adapt to adult life. 80 percent to 86 percent.

Generally it takes the patient the same amount of time to traverse each stage of recovery, though this depends on how soon and how well the patient can grasp the concepts that the counselors and staff teach. How closely the patient adheres to and understands these concepts depends, as well, on her inherent courage and confidence to try new things.

The Montreux Life Wellness Scale serves as a marker of recovery to victims and their families. To the victim, it gives a road map to understanding how her disorder can be reversed each step of the way. To the family, it provides a greater vision of their supportive role and helps them achieve greater tolerance of their child in her emotional journey. Watching a child or loved one disappear into an eating disorder without adequate recourse or explanation can make a parent go mad. The Scale provides a sense of order and purpose in the recovery process.

To ensure against relapse, treatment should not be interrupted until it is completed. Consider the analogy of building a house. Weather will destroy the interior unless a roof is put on. You might then think of the basement as the Acute Stage, where only the builder or architect rather than the owner can visualize the potential completed house. Someone uninvolved in its construction can only assume and respect that the architect has made plans to follow.

A basement is not a house. Neither are three or four months of treatment a cure. It is simply the essential first step that establishes a platform for building upon. So refeeding a patient is a necessary first step in the treatment of an eating disorder. Physical stabilization must occur before one can work with the mind. If a patient is agitated and distracted by inadequate nutrition, her concentration will be scattered.

However, physical stabilization does not equal cure. Otherwise, all of the patients released from traditional hospital settings which merely focus on refeeding would be "cured" after having reached their target weight. In fact, we can almost surely predict relapse or failure in many cases if treatment is interrupted too soon. An acute eating disorder has taken a long time to develop; it can require up to two years and sometimes longer to reverse.

Of course, each person's recovery depends upon the individual and her inherent predisposition to trust. As well, each patient will adapt to treatment differently, depending on:

- the length of time she has been enslaved by the CNC (although not necessarily the degree of severity of the eating disorder).
- the degree of inherent sensitivity.
- the guilt and trauma she may have felt over time in hurting those around her whom she loves.
- what nurturing is available to her when she returns to her home during the Environmental Integration Stage.

• how her relationship has developed with her family and friends throughout treatment.

Each individual will take her own time for recovery. As with any growing child, one can predict the normal time for each stage of development, yet allow for variation depending on individual makeup. This is also true for the eating disorder victim. Each person will interpret her world in her own way as her identity emerges. Each child will determine her own schedule of recovery. It is inadvisable to push a patient more quickly than she indicates is possible because the work to that point could become partially undone.

THE ACUTE STAGE: 1 PERCENT TO 30 PERCENT

The acute anorexic or bulimic patient believes she is responsible for everything. Just the opposite is true in treatment. The Acute Stage of treatment is synonymous with infancy. The patient needs to be totally without responsibility either for herself or for anyone else in order to begin growth.

It would seem the only way to correct an eating disorder and ultimately CNC is to enable the patient to start with a fresh interpretation of life. Therefore, the Acute Stage must allow a patient's total dependency until she no longer needs or desires it. Just as an infant needs twenty-four-hour care to protect her from herself and minister to her needs, so does the victim of an eating disorder.

Ideally, the patient must live in this unreal environment until she feels protected enough to emerge and begin to fight back for her life. Trusting in that environment is mandatory to initiate effective treatment. The patient is so subjective that the staff must be trained to be on top of the Negative Mind at all times.

It is therefore imperative during this stage to reiterate ad infinitum that the individual means much to the world and that she is cherished by her loved ones and the clinic staff. The victim will repeatedly deny her worthiness on one hand, yet demand attention and love on the other. Her needs are basic and all-consuming. Constant, loving care and reassurance accompany her return to physical stability.

The victim must necessarily have her physical self restored. At some level, she is aware of this, though she cannot yet admit it to herself or others. Neither is it essential that she admit it until later, when her mind has eased into an acceptance of her need to eat and she is able to argue with logic against the Negative Mind.

Once a person has been put under care, she is able to begin to relax into letting go of the negativity she has constructed against herself. Though she is still quite fearful of her mind's agility in attempting to trap her and trick her, she wishes to believe she is safe.

In twenty-four-hour care, the patient begins to test her boundaries (she hides food down her sleeve rather than eating it, for instance) gently and warily, hoping everyone is aware of her incredible need for protection but not yet quite able to voice it because of the trouble her Negative Mind will give her once she makes that need known. It may not allow her to read, to sleep, to drink, to lie on a bed, to use a pillow, to be kind to her parents or friends, to eat with other children, to play with them, to laugh, to talk, to sing, to complain.

At that point, the onus is on the careworker to let the patient know she is good enough to sleep on a bed, to use a pillow, to sing, to laugh. She has the same rights any of us has as a human being.

It is also important at this stage to create a structure of support for the patient to grow from. As the structure of careworkers and activities forms around the patient, she will begin to rely upon it. This is an interim, though a terribly important, stage. What appears as dependency provides a bulwark for the Actual Mind to defend itself from the persecution of the Negative Mind. This is the key to unconditional support. If we fail to give the Actual Mind the correct ways in which to enlist our alliance, the patient will be in grave danger.

Ideally, the patient will have the same staff team throughout her first stage of treatment because this helps fulfill her need for stability. When keeping the same staff team is impossible, the patient may have to be reassured that a particular staff member did not move elsewhere because of her. The patient is at a very subjective stage of her development, and she may interpret any change as a reproach against her.

We create a food list/mini-menu for added structure. The patient, who at the Acute Stage doubts everything about herself, suddenly can see that her meals are the same every day, served two and a half hours apart. This structure, again, gives her a platform of consistency to grow from. Both her food and her weight are no longer her responsibility. Not having to think about her meals because she needn't think about her weight leaves her freer to begin learning that she is valid.

Still, during the Acute Stage and early on in the Emergent Stage, the patient inevitably pretends to resist some efforts to feed her in order to save herself from being unduly beaten in her mind. There have been times when it has taken three hours, immense concern, and reassurance in order for the victim to brave a small bowl of beans, after which it took more hours of rocking and talking to assure her that she does not need to exercise frantically to burn off the just-consumed calories.

We don't change a patient's meal plan until she begins to become impatient with her existing one. This will indicate her need to move on in the program.

Initially, the patient will be relieved to feel "safe," to be at a place where she is absolved of responsibility for her own well-being. Simultaneously, however, she will become more anxious because at this point her condition will realize it is trapped and increase the negative activity in her head.

Now, as the Negative Mind becomes desperate and begins to lose control of the Actual Mind, the "civil war" will deepen. Her Negative Mind issues increasingly intense orders, instructing her to refuse food or supplements because she is unworthy. It commands her to run into traffic, cut herself, or exercise any calorie from her body. Her Negative Mind tells her to take too many pills or to put poison into her food because she does not deserve any unadulterated form of pleasure.

At this critical stage, the careworkers are constantly alert and ever-conscious of the devious nature of the Negative Mind. At times the patient will become agitated and may wish to act on the Negative Mind's orders, thereby lessening the mental pressure. This behavior is usually apparent only in the first few months of treatment.

As the victim begins to feel more comfortable in her surroundings, she will verbalize what her Negative Mind is saying to her and accept her careworker's dissuasion of its importance. Slowly thereafter she begins to experience some hope.

At twenty-two, Catherine had weighed forty-one pounds when her doctor contacted us. She weighed sixty-six pounds when we took her into the clinic. This is what she wrote at her sixth week of treatment.

> Dear Spirit:
>
> After 12 years of torment, turmoil, and never-ending sadness, I feel like I am slowly surrendering or rather my Anorexic counterpart is slowly getting tired. I am petrified, however, to live my life free of a familiar entity. Years of starving myself, vomiting the little I did ingest, haunting thoughts of fear, anguish, despair, and thoughts of self-hatred paralyzed my being. . . . Fear houses itself throughout my soul. However, despite indescribable fears associated with living "Life" and being "Free" from this terrible separate identity, I persevere.

THE EMERGENT STAGE: 30 PERCENT TO 50 PERCENT

As the Acute Stage begins to give way to the Emergent Stage, the eating disorder victim becomes more mentally available. Because of the physical stabilization that occurs during the Acute Stage, serious counseling can now begin. The Actual Mind can listen for short periods of time, and careworkers will note that the patient is able to concentrate on events in the external world. This stage is basically a bridge between the Acute Stage and Reality Stage. It consists of confirmation of positivity and reiteration of worth.

The battle that was primarily between the patient and her condition now shifts noticeably to a battle between the condition and the staff. The patient hands over the problems in her head to staff members more readily and easily. At this juncture, she has gentle assurance in her own mind that she is sometimes worthy to be loved.

During the Emergent Stage, the patient is still dependent but now hunts desperately for an identity. She begins to question her values and everyone else's. The search for self begins, and it's not unusual for patients to experiment, "trying on" different personalities as they struggle to find their essentialness. Brian came to the program wearing a woman's wig. He was acutely anorexic and was not expected to live past adolescence. His voice was high and quiet. In the following six months, he changed his outward appearance as many times. When we asked what he wanted to be when he was older, he said, "I want to cure people who are sick in the world." His external identity was that of a caregiver. Beyond that, his personality was all confusion, and remained so for several months until he began to sense and embrace his core self.

Depending on the patient's level of emotional stability on any given day, she begins to attend three-hour class sessions in our afternoon Educational Program. During this time, a patient will participate in class discussions. This reflects her sense of individuality. Students' opinions and comments are always valid and encouraged. As a patient lends her self to a group, her identity becomes more defined to herself. School becomes a microcosm of the macrocosm of society. It is also an opportunity for patients to discover and "own" their own interests, motivations, and passions, rather than assuming those they believe the world wants for them.

At this delicate stage of self-construction, caregivers must avoid deciding who the patient is to become. Therapy is not about creating a person—that individual already exists—but rather about allowing one to develop with unconditional guidance and caring.

This stage can prove confusing to the unschooled because the patient will continually be looking for behavior to copy. Therefore it is essential that caregivers are as emotionally stable as possible to ensure that they are in control of themselves when working with such fragile minds.

The mind of the patient during the Emergent Stage is extremely receptive to suggestion. Given the patient's old habits of adhering to others' needs, the caregiver takes pains to present nothing but kindness and compassion in dealing with every subject matter. Victims sort out their life philosophies based upon their own observations; they must not borrow these philosophies from their caregivers' opinions. When asked their opinions, caregivers are apt to reply, "Tell me what you think. I'm interested," or use other such gentle encouragement. Indeed, caregivers must keep their personal lives confidential, sharing only happy or humorous anecdotes.

Though the patient is still tentative and desperately in need of her boundaries, she is necessarily demanding during this stage. Soon, the "terrible twos" appear. The patient has found herself surrounded by unconditional loving attention. In order to prove herself worthy of being so loved, she tests the staff daily and subjectively for motive. Initially, she suspects ulterior motives are behind the acts of loving kindness. She may throw tantrums if we do not give in to unreasonable requests but we must remain steadfast for her security or she will start to lose ground in her support system and begin to regress, as would a two-year-old.

She begins to make her identity known. She wishes variation in her food plan; she asks for some new workers; she wants changes in outings and direction in activities. The patient is creating her own identity within a safe structure. Her actual self is beginning to evolve and emerge. Selfishness is a natural and welcome part of that growth. While the staff cannot seem to jump high enough in the Emergent Stage it also must gently provide guidelines and reassurance.

This is a time when a patient becomes curious about her world, a welcome development because it means she is turning her focus outward and taking an interest in other things for their own sake. It is a time for learning by trial and error. One young girl apologized to me for a tantrum she had during this phase. "I'm sorry I acted so immaturely," she wrote, "I want to be like a normal thirteen-year-old and normal thirteen-year-olds don't get so upset if they can't go for a walk."

Then she went on to say:

> I know that you can tell the difference between me or my head, so I listed the reasons why I want to go on walks and why my head wants me to. The reasons why he wants me to are:
> I'll gain weight if I don't keep going.
> I need to burn more calories.
> I'm lazy if I don't go.
> Everyone including clients do way more than me.
> I must do the same amount of activity that I did
>   yesterday.
> The reasons why I would like to go on a walk are:
> I'm 13 and like to get out and do things.
> I love to get fresh air and be outside.
> I have a lot of fun looking in stores.
> It's summer and the weather is getting warm and sunny.
> It really distracts me and takes me away from most of
>   my problems into the real world for a while.

As the patient comes to trust her surroundings, she gives clues to the counselor about what is going on in her head. If the counselor is trained to interpret the secret language of the Negative Mind, the patient will be relieved and will lean more heavily on him.

For instance, we had given a food list consisting of six eating times in a twenty-four-hour period to an eleven-year-old boy in the Emergent Stage. Tim's Negative Mind had instructed him not to comply. His caregiver phoned me and asked how to address this situation.

I spent time on the phone with Tim, who asked, "Did you say that there was no option to eating this yam?"

I knew that I had never made that statement, but I quickly realized Tim needed me to insist on it.

"Yes," I replied. "There is absolutely no option."

Tim said, "I thought so. I was just checking." He wanted the yam but could not bring himself to eat it without permission from an authority figure. He was not yet at the point at which he felt he deserved the food and his Negative Mind was strongly disallowing it.

Tim was prohibited from expressing his desire for the yam because if he did, the increased negativity would be unbearable. He could only hope that he would be understood and I would respond as I did.

The patient's outward behavior may not indicate what is really happening at this stage. She is eager to allow someone to side with her against the condition. But until she comes to this point, there are severe ramifications from the Negative Mind for cooperating with the caregivers. So it is indeed an exceedingly brave thing for the patient to ask for help.

Distraction continues to be the best way to offset the ceaseless negative chatter the patient must endure immediately after eating. Telling stories or playing board games such as Scrabble and Monopoly that require a redirection of the patient's concentration are great diversionary tactics. Before the Reality Stage (see page 155), the patient's concentration is at best is sporadic. However, most of the time, distraction serves to bring the patient past the hardest moment.

In the Emergent Stage, a victim's relationship with her parents (if she is on twenty-four-hour care) is tentative. She is so conditioned to feel pain vicariously that she uses her best virtue—her sensitivity—against herself. She may wait for any nuance of projected need from loved ones. The internal mental battle waging inside the patient's head is difficult to objectify and understand for parents and family who love their child and are ever present to her emotional needs.

Parents often do not understand why their children do not want to see them, though they can easily communicate by phone. As I've mentioned in the last chapter, the reason is obscure but valid. Parents are the people who mean most to the victim and whose opinion is paramount to her. Victims generally love their parents so much that they feel guilty for allowing themselves to eat in front of them. They still see themselves as unworthy and find it extremely difficult to permit themselves any pleasure since they have surely not protected their parents from all earthly ills, and in fact have brought them anguish by becoming ill.

It seems selfish to patients to admit openly that they are allowing themselves to partake of life. They still believe they have disappointed their parents, although generally, parents have not encouraged their children to think this way.

Patients may display much anger in the Emergent Stage, lashing out at times, and then immediately becoming repentant and self-abusive. It is imperative for caregivers to respond kindly and supportively, explaining the behavior to patients with no sense of judgment or reward and punishment. The Negative Mind will use any reproof against its victim. Further castigation is counterproductive since it confirms the CNC mindset.

Patients may swing from despair to hope as the Actual Mind begins to emerge from the shadows. As Marci wrote in her diary at this stage:

> Life sucks and then you die! This is the saying that keeps running through my mind continuously every day now. It's getting harder. I'm having a very hard time right now having to accept the changes that are going on. Sometimes I feel like

I'm ready to quit this fight but I know I can't give up because I have quite a long life ahead of me and I feel like I have a lot that I could offer to others. It's the day-to-day struggles that are difficult and hard to face sometimes, but I know that I'm going to make it, and I'll be happy and stronger because of it.

THE REALITY STAGE: 50 PERCENT TO 68 PERCENT

The Reality Stage begins at 50 percent on the Life Wellness Scale. At this point, the Actual Mind is equally as strong as the Negative Mind. And though the patient generally continues to hear a voice, albeit subdued in her head, as often as not, she has the strength to veto the negative mental activity.

As the patient continues through the Reality Stage, she will grow more accustomed to trying new things in the world. As she realizes she is capable of these small maneuvers, her confidence and identity grow.

Somewhere between 50 and 60 percent, the patient is likely to change her demeanor. The tentative, anxious mood will become assured and generally happy. The patient will be able to talk of her attitudes and perceived issues without as much subjectivity. The world will no longer seem an unfriendly, frightening, and foreign place. The patient will no longer perceive her past to have been in vain and her future impossible. This is a glorious thing to see. Witnessing a person's wonderful uniqueness emerge from the dampened spirit that first entered the clinic is simply amazing.

Though patients will be on care for most of this stage, the constant monitoring will ease radically and they will experience some planned free time. Now, they look forward to parental visits and even enjoy them.

The patient is beginning to respond normally and is gently able to put the world into perspective a better part of the time.

She starts to enjoy small parts of life without too much guilt. Even desires and wants can be discovered and fulfilled successfully.

One patient wrote to me, "I just want to let you know I'm so happy being in my new room. It's great. Life is almost a bed of roses. There are just a few odds and sods, and a few weeds to be dug up. Every day is a learning experience. Last night I went on my first big major solo voyage to town. It may not be the best sightseeing spot, but it was like the Bahamas to me. . . . Well, I must go now. My snack is calling me."

Many victims have lived in fear for so long that they are used to being anxious. Soft and firm encouragement, always with unconditional support, lends them a structure to fall back on if they attempt to move forward sooner than they are able.

During this period patients begin to venture out for one of six or seven daily snacks. They will make these restaurant visits initially with counselors or team leaders who are completely aware of how to interpret every nuance or innuendo patients suggest. The staff is well-schooled in eating disorder behavior and therefore adept at averting any of the patient's negativity.

A careworker and I accompanied Abbie to a restaurant. It was the first time she had eaten a normal dinner in a setting outside the clinic. The careworker and I ordered the identical meal of salmon, vegetables, and mashed potatoes. After Abbie had ordered, she became increasingly agitated waiting for the food to arrive.

Suddenly she leaned over in her chair and whispered quietly to me, "When the food comes, please insist that I eat it, no matter what I say out loud."

The waiter brought our meals, and almost on cue, Abbie announced forcefully, "I'm not going to eat that. You better not try to make me."

I replied firmly yet gently, "Yes, you are, darling. There's no argument here."

Abbie gratefully ate her salmon, her eyes swimming from the success of the battle.

The courage to appear normal by eating in a restaurant poses two problems for the tentative patient. The first is that she is afraid that others will see her as being recovered. She will appear physically well before her head has joined her. She is afraid that if others perceive her as cured before she is able to accept responsibility, she will feel overwhelmed, less protected, and will crash again. A patient will generally give many indications whether she needs care or is "safe" without it. At this point, she is able to verbally and physically ask for help.

"Safety" depends on whether the patient is able to effect her will without the instructions of the Negative Mind overriding it.

One of the main focuses during the Reality Stage is to continue to help the patient develop her identity. The Negative Mind robs the patient of her ability to make decisions about likes and dislikes. Now she begins to ask her careworker for help in choosing among options. The careworker need only guide and perhaps reinforce likes or dislikes of the person he sees emerging by throwing the question back to the patient. "What would you like to do?" he might ask, or "How does that feel to you?"

The Reality Stage invites reason. Finally the emotions keep pace with the intellect. One of my patients wrote to me as he was reaching the end of this stage: "Montreux is all about challenges, yours as well as mine. It is no small task that you've set yourself, and you must have hard days as well as good ones too. But as I am learning daily, nothing valuable in life comes easily or without work."

The patient becomes much more responsive in counseling sessions. It is during these sessions that we begin to focus on the Objectivity Training and role-playing that I described in the previous chapter. We might discuss how the patient can put a parent's divorce or other stressful trigger into the appropriate context. The preoccupation that formerly existed with the Negative Mind is subsiding. Between 55 and 65 percent of the patient's Actual Mind is present enough to begin understanding her own preferences and choices. She starts taking an interest in her clothes. Rather than the layered look, which patients wear in the Acute Stage to avoid detection of the seriousness of their illness, clothes begin to have a style, an identity, a definition, a color.

As well, other tendencies for honing one's personality will appear. Michelle likes the piano and tennis. She is doing it for the sheer enjoyment of it, no longer chased into "having to." Robin is taking a veterinarian course at the local college. "Animals are more dependable than people," she says and grins impishly. Sophia is a poetess and actress of the best order. Chuck plays violin. Andy skates and makes pottery.

Everyone loves art—and what these patients create is amazingly observant and representative of the human condition. The Reality Stage is exciting because the patient's personality is beginning to emerge and establish itself with more than a hint of independence.

As this stage progresses, the individual's confidence increases (as in adolescence) until it grows to a false sense of ability—a confidence necessary for emotional establishment different from whatever the status quo indicates as imperative. The patient rebels. She chooses anything different than what is the norm. She is trying her wings, her independence.

This pendulum swing (at 65 percent) is a wonderful sight to caregivers and counselors, who can have a hard time comprehending that this manifestation could occur within the same year and in the same body that offered no hope earlier.

If the patient is not actually a teenager, the pendulum swing lasts for no more than two or three months—a relatively short period for adolescence. If she is, it seems (though there are many variables involved) the teenager has no need to engage in extreme normal teenage behavior, such as breaking rules. It is possible she feels she has already "done it." Of course, this is not true of all cases.

There is an interesting point to be noted at this juncture concerning parental attitudes when a child is released to them. Before the manifestation of anorexia, parents generally had a view of their child as being incredibly agreeable all of the time.

Remember that most patients have spent their conscious pre-anorexia hours in consideration of others. Unconsciously, parents may take this attitude for granted and assume the extremely cooperative individual they knew before will come home again in exactly the same way, minus the eating disorder symptoms. In some cases, particularly when the patients are children, this will not be the case.

However, if parents think about it, they will realize that all they really wanted earlier was a healthy, normal, sometimes selfish and rambunctious teenager. What they had to endure was a living nightmare. It sometimes comes as a shock to them that the effects of "curing" an individual necessarily result in her becoming "normalized." In other words, the recovering anorexia patient will become a healthy person and occasionally an unreasonable and demanding one. Though she will always be caring of others' needs, she will allow her needs to take precedence some of the time.

This is as it should be. Balance is sanity.

During the first two stages of therapy, it is important to maintain the consistency of whatever caregiving team was in place when the patient arrived. As the patient moves into the Reality Stage, it now becomes productive to change counselors and even careworkers. These new people bring a refreshing vision and avert dependency, both for the sake of the patient and the counselor.

Before any change is made, however, the intermediate counselor gets to know the patient so that the transition is smooth and nonthreatening. He does this by joining the acute counselor in some session work at the end of the Emergent Stage. By the time the patient lets go of the acute counselor, she is generally eager to move on and confident that her former counselor will never close his door to her should she have a concern or a question.

The Reality Stage requires a quick mind in the intermediate counselor. He becomes an instructor and teacher of the first order. He has different guidelines than that of his previous colleague, but he need be at least as alert.

The patient, though she will be feeling her own way, will be looking for approval or boundaries. The counselor is in the same precarious position that a parent would be at this stage—guiding wisely, gently, yet firmly if it becomes necessary.

Because the counselor must prepare the patient for the world, his will be a trial-and-error role. The patient will need and want the safe structure of a reference point as she ventures to test her identity and her world. Given that the Negative Mind still has a healthy portion of control, it behooves the counselor to persuade the patient away from it. She will quickly accept his advice because she is not as frightened of the negative voice. She can now regard the Negative Mind more as a nuisance.

The danger during the middle of this stage, roughly around 60 to 65 percent, is that the individual may feel a false sense of courage, as does an adolescent, and may strive to be off care before she is capable of doing so. Again, we can compare her behavior to someone who is fifteen or sixteen, still needing guidelines yet eager to try things in the world.

If the patient continues to insist, "I am fine and can deal with everything now," then we may give her a trial period to prove whether she is correct.

The danger of stopping treatment is obvious. The Negative Mind could gain ground, and the patient might regress. Erring on the side of caution leads to a quicker recovery in the long run.

This is a time when positive self-esteem or "self-regard"—self-acknowledgment and acceptance of who one is—begins to develop. However, "Who I am" may not be at all what the family, loved ones, or even the patient expect.

Ironically, most of my patients discover that at a time when they are truly able to appreciate their external achievement—good grades, trophies, awards, which they had previously garnered only to please others—they find that their achievements do not matter as much to them.

One acute patient had qualified for the Olympics as a runner. When she got better, she stopped running entirely; it was no longer important to her. Another, who had set herself on the path of gymnastics, discovered after her recovery that the sport did not interest her.

THE INTERACTIVE STAGE:
68 PERCENT TO 80 PERCENT

By the time the patient moves from the Reality Stage into the Interactive Stage, she feels as if blinders have been lifted from her eyes. One of the comments I hear frequently now is, "I feel as if I am conscious, living again, whereas I was in a surreal daze before." In the Interactive Stage, Marci wrote to me:

> I'm so happy today. While I was on my way to my session, I felt like I was going to burst because I was just so full of happiness. I had just come from my interview and was thinking about what I said and how far I've come. And I just felt like Yes! Look at me now. I'm so proud of myself and the person I've become. Basically you could say that I'm Lovin' Life. This feeling is amazing. I'm high on life. . . .
>
> The person I've become, or should I say, the person that was never let out is also amazing. I feel so energetic inside. I'm more outgoing and less self-conscious or worried about what everyone else will think of me. There are still things that I am working on but it's like a lot of things in life. They take time. Besides, I had been sick for as long as I could remember.

This, from someone who just a scant few months earlier had proclaimed, "Life sucks and then you die!" The Negative Mind has little jurisdiction at this time. Indeed, as we can see from Marci's letter, at this stage, the Negative Mind has mostly seeped away, and certainly the eating disorder manifestation is gone. Another patient said to me, "It's not about anorexia now; it's about learning confidence." At its worst, in the beginning of the stage, the CNC has a little less than 35 percent clout.

Even so, the patient still needs support. There are things to work on. We cannot regard the fact that she is doing well in her battle against CNC as a sign of complete safety. As CNC grew initially, then subsided, so could it grow again without proper attention. The patient has a better chance to outwit CNC now that she has the tools of understanding to work with. However, after all that labor, why take the chance?

The danger is of course, now that the patient feels as well as she does—probably better than she has in her lifetime—she is eager to surge forward without help. If she does this prematurely, she is risking everything she strove for. In order to prevent a relapse, the counselor must teach her as much as she can learn in the time allotted.

One of the counselor's main goals is to help her understand her options in the outside world and the consequences of her choices. She is learning how to live responsibly. Like a young bird learning to fly from its nest, the patient wants to step away from her safety net a little. She is exploring with her counselors exactly what this may mean to her.

The patient learns to understand motivation from an objective, rational, humanistic perspective. She can then accept varying points of view, without being self-righteous about her own. As one patient wrote to me, "I've come to learn, for instance, patience. By learning that patience, I am a lot more content inside and with others." The patient will spend this period of time researching her personal needs in an effort to comprehend what brought her to the eating disorder manifestation.

The counselor will ask the patient, "What do you think you might be afraid of? Who will your friends be? How will your family react to your wellness?" Though the patient is familiar with her home environment, she will eventually be facing it with a completely different interpretation of herself in it. This thought can be at the same time exciting and alarming. Confidence of her "new" identity will take time and testing.

Fears about how to be in the world will be addressed in many ways. Gentle discussions of rationality will be the subject of many sessions. If a patient is concerned about her interactive skills—after all, the eating disorder may have stalled her social life for a long time—the counselor can place her in an atmosphere of her choice, to work on them. Often this involves volunteer work outside the clinic. At other times, it can be doing puzzles with or reading stories to people in the Acute Stage. These interactions depend on the individual's nature and desires.

One patient who became involved in helping others at the clinic wrote to me, "Work has been a great experience for me. I don't even like to call it work, because I don't feel like I'm working. I just feel like I'm being a friend who is giving support to a friend in need."

During this period of intensive learning, an adult patient becomes a "residential outpatient." Although she still lives mostly in the clinic, as she reaches the end of the Interactive Stage, she moves out. She is encouraged to live with one or two other adult patients in the same stage of care in an apartment near the clinic. She learns how to exist in the community and how to make her own choices without fear. She develops as many friends outside the clinic as within.

Many outlets become available to the patient at this juncture. The Educational Program classes of afternoon school are usually about subjects the patients-students do not learn in the normal school setting. Comparing societies and their value systems, for instance, teaches patients not to take any one society too seriously. Studying habits that explain other peoples and societies as well as the microcosm of their personal circumstances teaches patients not to take themselves so seriously either.

Patients do amazing project studies and submit reports. They are remarkably wonderful students who are leaving their negativity behind them and reaching out with a curiosity unhampered by worrying about what everyone thinks. By this stage, patients can have extra tutoring with specific help from home if they want to continue with studies that may have been interrupted by illness.

Patients in the Interactive Stage sometimes study an instrument they enjoyed while they were on full care in the program.

They study art, opera, museums, or architecture if that is their wish. One or two patients decided to write a play on the anorexic condition. Other patients joined outside poetry classes and put their art into displays. If patients are of age, they are able to get driver's licenses. Some take classes at a local junior college. By this time, each person indicates her personal interests, and we support her as much as possible.

The interactive patient must prove to herself and her counselors that she is ready for almost anything. The body language and gentle confidence of this stage are wonderful to see. From the once desolate, fearful patient has emerged a courageous, self-assured, aware individual fully able to take her place in society. Her gait is no longer downcast with humility. She makes eye contact with no hesitation and walks with assurance.

During the Interactive Stage, the patient spends much time forming and honing her identity. Toward the end, she often expresses a wish to try short visits at home to prepare for the final phase, that of Environmental Integration.

The patient will spend much session time with the companionship of her family, studying and explaining points of similarity and differences in family members' attitudes and deeds, past and present. For this session work, parents come to the clinic. Before the patient goes into the last phase of therapy, she will theoretically have figured out a way to live compatibly with her family. The theory will be put into practice once she gets home.

It is important, though, to remind parents that their children are returning to them as they would and should have been, had they followed their natural road to development. Surely, then, they will not be perfect. We would not want them to be.

THE ENVIRONMENTAL
INTEGRATION STAGE: 80 PERCENT TO 86 PERCENT

As the patient readies for her home trial period, the last part of therapy, she feels both excitement and trepidation. She has built up home in her mind and despite how wonderful it may be, it is almost always initially anticlimactic to get back to reality. The first month or two are anxiety-ridden for families, who struggle to absorb this "new" individual into their conception of the way things are.

Counselors instruct parents and siblings in sessions, in front of the patient, not to walk on eggshells around her but to have gentle understanding that her world is as new to her as she is to them.

Usually the well-being and acclimatization of the individual depends on the character of her home environment. Ideally, she will return to a supportive, positive environment. Ideally, family and loved ones realize the deep journey the patient has just made and are prepared to gently accommodate her first year at home where she will glean more stability in her environment. This can be likened to a convalescent period after a long hospital stay. Or one might compare it to bringing home a new baby. It takes a while for everyone to get used to the new arrival. Parents who have returned from the edge of the abyss will naturally be worried, and they are bound to misconstrue some of the signs when they see their child acting in normal ways—being a teenager, for example. Teenagers typically magnify the degree to which others notice and criticize them. A teen's lament that "Everybody in school hates me" need not prefigure a relapse into an eating disorder.

While the recovered patient is not the emotionally frail person she once was, it is nevertheless important that families seek appropriate therapy to resolve the stressful situations that act as barriers to caring.

After two months at home, the patient returns to the clinic for her first last-phase assessment, the duration of which will depend entirely on her stability during the time that has elapsed. Generally she will discuss things that did or didn't create problems for her on the home front.

If the counselor deems his patient safe to continue her home phase, she will return home after eight or twelve days of daily double sessions. If, on the other hand, the patient seems unprepared for the Environmental Integration phase, then she will continue her objectivity training as an outpatient at the clinic. This extension can last anywhere from two to three months except under unusual circumstances.

If things go well, the patient will return home after a normal assessment period to continue her second phase of adjustment, which lasts four months unless otherwise indicated. At this time, the patient generally makes a remarkable positive leap ahead and sets aside all wariness. She begins living in full swing.

Generally there is great variation in what happens after this point in therapy. During the whole time that the patient has been home, she can phone the counselors as needed, who will troubleshoot any problems as they arise. It is usually a shock to families to find that their children are establishing their needs, sometimes, necessarily, before those of their parents. However, most families are delighted with their child's growth and desire to grow, and interactions with siblings are a great relief, even if they involve "normal" squabbles.

After the first two visits back to the clinic for assessment, the patient is eager to get on with her life and would rather keep in contact by phone even though the program asks that she come back again in six months. In roughly half the cases, the patient returns on the six-month visit period merely to prove, with a grin, that she needn't have. This visit provides her time to catch up with patients who were just entering the clinic during her assessment times. The time is enlightening to all and much fun.

Some of the patients who entered the program at the same time as others ask to schedule their return assessment times together for an "old home" week. They compare tales as any normal graduates would. One of the most gratifying experiences is that they always want to encourage the patients new to the program. The interactions between new and former patients bring tears to many eyes. The former patients are, after all, proof of incredible potential, patience, and humanism.

It generally takes a year in the home environment for the "patient" to feel comfortable and at peace with her new identity. During that time, she is getting used to her new sense of self and may be more vulnerable to disturbances around her such as a parent's or a friend's divorce or substance abuse, or an upset at school or at work. She may well find it helpful to work with a therapist at home in order to come to terms with any such issues.

Patients in the process of recovery discover their actual, potential self, what some might call their true self. They achieve what humanistic psychologist Abraham Maslow referred to as "self-actualization."

Self-love and acceptance appear to be a natural evolution in development. When a person realizes her self outside of what she perceives the needs of others to be, she finds it very natural to love and take joy in living.

WHY 86 PERCENT AND NOT 100 PERCENT?

Readers will note that our Montreux Life Wellness Scale ends at 86 percent, not 100 percent. This underscores our core philosophy at the clinic: our stress on human limitations. No one can ever be 100 percent anything; nor should we strive to be. Every aspect of this therapy stresses acceptance and compassion for our imperfections. How better to arm anyone for the hurdles of life than to teach her to ask nothing from others except mutual respect and kindness. Understanding this concept allows objectivity and compassion.

The very nature of the percentile scale indicates the imperfectability of mankind. Eighty-six percent allows for 14 percent imperfection. Eighty-six percent represents that this is as perfect as we can or ought to be. To quote Robert Browning:

What I aspired to be,
And was not, comforts me.

. . .
Ah, but a man's reach
should exceed his grasp,
Or what's a heaven for?

No matter how deeply or thoroughly we strive to understand ourselves, we still have our human moments. Learning how to be objective, how to see the good of life rather than what is not wonderful will help the journey. I clearly remember one of my first lessons. One hot summer day when I was a child, I had fallen off my bike; a very sweaty woman had hugged me; and I had lost my silver locket in the stream ALL IN THE SAME DAY. I was crying when a wise man I knew stopped to ask me what was the matter.

I answered, "Not one but three bad things happened to me today, and I don't know that I can bear it."

"Bear it! Three things! Only three?" he asked incredulously, shaking his head. "Here, wipe your tears, and when twelve things happen in your day that aren't pleasing to you, come to me, and cry."

Twelve bad things have never happened to me in one day. No day has ever been that bad, and that was a long time ago, several lifetimes, I think. Life is, finally, only pertinent in our translation of it.

Our program is about teaching objectivity: seeing the world as it really is rather than as it appears. That is its essential component. Objectivity allows a "no-fault," "no-blame" situation. Its purpose is to allow a person to reinterpret the world so that she can appreciate what motivates others' behavior rather than seeing herself as the cause or blame for it. Her attitude will naturally then become one of understanding and caringness in a positive way.

CNC victims are naturally frightened of the world because it presents to them negative responsibility. Patients who have recovered have learned not to take things personally or demonize those who seem to harm them. They do not lose their sense of caring or compassion for others. They do not lose their essential kind nature; they are merely able to put it into better perspective. They are more able to create a balance between themselves and others.

An acute anorexic stands like a willow wand buffeted by the winds of others' needs, blowing back and forth in accordance with what she perceives others demand of her; this is naturally an exhausting process. When she has recovered, she finds that she can stand anchored in place, able to reach out and choose for herself what she needs and how she wants to respond to the needs of others. She has more energy to respond to those needs because she has more physical wellness, emotional balance, and a secure sense of self.

7

❧

On Love and Healing:
The Challenges at Home

How do you know if your child or loved one is on the road toward developing an eating disorder? How do you recognize the warning signs? What can you do if your loved one develops anorexia or bulimia? Can you prevent the condition from becoming acute? In this chapter I will attempt to answer some of these important questions.

But first a few caveats. If you suspect that your child has a predisposition for Confirmed Negativity Condition, it may be possible to prevent it from developing into an eating disorder. However, bear in mind that I am not fully convinced it is always possible to do so, even if parents and loved ones do everything in their power. I am reluctant to provide the opportunity for parents and sufferers to shoulder any more blame than they have already experienced.

I want to reemphasize that as a parent or loved one, you are not to blame for the sufferer's condition. However, I need to draw a distinction between exemption from blame and responsibility.

As parents, you are responsible for your child while she is in your care. You did not cause your child's condition, but you have the responsibility for helping her get the right help. More than anything, you can offer hope, love, and optimism, if not understanding. When your child realizes that neither she nor you are to blame and that you are willing to understand what she is feeling, that in itself helps relieve the terrible pressure feeding her Negative Mind.

Allow me to offer some guidelines that may help sensitive children and their parents, friends, families, and other loved ones face the challenges at home.

DETECTING THE CNC PREDISPOSITION

There are certain character traits that may help us determine whether a person has a predisposition toward Confirmed Negativity Condition.

Often CNC dispositions become apparent at an early age. These young people develop a sense of responsibility well beyond their tender years. As I explained in Chapter 2, most parents tell me they knew almost from the beginning that something was different about their child. They recall how she was worried, concerned, or overly responsible at an unusually early age.

Also, in Chapter 3, I mentioned how highly sensitive CNC-predisposed youngsters are. They overreact to the slightest family squabble. Here I do not mean to minimize the misery caused by truly "dysfunctional" families, which certainly do exist and cause damage. But I am drawing a distinction between genuine dysfunction and how a child with CNC perceives the world.

Amanda, for instance, appeared outwardly cheerful and sociable. All during her childhood, however, she grew up listening to her big sister, Eileen, complain about how Amanda received favored treatment at her expense. I did not find this demonstrably so, but apparently Amanda accepted her sister's interpretation of events. She later developed anorexia and moved out of the house so that Eileen "could have it all."

As I mentioned in Chapter 2, many have suggested that eating disorders develop in children after they experience some stressful or traumatic event. I have found it far more common, however, for sensitive children in these situations to be affected by the stress and trauma that befall their loved ones. They worry much more about others than they do themselves.

Although I believe these children will perceive a crisis where there is none, real crises can cause the CNC to manifest itself as an eating disorder that much more quickly. A parent's or sibling's physical ailment—and the child's inability to cure it—are obvious triggers. Tricia's mother had cancer; Claire's father had heart surgery; Meg's sister had been in a car accident. One little girl watched her two older siblings go into intensive care because of physical crises; she held her breath searching her parents' faces for a sign of relief indicating her siblings might survive. Three years later, at age eight, she developed anorexia. Another anorexic girl I treated asked me, "How is it that my being born caused my mother's cancer?"

These children all responded to crisis by trying to parent their parents. In their caringness and kindness, they immediately made themselves responsible, equally, at least to their parents—and vulnerable.

Children with a predisposition to CNC also seem to find doom everywhere. Of course, in our society, it's not hard to find: Think of the headline news on the radio and TV and in the newspapers death and destruction everywhere. It seems not to be a coincidence that so many of my patients have been exposed to soap operas. Here they ingest a steady diet of betrayal, rape, and even murder in the afternoon. But what appears as escapist fare to us is the stuff of nightmares to them. These children work diligently trying to offset the pessimistic view of life gleaned from such shows by attempting to make their own families that much safer.

Most parents describe children with the CNC predisposition as uncommonly selfless, altruistic, and sensitive. They are deferential and compliant toward others to a fault. They live with their antennae alert to everyone around them even as, it seems, they cannot receive transmissions of their own needs.

Thus, CNC may evolve into an eating disorder after some traumatic event in the family when subjectivity has the upper hand.

PREVENTING AN EATING
DISORDER FROM DEVELOPING

As I explained earlier, it may be impossible to prevent an eating disorder from manifesting. However, there are some precautions parents can take with their CNC-predisposed youngsters that may help.

Insist That Kids Be Kids

It is perhaps too easy to allow a competent, intelligent child to take responsibility when it is actually inappropriate for her to do so. If it makes our busy, stressful lives easier, how can we turn down her heartfelt offers of help?

Nevertheless, we must. It is imperative for parents to be parents. A child should not take on adult roles and responsibilities even though she may—in fact, probably will—possess extraordinary capabilities to do so. Nor should we unwittingly allow her to become our confidante. Our children are not and must not be our best friends, therapists, or marriage counselors. The CNC-predisposed individual will assume need if parents ache, and will naturally try to fix any problem that she perceives. But in so doing, she may set aside her own developmental needs and in her mind necessarily become a full-fledged counselor. It sounds like such a cliché, but it is vital to let our children be children. It is helpful to encourage normal childlike behavior and discourage adult behavior such as taking undue responsibility.

Seek Outside Help for Family Troubles

Families with marital strife or other anxieties and tensions would benefit from seeking appropriate counseling from qualified professionals or friends and adult extended-family members. This serves several purposes:

It provides families the help they need.
It relieves the child's anxiety and distress about the family's troubles.
It takes the responsibility for "fixing" the problem from the child's hands.
It demonstrates to the child that her parents are in charge.
It sends the message that it is okay to get help when it is needed.

A vulnerable person with CNC will use family strife to feed her Negative Mind. And while these triggers do not cause an eating disorder, they add to the victim's stress, and they will impede the progress of her recovery. They are more fuel for her self-consuming fire. As a parent or loved one, it is imperative for you to take a searching look at your life with the victim and identify those triggers. I say this with trepidation because I do not want parents to waste their precious energy blaming themselves instead of giving a victim the help she needs. Here again, it is important to draw a distinction between the laying of blame and the responsibility to change a harmful situation. That responsibility is yours. The challenge of addressing an eating disorder is great enough without putting more impediments in the way of healing.

We are all human. We have all made mistakes, advertently or not. As you'll see, it is a parent's role to teach his or her child about the imperfectability of human nature. When your loved one has progressed to a stage at which she can judge the situation objectively, you and she will most likely need to work through the issues with the help of a qualified therapist.

Encourage Your Child to Accept Imperfection

In addition, we must allow our children the imperfections of childhood. We can point out often that we are all human, while we remember to have patience with their mistakes. When we teach CNC-predisposed youngsters that childhood and adolescence are a necessary time of trial and error, we can help them let go of some of their overwhelming sense of perfection and responsibility.

When your child makes a mistake and is upset about it, gently remind him that it's okay to make mistakes, that you love him no matter what, that no one can or ever should try to be perfect. Encourage your child to try things for the love of it. Many children with CNC are reluctant to try something if they can't do it perfectly from the start; for them it's all or nothing. Try to coax them gently from a world of black and white to a rainbow of grays. If a child seems dead set on achievement, discuss with her what she finds meaningful in the effort and help her realize that you don't have any expectations of her. I would be concerned about a child who frets constantly over grades, who overstudies for every exam, and who is crushed by anything less than an A+.

Set Respectful Boundaries

Children also need to know that their parents will rationally and respectfully provide structure and boundaries. Extremely sensitive children benefit from households in which the adults have set reasonable rules rather than having everything decided by committee. The parents of CNC-predisposed children should be mindful of their offspring's greater need for security in the form of adults' respectful authority. These children need a firm platform, even if it is not the one they ultimately choose. In fact, healthy growth can include a child's opposition to the status quo, whatever it may be, simply for the sake of establishing her own identity. Moderation comes with maturity, not necessarily adulthood.

Children and youth need the encouragement of being believed in despite their differences in personality from their parents. Children also need to believe in their parents' strength and the stability of their circumstances, even in today's age of divorce and anxiety. The more adult friends, family, and counselors who support parents through the stumbling blocks of life, the more relatives who provide other perspectives that can influence the child, perhaps the more able the child will be to grasp an objective reality.

Put Problems into Perspective

Because the CNC-predisposed child is so sensitive to trauma and crisis, it is crucial not to blow up small problems into big ones. Parents can make clear to their child that life's annoyances are, after all, just annoyances. We can say, for example, "Oh, well, we missed the bus. We'll just wait for the next one," rather than "Oh my heavens. We missed the bus. Now what will we do?" It may also be helpful to point out that the pessimistic news that grabs the headlines may not be an accurate reflection of reality. Discuss with your child how the media use negativity to capture our attention. I am not advocating that you sugarcoat the world's woes, only that you give your children a context for understanding them. Always make it clear that these are adult problems requiring adult solutions. For those children too young to appreciate the context (recall the preschooler I counseled who absorbed daily negativity from TV news coverage while sitting on his mother's lap), I would recommend keeping the radio and TV off while the child is within earshot.

Help Your Child Cope with Life's Issues

If we address "issues" with optimism, hopefulness, and objectivity, the CNC-predisposed child will have fewer long-lasting effects than if she were convinced that she has been wronged and she lives with the fear that life is out to get her. A person with CNC will enlarge her problems to include whatever her parents did not do for her when she was young, whether it be buying her enough clothes in high school or concerning themselves adequately with needed orthodontia. Such "wrongs" will sometimes border on the ridiculous.

Intervene When Your Child Puts Herself Down

When you hear your child making self-deprecating remarks ("I can't do anything right"; "That was a horrible drawing"; "I'm the worst batter in the whole world"), step in and gently try to correct your child's perspective. Don't let your child blow up a single specific incident to a global indictment of himself ("I'm always screwing up"). Say things like, "Well, you missed that pitch, but that's no big deal. Everybody misses sometime. If it's not fun, why not try something else?" Encourage her to focus on the positives about herself instead of beating herself up for perceived or even real flaws.

Encourage Your Child to Explore Her Interests—Not Yours

If a CNC-predisposed child shows interest in any given subject, it is important that parents work with this interest in a moderate way without giving the youngster the idea that they have expectations about her level of attainment. It would be helpful to repeat, "You're fine the way you are." I would be watchful for children who pursue something with the hope of pleasing you rather than themselves.

Be wary of presenting an expectation to excel. If a child guesses that her parents have high expectations—"We want you to be the best"—she will do her utmost to please them. Indeed, I even become nervous saying to one of my own children or patients, "Good for you; you make me so proud." I prefer, "I really enjoyed looking at that. Thanks for showing it to me."

Many of us were raised to believe that one should finish what one starts, that quitting is failure. I have seen many people with CNC doggedly pursue perfection in a field, regardless of how truly interested in it they are. It may help parents to remind their sensitive children that they should feel free to drop something if its pursuit doesn't bring them real pleasure, that they should follow their true passions, lest they be seduced into fulfilling the perceived expectations of others.

The consistent message should be "Whatever you do is okay by me, as long as it is done with respect to yourself and others." However, there is a fine line here. When a patient asks me, "Are you proud of me?" I always reply, "It's not my place to be proud of anybody. I am me and you are you. I love you no matter what you do or don't do. You're not living for me." I do not want to buy into a patient's living to please me rather than herself.

This is not as easy as it sounds. Sometimes parents work very hard not to create expectations of their children, yet sensitive youngsters perceive them nonetheless. The parenting that works for children of normal sensitivity may not accommodate the needs of hypersensitive children. A thoughtless remark from a parent ("I expect better from you" or "Why can't you try a little harder?") might be shrugged off by the first child, while the hypersensitive one would take it wholly to heart and dwell on it for months.

Myra and Jonathan, two loving parents who were highly successful in their careers, brought their daughter to my clinic and said, "We love Stephanie just the way she is. We don't care what she does. We don't care if she's rich or famous or adheres to our values, as long as she's alive."

"Tell her that," I replied. "Perhaps you have never felt you had to, but she has developed expectations of herself, based not on what you've said to her, but on who you are, your professions. She believes you expect the same of her without your having said a word."

Naturally, we wish our children well in the world and will encourage them in their natural talents, but while we do this, we must explain to them that if following their talents into a career is their choice, that is wonderful, but if they do not choose to do this, but wish to choose an alternative profession or lifestyle, it is just as wonderful. And we have to mean what we say.

If your child fails to get a part in the school play or a spot on the team, you might say, "It doesn't matter. Did you have fun trying out?" I would even be wary of statements such as "Don't worry. You did your best." These set up an expectation that the child has to do his or her best for you or that her best was not good enough.

I counseled one family whose son had been sick for many years. I told them, "Jeffrey is going to be a wonderful person. I can't tell you what his likes and dislikes will be. I cannot tell you who he is going to be; I can only tell you that he is going to be terrific."

After eight months, as Jeff's marvelous and unique personality began to emerge, his parents started to express plans for their son, what he was and was not allowed to do, and so on. They were both creating expectations and putting conditions on their love. This was counterproductive because Jeff could be only who he was meant to be.

The only thing that saved Jeff was that he had learned enough objectivity by then to understand his parents as people with their own fallibilities rather than as authorities of anyone else's direction.

It is imperative to accept our children and let them exist on their own terms, no matter what their values, sexual orientation, beliefs, or preferences. These need not match ours. We cannot assume that our own values are the only right ones or impose them on anyone else. Our children are not our property; we have merely the right and the responsibility to guide them and interact with them. Ultimately, they are who they are. In the words of poet Kahlil Gibran,

> They come through you but not from you,
> And though they are with you yet they belong not to you.
> You may give them your love but not your thoughts,
> For they have their own thoughts.

WARNING SIGNS OF EATING DISORDERS

A child with Confirmed Negativity Condition is set up for an eating disorder before he or she ever manifests it. Sometimes the signs are obvious; sometimes they are subtle. As I explained in Chapter 4, not all anorexics or bulimics are underweight, so family and friends must be attentive to other signs.

Many parents are understandably concerned when their children go on diets, particularly if they are a normal weight to begin with. But how does one distinguish between a child's "normal"—if misguided—attempt at weight loss and the manifestation of an eating disorder? After all, eating disorders are common in teenagers and people in their twenties, particularly among females (although I see many patients in my clinic, male and female, well past these ages), and every magazine and bestseller aimed at them trumpets the latest miracle diet. Does someone caught up in the enthusiasm of the latest diet fad necessarily have an eating disorder?

Look at the history of your child. The sensitive child will be affected by everything and will try to adhere to the norm. If the norm around her is that everyone is on a diet, she will go on a diet and be the best at it. If she has CNC, she will always take it to an extreme. A "normal" child will stop when she feels she is thin enough; a CNC child will not.

As a parent, I would be wary of any child who always seems to be on a diet, regardless of his or her weight. Take note if your child begins to fret excessively about fat content, calories, and the like. I would be sure never to have diet products around the house, although I would keep the cupboards stocked with nutritious foods. Diet drinks are a particular problem. It has been suggested that some artificial sweeteners in them cause hyperactivity and other mood alterations in children. Many patients I see are literally addicted to them and experience acute anxiety when withdrawn from them. I would also be on the alert if your child begins making excuses to avoid mealtimes, constantly suggesting she ate too much at lunch and wants to skip dinner, that she ate at a friend's house, and so on.

A child with an eating disorder will generally manifest other signs beyond the dieting itself. I would be particularly alert if your child, always so deferential to others, becomes increasingly indecisive. Simple decisions about what to eat, what to wear, what movie to see become torturous. What may have evinced itself previously as kindness to others becomes an imperative for all action.

When asked what she wants to do, the child may seem abject. "I don't care, what do you want to do?" might be her response. Or "It doesn't matter what I want. What do *you* want?" These are warning signs that should be heeded. As I mentioned earlier, take notice if you hear your child continually putting herself down. I realize in retrospect I had done that myself as a child. When my mother heard my self-deprecating remarks, she would say to me, "Peggy, charity begins in the home. You have to love yourself more than other people." And I thought, "How can I love myself?" Attitudes such as these are important to watch for if we suspect an eating disorder.

SIGNS OF BULIMIA

One need not be thin to be bulimic. This makes it a doubly devious condition because it often goes undetected. Yet, as many bulimics die from chemical imbalances and suicide as do anorexics.

Bulimics who are purgers seldom eat a comfortable amount of food at the dinner table and then stay for conversation. They will generally make a trip to the bathroom immediately following the meal to get rid of what they ate. They may turn the shower on to drown out the sounds of vomiting.

Many bulimics abuse laxatives and complain to the doctor of constipation in the hope of getting a prescription for the strongest possible preparation.

Some bulimics have scars on the backs of their fingers from scraping them on their teeth as they stick their fingers down their throats. They may have poor gums, sallow complexions, and pitted, yellow teeth eaten away by stomach acid.

Many bulimics exercise constantly (basically, another form of purging) to burn off the pounds and pounds of food they can eat at a single sitting. They gradually exclude friends and family and spend more and more time on their single-minded quest for food. Groceries and money disappear from home; there may be reports of kleptomania as the bulimic searches out more supplies for a binge-and-purge.

Bulimics generally appear constantly physically agitated.

SIGNS OF ANOREXIA

Anorexics generally have strange eating habits. Many refuse food outright. Others consume it in a ritualized, almost robotic way. It is common for anorexics to be deeply anxious while eating or shortly afterward. They often disguise the fact that they are eating at all, going to the refrigerator at night when no one else can see them. I believe this is an effort to fool the Negative Mind. When my daughter Nikki was sick, she would pretend to be writing, then sneak a piece of food.

Anorexics are generally obsessed with food, even if they are not getting enough of it. They might prepare grand dinner parties, not consuming any food at the time, but allowing themselves leftover table scraps once the guests have gone. Eating out of garbage cans is common. Sufferers believe they are unworthy of good food, but worthy of any illness they might pick up by eating spoiled, discarded offal.

Anorexics have a marked pallor and black pools under their eyes; their fingernails are cracked, and their skin, particularly on their hands, often becomes dry. They experience a profound insomnia, and have difficulty concentrating and making eye contact. (See Chapter 4.)

There are other secret clues that people in the throes of an eating disorder might leave, awaiting translation by those aware enough to detect them. In Chapter 4, I mentioned that evocative artwork and tiny handwriting provide such clues.

I also find that depression goes hand in hand with an eating disorder. This can come as a result of the nutritional imbalance and an unhealthy emotional focus on food. Imagine not being able to do anything else but focus on food. As one sufferer described it, "Food is my only friend, but it's also my enemy." I find that such people are generally listless and apathetic, unable to take any joy in their surroundings. They have what psychiatrists might call "flat affect."

Given their intense mental suffering, it is not surprising that bulimics and anorexics will often mask their pain with alcohol or substance abuse.

I would seek professional help as soon as you suspect a loved one has an eating disorder. Take your child to the doctor for an evaluation. Do not attempt to treat the condition yourself. You will need all the help you can get.

WHAT TO DO WHEN SOMEONE YOU LOVE
IS DIAGNOSED WITH AN EATING DISORDER

If your child has been diagnosed with an eating disorder that has not yet reached an acute stage, her situation cannot be ignored. Just because this is not an emergency, it does not mean that you should not take immediate action. Be aware of your child's growing subjectivity. If she becomes exceedingly negative, her condition will only worsen without appropriate intervention. The severity of her condition depends not on her weight but on the entrenchment of CNC—something that cannot be as easily measured. While the severity of the eating disorder lies on a continuum, I believe that we must combat the underlying CNC in the same way for both an acutely ill person and one who is only at the beginning of the slide. Both people must traverse the five stages of recovery; the difference lies in the relative ease with which someone with greater access to her Actual Mind can absorb the recovery process.

Moderately ill eating disorder patients can be helped with outpatient therapeutic care, as long as their families participate in a loving manner. But first we must get these people into care. At this earlier stage, they may have more of their own "head space" intact—the Negative Mind may still not predominate. In that case, parents or other loved ones can explain to victims where they are now and what could happen to them if there is no therapeutic intervention.

You might say to your child, "I know you are trying to manage a difficult situation in your head and that you are afraid you are ruining the family. We love you and we know this isn't your fault. It's happening because you're such a good, kind person. If we don't get the right help now, the problem will just get worse. We're all going to get through this together. We are going to get a therapist for you so you won't have to worry anymore."

The key here is early intervention. Remember, no matter where a patient is on the eating disorder continuum—in the early stages or acutely ill—the steps for recovery must adhere to the guidelines and principles I have set forth below and in Chapters 5 and 6. We must always begin to reverse the confirmed negativity from the bottom up.

Eating disorders are insidious and difficult to treat once they become acute, and they can become acute alarmingly quickly. Reversing them requires a high degree of commitment, understanding, and training that is beyond many. The firmly entrenched Negative Mind is determined to sabotage every attempt of a helping person.

Once a person manifests an acute eating disorder, the circumstances which determine its progression are much more difficult to control. As I discussed in Chapter 2, at this point the victim takes a highly subjective and negative view of life, and will work overtime to translate any event or circumstance in a negative way.

From this juncture, it is not impossible, but certainly difficult, to reverse the Negative Mind without appropriate intervention. A victim's Negative Mind will be confirmed much more easily than not. As she heads toward self-destruction, her Negative Mind grows in importance and magnitude. As Julie wrote to me early in her illness, "I hate myself all the more and I feel more alone (rightly so) than ever before."

The victim's mind does not allow her to ask for help, as badly as she wants and needs it. And she cannot be treated by the ones who love her most and whom she loves because of the added burdens of guilt and sense of responsibility to care for her parents. Julie writes of this terrible dilemma: "It pains me to torment my mother so and despite all requests of me to speak, to divulge my thoughts, it is too dangerous for I increase my burden upon her too often. So many times I speak without regret and further aggravate my own mind. And too many times my wordless tears bring on her tears. And so the terror and pity, sorrow and hatred intensifies within me. Each utterance I make is done with overwhelming trepidation. I engage in a vicious cycle in my head, pleading for my silence, praying for her peace, knowing only death as an answer."

In a perfect world, every victim of an eating disorder would have full access to a treatment facility that could treat not just the symptoms of the disorder but the patient's interpretation of her role in life, thereby restoring her sense of self and worth.

However, I am all too aware that access to such facilities are few and far between, or beyond the reach of most people. Many lack the financial resources, and unfortunately, insurance companies have been slow to appreciate the severity of the disorder and the length of time required to treat it fully; they therefore do not offer the kind of full coverage many families need to have a loved one treated effectively.

Other families may have access only to treatment programs that they have either tried and found wanting or that they intuitively recognize will not meet the needs of the sufferer. Still others may be unable to convince a loved one that she needs help.

What, then, can families and friends do to help the victim of an eating disorder? As a first step, I feel it is essential to ally yourself with a caring medical doctor and other health professionals to work as a team, a united front, to help your loved one.

As you have read in the last chapter, the care offered by our clinic is not something that one can readily replicate at home. I wish I could lay out a linear, step-by-step program for helping your loved one; I wish it were that easy. Critically ill people with eating disorders are in dire danger; their bodies are almost completely depleted and they are often suicidal.

You need help getting your loved one through this acute stage and on the road to recovery. In the next chapter I will offer some advice about seeking professional help. Here I can share with you the guidelines that I have found so helpful in my practice. I hope that you can use them as you work as part of a team with medical professionals to help your loved one.

I applaud you for your bravery and tenacity.

TAKE RESPONSIBILITY FOR RECOVERY FROM THE VICTIM

As is clear by now, sufferers of eating disorders cannot take responsibility for their condition. They have already taken responsibility for much of the world and have been exhausted by their failure to make a significant difference. They desperately need for you and the rest of the health care team to take the burden from their shoulders.

I generally tell my patients, "Imagine a place where people worry about you and you don't have to worry about anyone. Can you think that maybe it's time you had a turn to be first? I know that you want help. I know that you can't ask for it. I am going to give you what you need without your having to ask for it." The patient needs to be relieved of this crushing burden.

You might tell your loved one that you and the doctors will be fully responsible for her recovery. You will make all the decisions for now. Your loved one will no longer have to worry about preparing or eating meals. You will schedule doctor's appointments. You will take care of food.

At this point, sufferers are usually both enormously relieved and terribly frightened and anxious. They will protest continually, "I've got things under control; I don't need your help," "I'm not worthy of your help." "You are going to make me fat." "I don't deserve to live."

You may answer each time by saying, "I love you and I know that you deserve to live. I am not going to let you go until I know you are better. I am not going to let you get fat; the doctors and I are going to get you well. You can trust me. I am in charge and I'm going to take care of you."

OFFER UNCONDITIONAL LOVE AND SUPPORT

When our children are infants, it is easy and natural to love them unconditionally. We do not blame them when they cry or keep us awake. We know that they are not responsible for the hard work required to raise them. We love them no matter what.

You need to recapture that same sense of unconditional love and support while helping a person with an eating disorder. It might be helpful for you to see the victim as an emotional child. That may be a way to connect with the feeling of unconditional love and support you would naturally give a baby.

Why unconditional love? As I explained in Chapter 5, unconditional love counteracts the harsh voice of the Negative Mind and allows the possibility of connecting with the Actual Mind.

In the early as well as the acute stages, the patient must be bathed in unconditional love. A harsh word should never be spoken because the Negative Mind will seize on it and use it against the patient. Not reproaching the victim can be extremely difficult, especially if the victim is behaving badly—cursing, throwing dishes, or having a tantrum. In these instances, draw a firm boundary between the person and her bizarre and distressing behavior. Instead of punishing or rejecting, I always say in a soft voice, "I know you're frightened. Can you sit by me?" Your challenge is to love your child no matter how upsetting her behavior.

Always treat your loved one with respect. From my experience, it stops the behavior more quickly than any other response.

Giving love as a reward for only good behavior actually reinforces the Negative Mind. Don't try to encourage someone to eat by saying, "If you loved me, you would try some of this." It is saying, "You are worthy of love only if you comply. There are terms to my love." This gives the Negative Mind leverage to explain to the victim her unworthiness. It might say to her, "See, they don't love you or they wouldn't have punished you." As the patient recovers, a healthy, realistic balance begins to establish itself between these polar opposites.

Sometimes our unconscious actions imply conditions on our love. Think about your own reactions toward the victim. Might you be praising only those efforts you consider to be her best? Are you more responsive to her when she behaves the way you want her to? Do you react negatively when she does something you find objectionable? Such actions might send signals that tell the victim your love is contingent on her meeting your expectations. You are striving for consistent, positive, loving support all the time—love and respect that depends in no way on how the victim behaves, but in honor of who the victim is.

While some people believe that "Tough Love" may be effective in moderating or controlling certain adolescent behaviors such as drug use, shoplifting, and so on, we have found it to be entirely counterproductive in treating eating disorders. Tough Love basically says, "My love for you has many conditions. You can't rely on me."

Using this approach, doctors might tell parents to set limits on their child—for example, to remove every source of pleasure for a child unless she agrees to eat. Here is a typical letter describing the failure of this approach:

The psychiatrist told us that they were "going to make Jane's life miserable until she chooses to eat." His behavioral approach of punishing Jane for not eating literally shattered our daughter's soul. She said in this hospital you have to eat to get love; she would not be able to see us unless she ate.

After a few weeks of hospitalization, where her phone calls were monitored so she could not confide in us, she was discharged having gained only a few pounds. She was returned to us and for the next several months, we began the work of repairing the damage they had done. . . . Needless to say, whatever sense of herself that she may have had before this trauma was gone.

DO NOT TAKE BEHAVIOR AT FACE VALUE

It is essential to separate a victim from her behavior. Remember that the child is plagued by the Negative Mind. She may become abusive, or she may engage in degrading, self-mutilating, or bizarre activities (see Chapter 4).

This negative behavior is not your child. When it occurs, attempt to ally yourself with your child against the Negative Mind. If you blame your child for that behavior or act repulsed by it, you are reaffirming and supporting the Negative Mind and confirming and strengthening the condition.

At this stage your child is extraordinarily suggestible and will twist everything you say into a negative to feed the condition. If you throw up your hands and say, "I can't take this anymore," the Negative Mind will have won. If your child tosses a dish at you, understand that she is doing it out of fear. She is operating on negative instructions to alienate the ones who love her the most. Indeed, the ones who love her best must be the first target.

How should you respond in the face of all this horrifying behavior? What I instinctively do is to put my arms around the patient, first to take away the fear, then to comfort her, to attempt to persuade her with logic, and most important, to convince her that I am stronger than the condition. I must convince her that I am not vulnerable to the pressure of the Negative Mind, and I am not going away, no matter what.

You might tell your child, "I know that wasn't you throwing that dish. I know the condition made you do that. No matter what the condition does to try to push me away from you, I'm not going to leave you. I'm here to stay."

Referring to the condition as a separate entity helps your child draw a distinction between that negative part of her and her Actual Mind.

Explain to your child about the Negative Mind. Tell her that she is not crazy, that what she is thinking and feeling is common among people with eating disorders. When you tell her that you know that she may be experiencing negative thoughts, even voices, music, or loud noises, that she is bound to be bewildered yet compelled by them, she knows that you understand, that she is not alone. To take away the stigma, liken it to a broken leg or pneumonia, except that it is an emotional condition rather than a physical one. Explain that you and she are going to be allies against this condition.

DON'T EVER JUDGE THE INDIVIDUAL

As an eating disorder wends its way to acuteness, parents and friends become increasingly lost about what to do. The horror at their helplessness only accentuates the plight of the victim who is becoming aware of her own inability to control or remedy her situation.

Within their fear, parents can react, usually against their child. Desperation persuades them to shout, demand, and lay on guilt. It seems inconceivable to them that their youngster is truly incapable of what is a most natural fact of living—eating. But remember, the victim of an eating disorder believes she is not permitted to eat because she has failed to save her parents or the world, and therefore does not deserve to live.

I cannot emphasize enough how easy it is to reconfirm the negative condition at this stage. The child already believes the worst possible about herself. Parents must be excessively kind. It takes great self-control to never react in the negative. It is unwise to tell a child, "You have a problem." Rather, say, "We have a problem, and we're going to fix it together."

BE PREPARED FOR IRRATIONAL
OR "MANIPULATIVE" BEHAVIORS

I've put "manipulative" in quotes because these behaviors are often misconstrued as a child's attempt to control others. In fact, they are the consequence of the Negative Mind controlling the child. As the Negative Mind attempts to control the child, so it attempts to control us through the child.

These children are terrified and confused. They intuitively know that their parents are their first source of help. Imagine the victims' turmoil when the Negative Mind tells them to push their parents away even as they pull their parents close.

It is helpful to regard these behaviors as the outcome of fear or the Negative Mind's internal manipulation, not the desire to control for its own sake. The child is loath to disrespect anybody.

Irrational behaviors in particular can appear as "control issues." Sufferers often attempt to structure their eating or sleeping habits based on illogical fears that harm might come to loved ones if they do not adhere to the Negative Mind's dictates. The Negative Mind threatens dire consequences to the sufferer's family members if she does not obey. "If you eat this, then your mother will die," it may say, or "If you don't run around the house a hundred times, your little brother will be harmed."

One patient could only prepare food between one and three in the morning. Another would not let her parents sleep together in the same bed; she kicked her father out so she could sleep with her mother and keep her as physically close as possible because she was afraid something would happen to her mom if she didn't watch her all the time. These behaviors are naturally exasperating to parents.

Kathleen had bought her daughter quart-size containers to store her food. Later she casually asked Mara if she had bought the correct item. Mara responded by sobbing uncontrollably, "What I really wanted was the gallon size." Mara acted as though it were the end of the world.

On the surface, this seemed like a bizarre overreaction, but it was a major crisis for Mara. She had desperately wanted the gallon size, but she was so grateful to her mother for purchasing any containers at all, she did not want to impose on her further. There was nothing she could do to redeem herself for not feeling utterly grateful and satisfied for the quart-size containers. She felt unworthy being asked to express a preference for herself.

EXPECT TO BE TESTED

Parents of children with eating disorders find that they are tested at every turn. If they are unaware of the workings of the Negative Mind, the destructive behavior will win, and the child will become immediately more agitated because she will be more fearful.

Your child might be hurtfully rude to you, and you may be tempted to break down and cry, a temptation you should do your best to resist. She might hide food she was supposed to eat to see how astute you are in finding it. (Some of my patients told me they have purposely hidden tidbits to see if I was smart enough to figure it out.) Conversely, a child might pretend to be overly cajoling or compliant so you will give in to something. "Well, I've eaten most of it," she might say when you are concerned about her nutrition. They may jump up and down in place doing exercise to see what you will do. In all cases, it is best to respond with distraction instead of anger. "Come, let's work on a puzzle together" or "Let me tell you about a funny thing that happened to me at work today."

Victims often present an illogical logic that draws parents in. "I need to exercise because it relieves my stress," they might say. Or "Yoga clears my mind." In Chapter 4, I presented many of the tricks the Negative Mind will use to further its condition. Victims will almost certainly know which foods have the most water, fat, and calories. And they may resort to hiding uneaten food or exercising in secret.

If you find your loved one engaging in these deceptive behaviors, it is important to refrain from anger, disgust, or resignation. Instead, you might say, "Hi, honey, I know your head is giving you a rough time. I know your head is making you do this. Come on, we will figure it out together."

The victim will usually be embarrassed and relieved at the same time. And you are proving that you can determine the difference between the person and the condition. My patients, once cured, generally laugh at how creative and inventive they were while in the grips of the disorder.

USE LOGIC TO COMBAT
EVERY NEGATIVE WITH A POSITIVE

Anorexia knows no logic as we understand it. Redirection of the child's mind depends, then, on reiteration of logic. It is therefore essential that you respond to each negative statement with a positive one.

IF YOUR CHILD SAYS: "I'm a burden on society."

YOU MIGHT ANSWER: "No, you're not. You are wonderful. You've never done an unkind thing in your life. If you were a bad person, you wouldn't worry about being a burden. Selfish people don't worry about being a burden."

IF YOUR CHILD SAYS: "I'm so selfish. I don't deserve to take up your time."

YOU MIGHT ANSWER: "If you were selfish, you wouldn't care about that."

Challenge subjectivity with objectivity. A victim will translate anything said, no matter how positive, into a negative. If you say, "Your hair looks so lovely today," she will think, "Oh, it must have been a mess yesterday." If you say, "Good morning, dear. Thanks for cleaning up the kitchen counter so well," the victim might translate this as, "The kitchen counter . . . the kitchen counter . . . didn't I do a good job dusting the living room? Or scrubbing the bathroom? Does she mean I didn't do enough? Or maybe she's just saying she liked the job; she doesn't really mean it."

Your child's words reflect the Negative Mind; your reply will be what her Actual Mind will one day will be able to tell her objectively. If she says, "black," you say "white." In many ways, this resembles the split-page journal exercise and the role-playing our patients do at the clinic (see Chapter 5).

Your messages should convey unmistakably that you will always be there:

"I will always listen to you if you get upset and cry."
"You aren't supposed to be perfect."
"You are not crazy, and you won't always feel this way."
"I have to know how you're feeling in order to help you, but if you can't tell me right now, I have a good idea anyway."
"Let's talk about it and work it out."
"I am nice to you because I love you a lot."
"Nothing you say or do could ever make me love you less."
"One day you'll be strong enough to be nice to others."
"I won't let your head hurt you."
"I know what I'm talking about. You can trust me."

DO NOT COMMENT ON BODY APPEARANCE

Anorexics will try to maneuver you into commenting on their appearance. This is the Negative Mind's attempt to collect more ammunition to use against the child. If you say they look fine, they will think they look normal. They will then think they have to lose weight to prove they are subnormal and unworthy.

If you say, "You look great," the normal dieter will feel a sense of satisfaction. But the person with the eating disorder will feel unworthy. The Negative Mind translates such a comment as, "You look fat and therefore unworthy."

If your child asks, "Do I look normal?" an unaware parent might respond, "You look just fine." The victim will translate this sadly as, "Now I have to lose more weight."

It is hard for any parent to "win" at this game; there is so little neutral territory. If you must, comment on hair or eye color.

DON'T PLAY A NUMBERS GAME

Parents or practitioners have been known to threaten anorexics with statements such as "If you lose seven more pounds, you'll have to go back into the hospital." Ironically, this is in fact giving the victim permission to lose six pounds, fifteen ounces. Numbers are best left unsaid.

Take the scale out of the house. Insist that your doctor weigh your child backward so she cannot see the result, because her Negative Mind will use any number, no matter how low, against her to lose yet more weight. Get rid of measuring cups because to the patient they are yet another means of determining her worth ("I'm only allowed to have two ounces of juice").

DISCOURAGE COMPETITION

Ideally, it is absurd to expect us all to compete with one another because we are all unique individuals. Yet society advertently and inadvertently demands that we do. Any concept that demands that some people be superior and some inferior has no place in a humanistic society, and certainly not in the home of someone with an eating disorder. This will only aggravate the condition; these children are already competing to make the world the best place for everybody else.

If possible, send your child to a school that gives written evaluations, where every child is an individual, instead of a letter grade. It would be hurtful for her to be in a position in which she would be ranked or measured, which again would measure worth. Refrain from bragging about your child in front of her, because you are sending her a message that you value her not as an individual but for her achievements. Avoid displaying artwork and essays that you or the teacher believe represent the child's best efforts. Consider talking with your child's teachers or principal about what they can do to reduce your child's pressure to compete.

Tell your child over and over that you love her for what she is, not just for what she does.

ENCOURAGE SELF-EXPRESSION

I would encourage self-expression that is individual and that by its very nature does not demand perfection. Painting, poetry, creative writing, and journal work are excellent tools. These are also a wonderful outlet and a way to enhance communication. You might discuss your child's creative output with her to gain a better understanding of how her mind works. Rather than impose your own interpretation, you might say, "Tell me more about this."

In fact, you might say, "I know your secret. There's someone inside telling you what to do, telling you to hurt yourself." It can help your child to let the Negative Mind out into the open because she will be reassured that the onus is not hers alone to bear. The enemy has been found out. It is imperative, however, not to ask your child to agree with you. In so doing, the Negative Mind will punish her.

If there is another adult the child respects, invite interaction with him or her too. Allowing your child other opinions will increase her ability to be objective.

FOOD AND YOUR CHILD

Work very closely with your doctor to design small, nutritious meals and monitor your child's progress. As I explained in Chapter 6, six small meals a day are less threatening than three large ones.

You might also ease the stress that follows eating with distraction, rocking, and holding to help your youngster accept the food and prevent her from disappearing into the Negative Mind.

There will be times when the dinner table seems like a battleground. Do your best to stay calm and supportive. Although proper nutrition is obviously vital to a victim's recovery, keep in mind that the focus should not be on food, but on helping the victim reinterpret her world.

HELPING SIBLINGS COPE

Siblings can make a confusing situation even more so. A normal family setting often involves rivalry between sisters and brothers. But it is difficult for children to make sense of something that makes no sense to adults. Suddenly, almost before they know it, parents start catering to everyone.

The parents' role is to ensure the well-being of their children. When they cope with a child who has an eating disorder, their energy is naturally focused toward that need. Because of this special direction of their time, the other children in the family may take on different roles. Some siblings have been the first in line to help, others have desensitized themselves to the problem in order to survive. A teenager in the family is likely to resent everything with little encouragement. A teenager with a sibling who has an eating disorder can become very resentful indeed. Some previously "well" siblings may even compromise their own development because of their anxiety.

Siblings are naturally concerned about the sufferer. To prevent their anxiety, it would be helpful to teach them that they are not to blame for their sister's condition, that she is in an illogical place, and that they should not judge her abnormal behavior or show anger toward her.

I would take all my children to a therapist, involving the entire family for two reasons: The children will realize that the family is a whole and that their parents are committed to maintaining that whole, and they will see that the problem is being addressed by the adults and it is not up to the children to mitigate their parents' frustration or anger.

Some siblings will be resentful that all the attention is sucked away from them, but in my experience, it is more often true that the "well" siblings are more concerned about the intensified emotions they see in their parents.

At the clinic we talk to siblings and allow them to express their feelings. They understand that the condition is not their responsibility, they did not cause it, but they can be part of the solution by not judging the victim's behavior. They must also realize that this is an interim time—that wellness will return to the sibling and balance to the family.

I often say, "The left arm is broken, so we have to pay attention to it. It doesn't mean that we don't value the right arm or the legs. It's just that the body will work best when every part is healed."

It is imperative that all is done with patience and with no blame. If you tell a sibling, "Can't you see that your sister needs my help now? Don't be so selfish," it can be damaging because the onus of negativity will land on that child. Moreover, if the victim sees her siblings suffering from what appears to be rejection or anger, she may feel more guilt as well. Remember, the eating disorder victim loves her whole family and would like nothing better than to have it work. Your goal is to try to achieve as much balance in the family as possible, discouraging siblings from stepping into adult roles.

COPING WITH BURNOUT

There can be nothing more frightening than the belief that your child might die. When my daughters were ill, I felt as if they had been kidnapped but no body could be found. I had the frantic sense that there had to be something I could do, but I did not know in which direction to run. I was terrified and at times immobilized with fear.

Never knowing which day might be their last was utterly draining. Would death come from heart failure or suicide? I weep inside when I remember the relentless fear of the not knowing.

The player of a potentially lethal chess game, you may have to be two moves ahead of your child's Negative Mind, aware of all of its possible countermoves. Such hypervigilance can also be exhausting.

As a parent, you may find yourself on an emotional roller coaster with no scheduled stops. I can empathize with the pain and courage you feel when your child is ill. For your own sake, remember that you are not to blame for your child's illness. This is a time when many parents set aside their own needs entirely and risk burnout. Be reassured that the time for balance will come later, but there are some things you can do now.

Support groups for parents, family members, and other loved ones can be helpful in avoiding burnout. Build a network of friends. You need to draw on anyone you know who is kind. Do not isolate yourself in shame or fear. Look to family and friends for support. Seek respite from the necessary intensity of the condition. You need adequate sleep to maintain your stability. Find a safe place where you can express your feelings. If you take better care of yourself, you will be a more effective caregiver for your child.

To hold your center, learn to not take CNC personally. It will pass. You cannot be the perfect careworker. Some people escape into their jobs. Find your spirituality, even if you are not necessarily religious. This will encourage faith, courage, and direction.

It is possible to work within your community to find the help you need. In the following chapter, I provide some guidelines for advocating for a new kind of care for your child. Although finding the right kind of help may be difficult, I know from experience that well-intentioned caring professionals do exist who want to do all they can to help victims of eating disorders become well again.

Last year a family from the eastern United States dropped in unexpectedly, hoping their child would be immediately admitted—an impossibility. However, given that the fourteen-year-old was so weak, we established communication with her doctor and her extended family at home. Together they are successfully bringing this child through her condition by fax contact with us. As the caring network of physicians who appreciate the role of CNC and the Negative Mind expands, I hope that all facilities will work with one another to help these victims.

8

Finding the
Help You Need

S ome people with eating disorders will, through luck in the form of inadvertent intervention and/or the attentiveness of others, find the help they need and reverse their condition before they have reached rock bottom. Those who are in the grip of acute eating disorders are in a potentially life-threatening situation. At the time they most need help, however, they will seldom be able to ask for it, much as they wish it. It will be up to family and friends to insist on that help. The acute victim must be kept safe until the crisis is over. Practically speaking at the present time, that means hospitalization.

If your loved one is not in immediate physical danger of collapse—something that only a medical doctor can determine, since physical appearance is not the only determinant of the health of someone with anorexia or bulimia—you may find it necessary to confront her with the need to get outpatient help. Explain to her that she must begin meeting with medical and/or mental health professionals. You might say, "We're concerned about you. We want you to get the help you need. This isn't your problem, it's our problem, and we'll all work together until you're better."

Remember, the victim is embarrassed at being a burden, so she will insist she is all right. If you know she is seriously ill and she appears adamant about wanting no care, you can be assured that the Negative Mind is in control and you must be strong for her. Her life may depend on it. Sometimes a dire situation demands that I feed a child when she refuses with almost anyone else. Even though she may resist feeding before I start, immediately afterward, she begs me not to let her go and insists on me convincing her she is not bad.

If your loved one is acutely ill, your first step must be to inform her that she needs help, and that she will have to go to a hospital to begin treatment. The victim is likely to react with anger, denial, or refusal. Perhaps she will tell you that she is worthless and does not deserve help, that no one can help her, that nothing will work. These protests are the work of the Negative Mind.

In response, it is helpful to say firmly but gently, "I love you and know you need help. I am going to see that you get the help you deserve, and we will all work together until you're well. You don't need to worry anymore; we will take care of everything for you." Reassure your loved one that you are not abandoning her by putting her in the hospital; you will be there for her no matter what her condition makes her say or do.

Given that an acute patient is more in the grip of the Negative Mind than the Actual Mind, she will typically react in two ways: the small Actual Mind will be both relieved at the possibility of help and terrified at the impending onslaught of unkindness that the Negative Mind will assail her with. When the status of the Negative Mind is threatened, it responds with horrifying determination to maintain itself.

WHILE YOUR LOVED ONE IS IN ACUTE CARE

The priority of acute hospital care is physical wellness, which comes down to feeding the patient to get her to a safe weight and rebalancing her electrolytes. We must save the person's physical life before attempting anything else. Normally, a patient in an acute care hospital is fed by means of a gastric-nasal (GN) tube inserted through the nose into her stomach. This is hardly pleasant, and it is not surprising that patients react to this first step in their hospitalization with anger, tears, fears, or depression.

Explain to your loved one that her body is so depleted that the GN tube is the only way to help her body for now so it can heal. Reassure her that this is a temporary measure.

The idea of feeding and weight gain is frightening for most patients, yet it is a necessary first step in acute care. Unfortunately, however, feeding can be such a battle and focus that the patient's emotional needs and the root of her problems—CNC—are often inadequately addressed in hospital care. As one person wrote to me, "Any program I've been in was a stop-gap measure. . . . I'd put on weight that I'd immediately drop as soon as I was released." Family and friends have a crucial role here, one that can make a big difference in a victim's recovery. Your loved one needs your careful and thoughtful intervention and advocacy on her behalf.

It would be difficult to overestimate how terrifying and overwhelming hospitalization can be for an acute patient. The letter below expresses this so eloquently. Reading it will help loved ones appreciate how crucial their support is at this time.

> *There was no way out. . . .*
> The room was cold and white, spotlessly clean. I sat on the edge of the window seat, alone. To my left stood the small, untouched, sterile chest of drawers, in front of me was the huge white pressed bed. To my right a vast television screen bulged out from the corner—empty and blank. The wardrobe was big, wide and bold. Everything—white. The door was shut tight. I listened and strained to hear a voice but there was nothing, just a buzzing electrical sound which seemed to become louder and louder as time went on. My bag leant against my right leg. I daren't move. Behind me the window was black. The curtains were drawn open. Outside I could see nothing but myself and again the same cold, hostile, white room. The smell was unlike anything my nostrils had ever

come across, I kept sniffing. I was certain there were people outside looking in, watching every twitch or move I made. I was scared and ready for attack. As the fear built up and up I could almost hear it grow louder. The voices in my head were calling out as loud as they could but nobody was there. Why had they left me here? Was this my punishment? I had screamed and cried all the way in the car, partly with fear but also with the pain, my whole body ached. As I sat in the stillness I wanted to move, to get out, to escape it all, but what would the nurses say? What would they do to me? What was I allowed to do? Nobody had told me anything, I'd just been told this was my room. My room? This cold, empty, silent room, was mine? There was no time, no clock ticking, nothing, just a deafening silence.

I stood, quickly, turning and saw my reflection. It wasn't me at all. I looked and studied the figure, as she did too. Her eyes were dark and hollowed out, her cheekbones had tight white skin stretched taut across them. She wore a huge woolly, green jumper on top of two other jumpers beneath, which poked untidily out at the neck—just like mine did. She looked drowned and hidden inside the many layers of clothes. The strange, emaciated girl turned with me as I looked down at my hands. They were raw and unfeeling, numbed with harsh, penetrating cold. What nightmares lay in front of me? The insecurity and uncertainty of it all were too much to bear. Despair, hopelessness and the prospect of eternal loneliness which lay before me were intolerable. I had been left, abandoned, isolated, deserted without anyone or anything. Although with these feelings there came the inevitability, a sense that it was deserved, a justified torture—but what for?—I did not know.

I was "killing myself" they had said but I hadn't cared. But now I had been caught and imprisoned. Strangely resigned to my fate, there was no way out. My control and power had been torn away from me. My coping mechanisms were to be stolen, and I'd be left vulnerable and open, naked. They would be able to do anything they wanted and there was nothing that I could do about it. Yes I was here in this isolated white cell but even worse, mentally I was condemned to the timeless void that was "treatment."

Having a good liaison with the doctor is imperative. Consider that you are building a care team. You might say to the head physician, "Our goal is to work with you as closely and as effectively as possible. We have insights into our daughter that we think will really help." Ideally, the doctor will be open to your perceptions.

Perhaps you can share a copy of this book with the doctor so that he or she will appreciate your approach and accommodate you wherever possible. You might wish to explain CNC and the Negative Mind to the medical personnel so they will understand that the victim is not "insane," noncompliant, or truly wishing for death. You could say, for example, "We feel very strongly that our child needs and wants help, but that a large part of her mind is preventing her from asking for it. She wants to comply, but the negativity in her makes it very difficult. We believe she wants very much to survive, but emotionally she doesn't feel she deserves it. We don't want her to be blamed as being uncooperative if she cannot follow through on your orders. She is simply not able to take responsibility for getting better; we need you to do that until she is strong enough to do it for herself. She needs positive reinforcement, no matter what. Here's a book that explains our viewpoint. Can you support us on this?"

It is also important for the physician to appreciate that while your child may be attempting to push you away at this stage, it is most likely because she does not want to be a further burden to you and already feels horribly guilty about putting you through this ordeal. It has been my experience that any reluctance disappears when CNC is reversed.

Ideally, at this stage, patients will receive twenty-four-hour care. Unfortunately, most hospitals are not set up for such intensive attention and will not provide it unless the family insists strongly; even then, it may be impossible. If a hospital does permit round-the-clock care, practically speaking it generally falls to the family members to fill in the gap themselves, although many hospitals may not allow this because of liability issues involved in family members coming and going or interfering with hospital routine.

Families need to be particularly vigilant at this point. I have come across many facilities that recognize that acute stage anorexics need round-the-clock care, but put the patients in five-point restraints because they do not have the manpower to offer one-on-one attention. This can prove devastating to patients, though it is unfortunately sometimes necessary if hospitals are short staffed and there are not enough family members or friends to help.

Saving the child's life is the immediate imperative. However, saving the child's spirit is imperative as well. Reiterate gentleness in everything you say and do.

I think that it is easy for us to underestimate the powerful effect that hospitalization can have on victims of eating disorders. I've received countless letters from parents detailing how their children felt traumatized or demoralized by the use of feeding tubes or restraints. Many of these children viewed their hospitalization experience as confirmation that they were worthless and misunderstood. They saw medical treatment not as a lifesaving measure but as a punishment. In these cases, I believe we need to do much more to change patients' perception of the hospitalization experience so that they don't divert so much of their energy to fighting it instead of working with health professionals toward a common goal. The key is better communication between parents and the health care team before, during, and after treatment.

Ideally, patients and their families will work with a staff that understands the Negative Mind, even if they don't identify it as such. When they do not, the consequences can be dire. I've had reports of desperate children running away from hospital programs and cutting themselves off from needed support.

In discussing your child's case with the medical personnel, be sure to explain which treatment approaches are totally unacceptable to you. You might say, "Punishing our daughter by withholding privileges if she can't follow orders will only reinforce her belief that she is worthless and unworthy of being helped. We also feel restraining her unkindly will have a terribly negative effect." You might then discuss how the staff should handle situations in which they would normally punish or restrain the patient. What will they do instead? I have found that people always respond eventually to unconditional caring.

As we have seen, the Negative Mind will make every attempt to foil treatments like gastric-nasal feeding, especially in the absence of one-on-one care. Patients sometimes pull out the tube, as Emma did, empty the gastric-nasal bag down the toilet or into a plant, or dilute the nutrition with water. They may also exercise through the night when the nursing staff is reduced. One patient pushed her gastric-nasal bag on a pole around and around the nurses' station, burning off every calorie she absorbed; another used the break between feedings to go up and down the stairs incessantly. The caregivers, so well intentioned but understaffed, simply could not keep up with these ploys.

Parents might want to ask the nursing staff for particular help. You might explain to them all the strategies your daughter might use to outwit them and all the bizarre requests she might make. You can say, for example, "Please understand that Mara's behavior is not her; please don't blame her for her actions because she can't be responsible for them until she's well. We believe that positive reinforcement and lack of blame are absolutely crucial for her recovery. She thrives on physical contact. Would you be able to rock and distract her after mealtime? If you're overburdened, may we come in and do that?" Most professionals who treat eating disorders are eager for any assistance in the task of saving lives from this tenacious condition, once they realize it can be productive.

Many hospitals make the mistake of giving patients a target weight and telling them that once they make that weight, they will be released. The patients' Negative Mind lets them put on the weight because its long-term goal is to get them out of the hospital and out of the reach of wellness, but once released patients usually go right back on track. The hospitals obviously must feed these critically ill patients; the task is to do this without letting the patient know any numbers.

Similarly, programs that specify a time limit for the patient, telling him or her, for example, "You'll be out of here in three months," can be counterproductive. In my experience, the patient dutifully "does time" in the facility, pretending compliance as she waits out the days until the Negative Mind can get back to business. As Camille, a twenty-eight-year-old woman wrote to me, "I have had an eating disorder for more than twelve years. I've been in and out of hospitals for this over eleven times. Each time, I just did what 'they' requested in order to get out and ended up right back where I was before I went in."

I prefer to tell my patients, "You will graduate to the next level of care when I know that you're not being directed by your Negative Mind." I am very clear with them that moving ahead does not depend in any way on weight or a number. I never give them a specific time line because each person progresses at her own pace. One must not to give the Negative Mind a structure to work with. Although my staff and I will have that number or structure in mind, the patient's Negative Mind will never be privy to it. This is a great relief to the patient's Actual Mind, because the Negative Mind has nothing to work with and cannot issue instructions based on it.

Consequently, it would be helpful for you to ask the hospital staff to weigh your child backwards and request that they refrain from revealing her weight to her, no matter how many times she demands to know it. Moreover, there should be no discussion with the victim regarding the length of her stay in a particular program.

In addition to the advocacy I have suggested, your chief role in this stage is to reassure your child and soothe her anxiety. Reassure her that she is not to blame for her illness, that you love her no matter what, and that you will stay by her for as long as it takes for her to get well.

Spend as much time by your child's bedside as the hospital permits, as long you are sure not to transfer your anxiety to her. At our clinic, parents stay away initially because their presence can cause the patients too much guilt and anxiety. After all, children generally have managed to *not* get better in their homes, so they don't initially know that their parents can help them. If parents are part of a "caregiving team," they can make a positive contribution to their loved one's healing.

If you find yourself incapable of handling this emotional burden, send other loving people in your child's life in your stead. She needs to feel positive that you are not abandoning her, and that you have a confident vision that she will recover. Where allowed and possible, I would use comforting touch, words, and rocking to soothe your child.

It is particularly important at this stage to distinguish between your child's needs and the demands of the Negative Mind. Children will typically ask their parents, "Tell them to stop putting so much food in my tube" or "Tell the doctors I need more medication." Parents naturally want to respond to their children's distress calls, but in this case, they need to realize that these requests are not in the child's best interests. They are coming from the Negative Mind. Explain to your loved one, "I know that the real you wants and needs help. I love you and you can trust me to work with the doctors to get you better. You don't need to worry; let us take care of you."

Depending on the nature of the acute care facility, patients who act particularly irrationally or suicidally—patients who are not "compliant"—may be put under psychiatric care. There are many different approaches: group therapy, one-on-one sessions with psychiatrists or psychologists, psychopharmacology. Some patients do very well under such care.

Ideally, patients and their families will have the opportunity to work with a professional who understands the Negative Mind, although they may use other descriptive terms for the concept. In reality, there are not yet enough therapists who realize that someone in the acute grip of an eating disorder is generally incapable of coming out of it without a very specific kind of help and support and so the course of treatment can be difficult. If you find that the doctors and nurses at the hospital are obviously uncooperative and unresponsive to your concerns and requests, you will need to look elsewhere for help.

THE ROLE OF PSYCHOPHARMACOLOGY

When most patients arrive at our clinic, they are generally on four or five psychoactive medications. They start out being prescribed one. Then the doctor adds a second to compensate for the side effects of the first, and a third to compensate for those of the second, and so on.

I do not want to stigmatize anorexia patients who are on medication; they bear enough stigma as it is. There are important reasons for acute patients to be given medication to treat their symptoms. Without twenty-four-hour care, they can be suicidal, and the drugs can help mitigate that deadly impulse. People with eating disorders who live at home are acting out continuously and may be suicidal. Drugs can help moderate their behavior and keep the household together. In an outpatient setting, medicating is understandable, because the doctor must keep the patient safe while dealing with her mind.

Antidepressants are commonly prescribed because depression comes along with anorexia and low nutrition. I have never seen a happy anorexic! People with eating disorders do respond to medication, but I would suggest that it is mainly their symptoms that are being addressed; the medications do not treat the underlying reason for the condition.

I believe that to correct the CNC, I need access to a person's unhindered mind. I am concerned that medication can mask or alter a patient's symptoms and behaviors, thereby reducing the effectiveness of psychotherapy to effectively treat the condition. In twenty-four-hour residential care as we provide it, in order to ascertain the severity and direction of the mindset in the patient, the fewer drugs used, the better. We work very closely and carefully with a number of medical doctors who make the decision to decrease the drugs depending on what they deem safe and necessary. When a negative mindset urges a patient to throw herself off a balcony or in front of traffic, sedation has an imperative role.

If patients indicate the need of medication for disorders other than those connected with eating disorders, our doctors will prescribe it. However, I would say that in well over 90 percent of the cases we see in our clinic, the symptoms for which the medication was initially prescribed disappear as we reverse the Confirmed Negativity Condition. We chart our patients' progress closely; if after two or three months it becomes clear to the doctor that the patient has been fed to the point that depression symptoms should have been abating but have not, and an antidepressant would be medically recommended, the doctor will involve it in her therapy.

A recent study suggests that Prozac can be effective in reducing occurrences of relapse, although it does not address the underlying cause. In our program, patients whose CNC has been successfully reversed are not likely to relapse. However, you may want to investigate the use of medication for this purpose.

As their children enter treatment programs, it is important for parents to discuss with their doctors whether they are considering prescribing medication. Hospitals have their own rules and reasons about these matters. I would ask about them, make sure I understand them, and state my preference. If children are already on medication, gradual, supervised withdrawal may also be an option worth exploring. But I cannot emphasize strongly enough that no one should *ever* withdraw from any medication unless under the close supervision of the prescribing doctor. Sudden withdrawal may have serious consequences.

It is also imperative to note that if, after a patient's CNC is reversed, he or she has another disorder that is not related to this condition, medication may well be necessary. This has been true of patients I have treated in my clinic. For example, our doctors discovered that a patient's underlying hormonal imbalance was contributing to her difficulty in keeping her emotions under control. In such a case, it is necessary to stabilize the hormonal imbalance before working further with the eating disorder.

OUTPATIENT THERAPY AFTER HOSPITALIZATION

After a patient has regained what the hospital considers an acceptable amount of weight, she is usually released. At this stage she appears physically well, but in fact she has taken only the first step toward total recovery. It is quite common for people with anorexia to leave acute care wards and immediately lose every pound they have gained, as in Camille's case. Most of the patients we see at the clinic have had multiple courses of unproductive treatment in acute care hospitals—sometimes dozens and dozens of visits. Remember, though, we are in the unhappy situation of seeing mostly worst-case, "tried everything" patients.

I do not want to denigrate the quality of care in such hospitals but I believe that treatment there usually has not been taken seriously enough because it has neither understood nor focused on the true nature of the underlying condition. This is what comes of defining eating disorders as primarily a medical problem whose cure is physiological repair or focusing on a single issue as "the cause." Many parents have written me that while they appreciated the caring efforts of the hospitals that treated their children, they felt the programs weren't getting to the heart of what compelled these victims to behave in such self-negating ways. Ideally, your enlightened advocacy and intervention will render hospital treatment more effective. I also believe that most hospitals and treatment centers fail to appreciate how long it takes for a patient to feel completely secure even after emotional healing. Recall that it took my daughter Kirsten over a year before she felt wholly at peace with her sense of self.

After hospital release, patients typically begin outpatient work. Outpatient psychotherapy can also be helpful—and necessary, I believe—for people with eating disorders who have not yet reached an acute stage.

Your first task should be to find a therapist or clinic that believes in and practices total recovery, not maintenance of the condition. Again, just as you allied yourself with the care team at the hospital, it would be helpful to take a team approach with the outpatient psychotherapist. Once more, it would be constructive to explain CNC and your frame of reference vis-à-vis the Negative Mind. You might explain that your child needs and wants help, but that the negativity prevents her from asking for it or complying with recommendations. Reiterate that she is unable to take responsibility for her actions and thus should not be blamed or labeled uncooperative. Insist on positive reinforcement and unconditional positive regard. You might suggest that the therapist read a copy of this book to better understand your position.

However, be forewarned that the magnitude of the Negative Mind is almost more than one would wish to believe. Its reversal can be more taxing than most people are prepared or willing to lend themselves to, even committed therapists. It is imperative that the battle of the loved one's life become your battle for the duration. If you embark on this mutual journey, keep focused on the destination in mind, expecting and accepting the waves and storms that will occur.

To effectively rid herself of the Negative Mind, a victim must feel protected all the time. The Actual Mind of patients who are acutely ill or who are long-term sufferers is already feeling so beaten and so exhausted from fighting that an outpatient situation can be counterproductive if not approached effectively. The patient feels guilty for money spent on her and for taking up the therapist's time. Or she feels needy for having had a touch of caring squeezed into a narrow time slot. She must then go home with her Negative Mind and be berated for her obvious selfishness.

The Actual Mind knows that to survive it must take advantage of any kindness extended to it. However, given the victim's incredible need, the Actual Mind must prove that the love and kindness is unconditional. Expect your loved one to test the therapist, and prepare the therapist for this. That means the victim may engage in bizarre behavior such as abusive language, throwing things, and other acting out in an attempt to alienate the therapist. Unfortunately, at this point, few people who do not understand the source of this need will cater to what they perceive as immature and irrational behavior.

It is imperative, therefore, that you find a therapist who understands that the onus of recovery cannot be placed on the patient, who will help the patient separate her Actual Mind from the condition, and who will offer unconditional love despite disturbing behavior. The treatment approach should be grounded in the conceptual framework of humanism rather than behaviorism.

Humanism is based on compassion, optimism, and positivity. Behavior modification techniques such as offering rewards (for eating) and imposing punishment (for not eating) are based on the idea that you are what you do—your actions are you. "Good" actions are rewarded, "bad" actions punished. By extension, the patient is perceived as "good" or "bad" depending on her responses. This is the antithesis of unconditional love.

Behaviorism may be effective for treating many conditions, but I do not believe it works for eating disorders, since a victim's actions are very much *not* who she is. One father wrote to me about his daughter's experiences with a "state of the art" cognitive/behavioral program:

> This program DOES NOT WORK FOR Amy. Amy weighs 72 pounds and is 5 feet 3 inches tall. Her nutritionist and physician are both telling me today that Amy must be admitted again to the hospital's eating disorder unit. When Amy was discharged from the hospital the last time, I told

myself that I would never admit her to a program again. When Amy is hospitalized she loses any sense of dignity that she has. She tells me, "Just shoot me now and get it over with." I'm afraid that if I do admit her, she'll find a way to kill herself.

I am not surprised that programs based on behavior modification are generally ineffective since the behavior they are designed to address is merely a symptom of the underlying condition, not the problem itself. If you are more or less saddled with such an approach because it is the only one available to you, make your preferences known that encouragement for "good" behavior is acceptable but there can be no punishment for "bad" behavior.

Unfortunately, there are many other approaches that I believe you must be wary of, as well. I recommend, for example, that you avoid programs that seek to explain the cause of the condition in terms of a single trauma, like sexual or physical abuse. While trauma *may* be a precipitating factor in an eating disorder, as I have explained in Chapter 3, it is not the underlying cause. Certainly, "issues" and their consequences need be addressed, but with a positive attitude to the continuing work toward reversal of CNC.

Similarly, from our experience, twelve-step programs that can be highly effective for drug or alcohol abuse may be ineffective in producing total recovery from CNC. At the core of this approach is a belief that eating disorders are "addictive behaviors," and the patient must remain constantly vigilant lest she "fall off the wagon." While this approach may indeed improve the victim's quality of life, it essentially reaffirms and maintains the condition, thus obstructing the path to full recovery.

As a middle-aged anorexia patient, a mother of three children, wrote to me, "I have been in therapy and have been to eating-disorder twelve-step settings. I've learned a lot, I think, about what it is . . . but frankly, it keeps getting worse."

I would also be wary of a treatment approach that blames parents and other loved ones or excludes them from the process. As I have said, most of the parents I have worked with are loving and dedicated to their child. Ill-intentioned parents are the exception, not the rule. When their attitudes make it evident that parents' first interest is *not* the child, nevertheless, of course, the child must come first. The situation must be tailored to serve the child's best interest. But blame of anybody or exclusion must not enter the equation verbally, lest the victim use it to feed the Negative Mind or the parents use it to exacerbate the situation.

Parents are their child's best support and source of structure. When therapists exclude parents, I worry that the Negative Mind will use either the therapist or the parents against the child. For example, if a mother tells her child, "You need to eat this meal," the child can reply, "Dr. Brady says I don't have to." The excluded parent, still in a position of having to care for her child, has lost all authority. When she calls the therapist to ask what's going on, the therapist may say, "Any communication between me and your son is private and confidential." This plays right into the hand of the Negative Mind, which sets up one adult against the other, to the demise of the child. The child needs a united front, a solid team. He has to know consistency so that the Negative Mind cannot play games.

Furthermore, excluding parents is unfair because they will eventually continue the therapy that has gone on before, once the therapist's role is over. If they are not a part of the treatment plan from the beginning, how can they continue it? And you surely do not want to find yourself in a situation in which you are unable to evaluate whether the therapist is the right one for your child.

If you are not happy with your child's therapist, continue to search for a therapist with a positive attitude. Remember, what the child needs to learn to survive the Negative Mind is a compassionate objectivity that will arm her against the eventual plights in life, of which there will be many.

SUPPORT GROUPS

I have found that support groups for victims may be detrimental if they consist of other victims alone. In such a group, I am concerned that sufferers will compare and reinforce notes of negativity. I would worry that each patient will try to "better" the next at being unworthy, whether it be at weight loss, number of times purging, hours of exercise, use of laxatives, and so on. Even if a positive leader monitors the group, that person might be overwhelmed by so many Negative Minds in one setting.

Group therapy situations can also be counterproductive. One girl said of them, "I was offered group therapy with other anorexics, but declined because I know they would be thinner than me, and then I'd feel even worse about myself."

In our clinic, we do not allow a dormitory situation for just this reason. We avoid putting two emaciated anorexics together. In those rare situations in which patients share a room, we will put an anorexic and bulimic together, and stress to them how their situations differ. At the same time, we emphasize that their one-on-one caregivers are an arm's length away if needed.

Many of my patients have grinned when talking about hospital programs where they exchanged "trade secrets" in their support groups on being better anorexics. They delighted in being able to outsmart whatever strategies the hospitals used. Small wonder that the word "manipulative" is so often used to describe the eating disorder victim.

A mixed support group—some members with eating disorders and some with other problems—can be helpful if it is positive. It can show the patient that other people have problems too, but the danger is that the patient will worry more about others than herself. Eating disorder patients automatically give themselves to other people's pain and therefore can tread water in such a group instead of progressing. I feel it is more than useful to have patients around healthy individuals as much as possible until they are better.

These are my observations based on my clinical experience. They are generalizations. Your loved one is very much an individual. If a program I am cautious about is working for your loved one, she should stay with it as long as it is effective. Whatever the approach, however, it is essential that victims know they are not alone. Parents and caregivers need to remind them of that again and again.

BE WARY OF LABELING

At the risk of denigrating the fine work of many reputable, well-intentioned mental health professionals, I must advise parents to be cautious about accepting diagnoses of mental disorders. Scores of patients have arrived at my clinic diagnosed variously as obsessive-compulsive, agoraphobic, schizophrenic, manic-depressive, and so on. Worse yet are the vague labels such as "borderline personality" and "undifferentiated schizophrenia" that could mean nothing or everything.

I do not in any way mean to suggest that any of these are not genuine conditions. However, in my practice, I have found that very few of the patients who come to me with these labels attached to them actually have these conditions, even though they may have had symptoms that matched them. As we treat the underlying condition of Confirmed Negativity Condition with love and respect, the symptoms fall away.

If your child receives such a diagnosis, you will obviously need to pursue further medical evaluation, but I would be careful not to discuss the diagnosis in front of her. The danger of emphasizing labeling to the eating disorders patient, even if it exists, is that she will further resign her worthiness, and it will arm the Negative Mind with the additional tool of stigma to use against her.

Instead, emphasize and celebrate your child's unique individuality as she begins slowly to describe it to you in moments of gentleness and truth. Ask your child what she is feeling, what her impressions of what is happening to her are, how her head is talking to her. Keep asking gently until she responds. As she comes further through the condition, she will be able to share things much more comfortably. If she tries to label herself or uses a label bestowed on her, you might say, "I'm not interested in labels. That's not how I see you. Let's talk about what you think, not what others do."

Say what comes from your heart. What works for me are terms of endearment. These are heartfelt and heart-meant for me and serve to soften the distance between me and my patients. Given the gentle, sensitive nature of this population, it comes naturally. You will find your own words as befits your character and ability.

It is imperative, however, not to appear anxious or nagging. Be unconditionally supportive and strong. Do not be afraid to lose your pride. Pride and ego have no place here; the road to recovery is a humbling journey.

BE WARY OF AUTHORITY
FOR AUTHORITY'S SAKE

As parents, we sometimes ignore our internal compass and cede our authority to the experts because we feel they must know better than we do, especially when we find ourselves in life-and-death situations. Parents inadvertently hone themselves to society's order, sometimes without question. But you know your loved one better than anyone else. Perhaps we should not honor authority for authority's sake alone, but consider what we intuitively feel in balance with it.

I feel saddened when I hear of what I consider atrocious behavior presented under the guise of Tough Love. Parents weep about how they have physically or mentally abused their child because it had been advised to them by an "authority." If I succeed in doing nothing more in this book than convincing you that your child is not in charge of what she is doing, that you must not abandon humanism for the sake of an unaware authority, that you must not follow the herd because it is there to follow—the path of least resistance—then I have not written it in vain.

I have heard from many parents who had terrible misgivings about the mismatch between a specific treatment modality and their child's needs. All too often, they went ahead and put their child in such a situation anyway, to disastrous results:

- One patient told me, "I was screaming because the windows were covered so I couldn't see my father in the parking lot. My father came in, saw the therapist actually sitting on me to get me to stop screaming, and said, 'Oh, okay,' and left again, shutting the door. I knew that my father, who knew me better than anybody except my mother, had decided to give up on me, that I was truly alone. I felt so betrayed, and never so frightened. I didn't know what was happening in my mind. I only knew that it was out of my control. Now my father had turned against me as well and I would have to find the answers myself or die."
- One therapist advised a couple to restrain their boy in a chair and force-feed him. They reluctantly did so, but when the boy's mouth began to bleed, they phoned the therapist to ask her advice. She responded, "Keep feeding him." These parents were frustrated with their child's resistance and could not understand that their child would not listen. They did not comprehend the dual mindset.
- Another therapist encouraged a mother to hit her anorexic child when the child refused food.
- A father was told to carry out a tough love intervention with a ten-year-old boy who had anorexia. If the child

did not eat, the father was instructed to punish him, deprive him of all his pleasures, including all toys, games, stuffed animals, and books in his room, and keep him in his now-empty room until he "complied." Needless to say, the Negative Mind had a heyday—here was more confirmation than the boy needed that he was entirely worthless—and the child got sicker.

- An anorexic child was placed in solitary confinement in a mental institution because she would not comply with the program. Incredibly shy, she finally found the courage to knock on the door and request a trip to the bathroom. The orderly made her wait another hour before releasing her.

Parents are always apologizing to me for "knowing better" but allowing their children to be treated in inappropriate ways anyway. If this has happened, please do not blame yourselves. Rather, proceed with the task of seeking out appropriate help.

Parents, listen to your hearts; do not forsake your children. Insist that your child be treated with respect and humanity. It will always continue to be my belief that man is inherently good. If all evidence shows an "authority" figure to be without compassion, do not inflict his or her insensitivity on your child. Search for a viable alternative.

I know that alternatives do exist. I am in the position, at this point in time, of having doctors and nurses worldwide contact me for advice. Most medical people in my current experience are eager to help this patient population which continues to baffle most of the contemporary world. They are searching for answers anywhere they appear to be available. You can help provide some of those answers.

AVOIDING RELAPSE

Relapse becomes a nonissue if CNC no longer exists. The "patient" has learned a different perspective on life and now has a mental road map to follow. She has more opportunity to make things happen, rather than have them happen to her. If ever her condition had been an issue of control, she is now in control as much as any mortal ever is. The many recovery stories in Chapter 9 will show you that full recovery without relapse is possible.

If your loved one's CNC has not been reversed, she is susceptible to relapse. If you see any of the warning signs, seek help immediately. You will need to begin again. Do not lose hope.

A TIME FOR PATIENCE

When we bring up any young child, we are tolerant of her fatigue, her hunger, her small fears of new things. We understand that to be gentle and to slowly explain life to a child is more conducive to her learning and her eventual adult mind than to be impatient and abrupt. Certainly there are moments in anyone's life when this does not happen as well as one may wish it. Nevertheless, it appears obvious that most parents care about the long-term results of their parenting.

Helping the anorexic victim is like bringing up a small child. The victim's emotional development has been arrested, so she may be an emotional infant. At some juncture, her subjective perspective and self-loathing culminated with the illness and immersion in total turmoil and confusion. She has lost her way and requires gentle redirection.

Society's response to the family's needs can cause either unity or disruption. When their child has an eating disorder, many families suffer enormous trepidation with no clear end in sight and are made to feel guilty without obvious reason. Many parents are told their child will never get better. This common societal dictum can only further paralyze their badly needed efforts to save their child.

It helps parents to remember that it took time for their loved one to develop Confirmed Negativity Condition; it will take time to recover from it. In my experience, it can require anywhere from six months to two years after a patient's physical condition has been stabilized for her to achieve total recovery.

One might naturally assume that someone who has had an eating disorder for only one year will "turn around" more quickly than someone who has had it for five years. Surprisingly, however, in my experience, recovery does not depend on how long a person has had the eating disorder, but rather on how long the person has had CNC and on how severely confirmed the condition is.

If you keep in mind the reparenting model of recovery I explained in Chapter 6—that your child will move from infancy to toddlerhood through adolescence and maturity as her condition improves—it will be easier for you to be patient with your child's recovery and to recognize the stages as she progresses toward wellness. Regard your child's reach for recovery as but one more way to prize her uniqueness and individuality.

9

The Poetry of Healing

Much to my dismay, I found out years ago when trying to cure my children of anorexia that the eating disorders as I had studied them in psychology books bore little resemblance to what unraveled before me. Years of relentless research have revealed that a much more sinister, malevolent, and predatory mental construct somehow coexists in and directs the minds of some of the most caring, gentle individuals in our society. The horror of the depth and complexity of this powerful negative mindset is daunting to its victims and families alike.

However intimidating this mindset is, it has proven to be completely reversible. Although it is a difficult and sometimes arduous task, with patience, compassion, and unconditional caring, loved ones and therapists can reverse the negativity and restore the self.

I have had the privilege of working with and talking to hundreds of victims of eating disorders. Some have lived four to eight years in mental institutions. They were told they were lost causes and could not get better because they did not want to. Others have had electroshock treatments in the hopes of changing their thought patterns. Many others, nursing a Negative Mind, have lived years in sedation, merely existing rather than living.

Some of my past patients wanted you to know what they now know—that life is worth living; that you can become well again completely and forever. I hope their words will help your healing.

Have courage and believe you are worth it—we do.

I was 20 when anorexia first manifested itself in me. Now I am 41. Half of my life (20 years) has been robbed from me. Anorexia is a lying thief that keeps you [chained] in a silent isolated prison. The years of my illness were like that.

Besides the obvious of denying myself food, everything else that was in the least way pleasurable or luxurious I could not allow myself. I wasn't "allowed" to listen to music, watch TV, use the air conditioner, have friends or fun. Life was serious and discipline excessively strict. Necessities were allowed with strict restrictions: 1 roll of toilet paper a month, use the shower only once a week, can't drive car more than a ridiculously low number of kilometers per month.

I could not allow myself friends. I wasn't good enough to be loved, though I craved it. If someone gave me a hug that I desperately wanted, I would stiffen and slither from their grasp. I didn't deserve it. I would keep the phone unplugged, then cry and cry out of loneliness. I *existed* for 20 years but didn't live.

Changes came about slowly, often unrecognized. Then one Sunday about 6 months ago, I was singing a hymn in church with the words, "My chains fell off. My heart was free!" It was at that moment I realized that I *had* happened. How did I know? I wasn't obeying that cruel taskmaster, anorexia, anymore. I no longer had all the rules to follow. I could drive my car as much as I wanted; I can use my shower as much as I wanted; I no longer have to put the "company" toilet paper out if someone comes over. I have bought myself "luxuries" that I quite enjoy—TV, VCR, CD player, microwave.

I guess my self-denial was pretty obvious. I was told about a remark made by someone who had visited my apartment here. "Stacy is normal now. She has a TV, VCR, answering machine!" And I have friends. Friends that love me for the person I am and I am able to accept that love. I am able to accept myself. I have become aware of areas of strength and talent in myself and am developing them. They are a better definition of who I am than the number on the scale. My confidence has increased 100%. I am more decisive and can stand up for myself and what I believe. I don't have to agree with everybody to gain their approval. Exercising no longer rules my life. Relaxing is a welcome part of my life now. People have become more important to me than my diet, exercise, and housework.

I have had my mind changed from hearing everything that's said sifted and rearranged into an "I hate Stacy; everything is Stacy's fault; Stacy is a failure" message. That's what caused such inner torment. Listening to the accusing, hateful, punishing, destructive voices all day and night was killing me. Now the messages are what is actually said. I can hear and accept words of love, encouragement, compliment, and even correction. It has brought peace of mind to me. I am enjoying life now. I have fun and laugh. I have an active social life. I have much more compassion toward others.

The recovery process has not only changed my life but given me a broader understanding of others which has definitely enhanced relationships with family and friends. I now see what a beautiful gift life is. I have been given the chance I thought was lost forever—to live that life.

I don't really remember a time in my childhood, adolescence when I didn't have an eating disorder. At age six, I remember looking in the mirror and thinking I was too fat, and so I began eating less and less. Severe food restrictions, obsessive exercising and vomiting were constants in my life. By age sixteen, my weight had dropped to 65 pounds. It is difficult to put into words for someone who has not been there, what it feels like to exist in this state. I wanted more than anything to be free of my eating disorders—I wanted to die. By age eighteen, I had gained some weight but inside me, nothing had changed. I attempted suicide, ended up in the hospital and was told by "professionals" that I was more or less a hopeless case.

I met Peggy later that year. After years of hearing therapists tell me I was "incurable," she was the first person to assert that I would in fact get better. Of course, I did not believe her. I insisted she did not know how "crazy" I was—I have to admit that I did not want to get better at first. My identity, the way I related to the world were all centered around my eating disorders. Stripped of those, who would I be? Through her continual patience, perseverance, and support, a slow change began within me. I see this as the beginning of my "living" life.

I have been out of "therapy" for about five years now. Each year I become increasingly healthier. I am far from the person I used to be and I have faith in my strength. I am happy. I have purpose. I have passion. I am alive.

I remember being suspicious and intimidated at every turn; I was hesitant and almost incapable of relating to anyone or anything. There was a time when I frantically looked up different psychological disorders and illnesses hoping to find a clue as to what could be wrong with me, and nothing in any book at that time alleviated my terror or my feeling of aloneness.

As a child, on the surface, I was very outgoing socially and a leader amongst my friends. I was always initiating new ideas and open to trying new things. I felt I had to be this way all the time to be noticed or acknowledged and sometimes living up to this role was exhausting because of the expectations this included.

I used to love sports and the competitive thrill. I cared very much about the outcome and would strive for first place desperately. I thought I would be less liked, less important even in second place and obviously it would state I had not trained hard enough.

School was quite stressful also because of the grading system and how I graded myself as an individual based on that system. The grading system did not appear to allow us room for human error but underlined the word "perfection," a word very popular in my vocabulary at the time.

I was always worrying about my family, especially my little sister. I thought I should be largely responsible for her well-being and happiness and if something caused her any harm, I would blame myself for not coming to the rescue quickly enough. I also remember as a child checking all the windows, doors, the stove and toaster when my family was in bed at night to ensure that everything was secured and turned off. My fears and paranoia were obviously already manifesting at an early age. I wasn't inhibited or ashamed of myself at that juncture, but then things started to slowly change.

I became quite reclusive. Rarely would I get out with friends or family unless coerced and felt there was no alternative. I dropped out of all sports quickly and made many excuses as to why. I had no motivation because I was afraid of failure, afraid that people would judge and criticize me and I felt it necessary to have universal acceptance regardless of circumstances, differing opinions, etc.

I always wanted to be a good, compassionate and kind individual but somehow I believed I had been severely overlooked. Every time I attempted to do something that apparently was kind and thoughtful, I thought for sure I must have another motive and it definitely wasn't enough always. If someone else did a similar thing, it was genuine of course and beyond reproach. I used to lie awake in bed many nights, imagining all the horrible things that would befall those I loved if I once again allowed myself to venture out and be part of the world.

I started to exercise obsessively and eat less well, narrowing down the types of food I allowed myself. All the foods I loved were no longer on my menu. I started hiding food, pretending I ate it and would only eat with my family when given no alternative. I was ashamed that they would wonder why I thought I deserved to eat and especially in the presence of others. I denied myself pleasure in this aspect as well as many others because I believed myself unworthy of partaking in anything remotely enjoyable, especially since I had not given enough of myself to others and was not capable of mending the horrors of the world. The happiness of others was far more important than my own at any time.

The pressures inside my head were driving me crazy and I didn't know how to cope with them. I quite often contemplated suicide and after a few failed attempts, my imperfections were once again confirmed. I thought I was an absolute failure, as I couldn't even get that right. I had already accepted the fact that I had failed at life.

It is difficult going back to the place I have described above, only because today, I feel so far removed from how I felt then. The contrast between then and now is astounding. It's almost as if it were another lifetime. I feel like I have described someone else's previous life.

I have learned to work through things as they arise. I no longer worry unnecessarily or "buy trouble" as some would say. I realize now that all things are not my responsibility, I can only do so much because I am imperfect. I have limitations and I do not have all the answers nor do I want them all. I have ceased caring about being the best at anything because it's irrelevant and only a matter of opinion.

I am still a sensitive human being but I can now put life in perspective. I am able to objectify situations quite well—well enough for me anyhow. I have a lot to offer the world but I can now balance that with my personal needs as well. Recognizing my potential has enabled me to love life again and I know without a doubt that there is no negative condition left. I am not coping or managing my life; I am truly living and intend to continue on in this vein.

I have now been well for seven years. It's hard to think back to when I was ill for I don't even remember who that person was. What I do know is how I feel now. I have greater understanding and acceptance of my uniqueness as a human being. I enjoy the small details of that that I never allowed myself to enjoy before.

I cannot express the difference of waking up in the morning and being glad that I am here, as opposed to waking and wishing that I was dead. It is as simple as that and there is nothing more astonishing than comparing my state of mentality today to what it was 3 years ago. Today I can honestly say that if it hadn't been for a miracle, I would be 6 feet under and not have the slightest element of regret because at that point I saw no need to continue with a pointless, meaningless existence that caused everyone pain and suffering. I had no reason to live and not an ounce of hope left in my body, let alone strength to keep it there. Starving my body at the time made me feel [like] a better person although in reality the strength that I was desperate for was being reduced to non-existence and so I was inflicting more pain on myself both mentally and physically.

I saw no need to try to defeat the negativity that was growing day by day; or hour by hour because whatever I was doing was never enough for me to concentrate on and time went past so painstakingly slowly that I lost interest in life. Nothing I did was good enough and although I craved praise and congratulation for everything, nothing ever reached the point of satisfaction. A feeling of emptiness became the only way of making sure that I had been "good" that day and in the end it became a feeling of comfort and reassurance that I had not rewarded myself undeservingly. I wished every day for some kind of triumph that would either take it all away and let me live without permanent punishment or kill me so that I wouldn't have to begin to deal with ridding myself of the negativity and never-ending hopelessness that filled the void that someone still called "life."

Today I finally have a "life" and I can honestly say that

every element of every arduous day of recovery has been worth the feelings I have now. The tantrums over eating another mouthful of chickpeas and the black depression that I hopelessly sank into having caught sight of my reflection in a mirror seem inconsequential compared to the happiness and joy that I can experience now.

I don't have to sit for hours calculating exactly how many calories I have eaten or when I next need to go to the gym in order to force my body to undergo more exercise and grueling calorie-burning activity. I no longer walk around supermarkets wishing that I could eat all the things on the shelves and putting things in my mouth to get the taste and spitting the whole lot out because I was not only going to look like more of a hideous balloon than I already did, but someone might see and think that I was obviously treating myself unnecessarily and without reason.

Not only does the difference within myself seem incomparable but the reaction of people around me, especially my family and close friends who instead of distancing themselves now ask me out to dinner and no longer feel worried about giving me a hug. Physically there are still good days and bad days but having the strength to deal with them is more than enough to pull through and realize that there are far better things to worry about.

For years the fashion industry has been accused of brainwashing women with its images of super-slim perfection, and being confronted with skinny models pasted on bus stops every day no longer affects me. Thanks to Peggy and Montreux I now accept the fact that if people can't like me for who I am rather than what I am or look like then they are valueless, hopeless people themselves.

The difference of being able to sit around the table and not have to worry about pushing food around my plate, make sure that I am interesting and ensure that everyone else looks happy is fantastic. And the biggest difference of all is being able to just sit down and relax because I am who I am, and in my mind I have acquired the strength that means I can learn to deal with almost anything at all!

It seems that the person that I was when I was sick did not resemble me as I knew myself to be. It has been ten years since I felt so pathetic, hopeless, and detached from the world as I knew it back then. I vividly remember cursing when I awoke each morning that I had to manage another day—not understanding what was wrong with me. I knew that others did not appear to feel the way that I did and I secretly wished to share my thoughts to know for sure. I remember watching others and wondering what made them so different from me.

Through the understanding that Peggy gave me, I learned that I saw myself in my life and the lives of those around me through clouded eyes and a shattered soul of mixed up feelings and distorted ideas. With her perspective, I was able to see that I was the person I always wanted to be but was unable to see it in myself.

Since then, I no longer feel I have been singled out to be punished but allow myself to be human, make mistakes, and learn along the way. I take life for what it is and play with it rather than always trying to "fix it." Most importantly, I accept myself for who I am and enjoy learning more about myself and the world I am part of with every year that has gone by since I have been well.

Four years ago I led a bleak existence; trapped in the living hell of a bulimic's life. My days were preoccupied with a series of private rituals and activities consisting of bingeing and purging, obsessive exercise, and laxative abuse. Obsessive concerns about my body, looks, and weight were just the tip of the iceberg; there was no aspect of my personality that didn't disgust me. I felt that who I was, was worthless and without this bulimic identity, I was nothing. Often, frustration and self-loathing would lead me to acts of self-abuse and violence against others, and the guilt I felt would reinforce my beliefs that I was a horrible person.

I used to wonder what I had done to deserve such torture, but the ugly voice in my head would tell me I was getting what was coming to me and that this is what my future held for me. Deep down in my heart, I knew that wasn't who I was and who I wanted to be. I wanted to see what my life would be like without that horrible negative voice screaming at me every day.

Then I met someone who made me realize that I wasn't worthless, that it wasn't my fault, and I certainly didn't deserve these things for the rest of my life.

Today I live a life free from anxieties about food and body image and I love myself unconditionally. I can now look in the mirror without wanting to smash my head against it in disgust for what I see there. I no longer live my life to please other people, I know who I am and I realize that I can be anything or do anything I want to do; I have no limitations or fears now. I am in control of my destiny and look forward to wherever my life may lead me and I am happy to know myself.

I feel a great sadness in my heart when I hear people say that eating disorders can't be fully cured, because I know that I am living proof that they can. I was no different from anyone else, no exception to the rule, and I know that there is hope for a life free from this terrible thing and hope for a future.

I wrote a final exam last night, and when I went for a drink of water, a whole wave of memories swept over me. Ten years ago, I'd been at the same fountain, having written my final. I recall having an incredible thirst, and the panic and terror I experienced when I accidentally actually swallowed some of the water I was so desperately swishing in a futile attempt to moisten my mouth. Terrified, I took off for the tallest building at the university where I spent the next hour or so running up and down the stairwell in an attempt to burn off the effects that water would have on me. (I had traveled up and down so often between classes that the details of the floor and walls along that staircase are indelibly etched into my mind. To this day, though I'm still not sure what lies beyond the top-floor doorway . . .)

The fear and depression and sadness of those last years of university are only memories now. As I attend lectures and write exams there once again, visions and events of those hellish years often flash through my mind. But that is all they are. That uncontrollable urge to exercise; that intense fear of food; the unceasing desperation and fear; they're all gone now. And Peggy saved me from that living hell. All the "specialists," psychologists, drugs, programs, and medical models used by these "professionals" only made the condition worse over time. Without Peggy's patience, understanding, and love, I know I would not be here today to experience the life I lead.

And what a wonderful life it is! My job is terrific. It's challenging, interesting, and I'm valued for the contribution I make. My employers and coworkers are the best of friends. Days are filled with laughter and fun. School is also going well; only three courses remain until I graduate. Exams are hard but I enter into them confident of my capabilities; the psychologist that ruined my confidence (the little that remained after anorexia stripped most of it away, that is) by repeatedly stating that the brain damage caused by malnutrition meant I would never again amount to anything (because I would be unable to pass such grueling exams) has been proven wrong. (Indeed, I received 98% on my last exam!)

Weekends and after-work time are spent reading, on the computer, and biking—a hobby I continue to love and enjoy.

It's such a relief to do it for fun again! (Those 12-hour-long sessions of non-stoppable pedaling are just a bad memory now.)
Better yet, I often go home at night and do nothing but watch a
movie or listen to music. Best of all, when I look at life, I can
think of nothing I would choose to change. There's a feeling of
laughter inside my chest that regularly erupts into laughter and
joy again. It's great! I can honestly say that I couldn't possibly
be happier. I have proven all the doctors wrong. I am happy
and I love life!

I have suffered from anorexia nervosa for almost fourteen
years. In those years I have tried to commit suicide many times
and have spent many years in different hospitals. I hated my life
and my only goal in life was to die. I lost my social life and contact with all my friends. I tried to look after other people but
did not care about myself. I went through years of depression.
My Life After Anorexia Nervosa
I have been recovered now for two years. I am enjoying my
life, have a social life back and spend a lot of time with my
friends. For over a year, I have taken care of my friend's baby,
as my friend went through a bad time of her own. I like helping
people and do what I can for them, and I care a lot more about
myself. I [want] to work with people with eating disorders or to
be able to work with children as I have always adored children.
At present, I am doing a lot of voluntary work which I really
enjoy doing.
I can't get back the years that I missed out on due to my
illness and I don't regret that as I am making up for those lost
years now.

I was eleven years old when anorexia entered my life.
Anorexia was a monster. He would never leave me alone.

Anorexia constantly told me I was fat and if I was skinny, people would like me. Instead the only friend I had in my mind was the scale. Each day I weighed myself about twenty times, hoping the scale would be less, thought if I did weigh less, anorexia was still not satisfied. I isolated myself from my family, consuming my head with calories, wanting to exercise constantly, and only seeing a massive image in the mirror. Doctors considered me a statistic; just waiting until I weighed sixty-five pounds so they could admit me to the hospital.

Suddenly my life instantly had a sense of hope when I met a lady named Peggy Claude-Pierre, who understood anorexia completely. I trusted her the first time I sat in her office because she looked into my eyes and told me, "I know why you are rubbing your hands up and down your legs: for exercise." That was a secret only anorexia and I knew. From that day on, I believed in Peggy. She took the responsibility of anorexia away from me, allowing myself to heal, so I could get strong and beat up anorexia until he vanished. Peggy also helped my parents understand anorexia, which brought me closer to them. Peggy became an angel because she saved my life.

I am now nineteen years old and going to the university. I have been able to go around schools and talk about anorexia so people have a better understanding of the monster that once lived in my head. I have been able to enjoy sports such as winning the county championships for rowing. Anorexia is no longer a part of me. I am never afraid of food and I am very happy. My family has become the most important part of me. I consider my mom and dad my best friends.

Before I came to Montreux, I was completely consumed by anorexia—it was my entire identity. The hooks of anorexia were embedded so deep in my mind and my body that I thought they would never loosen. I had no self-esteem, self-confidence, or sense of self-worth. The negative mindset and obsessive-compulsive behaviors of anorexia completely controlled every aspect of my life, as I lived according to a very strict and rigid set of rules created by anorexia to control every minute of the day, from my thoughts to exercising to my every action.

Suffering from frequent mood swings and depression, I was withdrawn and isolated from my family and society; I couldn't trust people, and was terrified of life and people. I felt completely unworthy of love and friendship because I was a failure as a person and could never be good enough to live up to the unrealistically high expectations I placed on myself and that I perceived were placed on me by others. I felt I had to be perfect at everything in my life, but constantly failed, and that I had to please everyone.

I was apathetic, not caring about life or living—I lived through and for other people, according to other people's expectations, because I wasn't worthy of living for myself and had to take responsibility for everyone else's life and problems, trying to solve everyone's problems and take away their pain.

Filled with self-loathing, I was on a path to self-destruction leading to death, constantly inflicting physical pain upon myself by bruising, burning myself with hot water, making myself bleed, and making my skin raw and sore. The anorexia filled me with an intense phobia of food, eating and weight gain (I weighed myself several times every day); constant nightmares and insomnia; defiant, secretive and manipulative behavior; frequent dizziness, fainting, and blackouts; constant never-ending inner and physical pain; constant, relentless daily exercising to the point of exhaustion and collapse, always working myself harder; atrophy of my muscles to the point of no longer being able to walk by the time I came to Montreux; and starvation to the point of severe emaciation and near death, looking like a skeleton.

I was in and out of hospitals for $2\frac{1}{2}$ years, becoming even more severely anorexic each time. By the time I came to Montreux, the doctors and hospitals had given up on me—I had no blood pressure, an almost undetectable pulse, no hope.

Coming to Montreux saved my life, without a doubt; I could not have survived if I hadn't come here. I was horrified when I came here and thought it would be the same as the hospitals. I was convinced that the people here would give up on me and send me home, but they never gave up on me in their battle to defeat anorexia, no matter what the "condition" did.

The whole atmosphere and treatment here is different from hospitals. At Montreux, I was under 24-hour care by people who understand the condition and are patient, loving, and caring. I was enveloped by *unconditional love,* positive reinforcement and objectivity in a home-like environment where I was totally made to feel safe and learn to trust people again. All my trust was put into the careworkers and the counselors.

I was on complete bed rest at first, and was not allowed to exercise or do any other self-destructive or self-harming behaviors. Responsibility for everything, including eating, was taken away from me and given to the careworkers to alleviate my guilt and shame. I was hand-fed by the careworkers for many months—liquid nutritional drinks at first, then slowly and gradually introduced to food. It was a long, hard battle but the careworkers were always there helping in the struggle and providing constant love, support, and encouragement. I was made to feel that I deserved and was worthy of love and friendship and happiness.

As time progressed, I went from being on 24-hour care to being in partial care to being off care and in counseling. Even though I was off care, my careworkers were still available for me to talk to. I had counseling sessions several times per week, at which we talked about many different topics, issues, and problems that I had to deal with, and how to conquer my many fears. I was given many projects to do, and taught many things—including how to live life again, and to discover myself. I've made many friends here.

At this point, I am living in my own place not far from the clinic; I am volunteering at a local charity and looking for a part-time job; I am going for weekend visits home to my family; and having sessions once a week, working on clearing the final hurdles.

I can't believe how far I've come and never thought it would ever be possible before I came to Montreux. Everyone here is so special, and the best thing to come out of my becoming anorexic was coming here and meeting all the neat people, making great friends, and being given a chance to live.

I started loathing myself when I was 11. It started by waking up every morning and picking apart every flaw I thought I had. This escalated to my cringing every time I heard my own voice. I thought I talked too much or not enough, I was evil or I was a doormat. It didn't seem to matter what I said or did, nothing was good enough.

If I ate, no matter what it was, it was too much and I had to get it out of my body. My knuckles were raw from stuffing them down my throat; my teeth scraped off skin. There was about five minutes after I purged where I felt a numbness. The pain inside subsided. Only to return stronger shortly thereafter.

Being sick was like being drunk for seven or eight years, although I was that too. I don't like to use the overused words "out of control." . . . I think "loss of being" is a better description. No sense of myself existed. I was what each different individual in my life wanted me to be. "I" had disappeared. All I wanted to do was die and even in that I saw myself as a failure.

When I entered into the program, I didn't even know who or what to believe. The more these people described this condition to me, the more at ease I felt. For the first time in my life I felt understood. I wasn't better overnight and it wasn't as though I woke up one morning and yelled, "Yay! I'M WELL!"

It took a lot of time and effort by both myself and those who helped me at the clinic. And slowly but surely I started to find out who I really was, and to my amazement, I began to accept myself.

Today, which is now 3½ years after I finished the program, I work 40+ hours per week, am living with someone, and am no longer a half of a whole. I feel complete inside and out. When I look back at what my life was like when I was sick, it only makes me look forward to all that I now have the chance to enjoy.

BEFORE
BEFORE I came here and during the times when I felt most TRAPPED, whilst I was here I was so SUICIDAL.

I was a BURDEN to the world, USELESS and an IMPOSITION on everyone. I felt GUILTY for living, for using ELECTRICITY. I WASN'T ALLOWED ANYTHING. NO LIGHT, NO HEAT, NO BED. NO SHELTER from a building, a BUSH was too GREEDY. NO MUSIC, NO TELEVISION. I was not allowed WARM baths or showers. NO WARM CLOTHES or COVERS. I felt GUILTY for the MONEY it cost to refrigerate my FOOD, when I was too FAT and too OBESE to ever need to eat another CALORIE in my life.

I was so INTRINSICALLY BLACK, so deeply, deeply EVIL I COULD NOT EVEN BE HUMAN. No human being could be so BLACK INSIDE, so INCREDIBLY EVIL.

I would CUT myself with RAZORS or KNIVES, 100s of times. Each time, the BLACK liquid within me, so much thicker than any tar, could NOT be RED. It could not be. There was ONLY BLACK inside me. WHY was it still RED? *WHY?*

IF I was even a little human, I wanted so badly to DONATE MY ORGANS, so that good people could live and do good things in the world. I NEVER could, despite wanting to HELP PEOPLE MORE THAN ANYTHING in the world.

I was a SELFISH, SELF-CENTERED, FAT BITCH. I didn't and COULDN'T even WANT TO WANT TO GET BETTER.

I was NEVER allowed to enjoy anything and must CONSTANTLY HURT MYSELF. I couldn't open letters as I enjoyed it but it might also confirm that SOMEONE OUT THERE MIGHT CARE. No I couldn't allow that. I must BURN, CUT, SCAR, STARVE, BINGE, PURGE, EXERCISE, ABUSE LAXATIVES, PAINKILLERS, ANTIDEPRESSANTS, ANTI-PSYCHOTICS, SEDATIVES, CALMING PILLS, anything to NUMB the PAIN. I would SHUT my EYES as I walked along, pretending LIFE WASN'T HAPPENING. I'd go to bed hoping and praying I'd be DEAD by morning. The SCALES were never low enough. The CUTS and BURNS, never NUMEROUS ENOUGH or DEEP ENOUGH. The clothes SIZE never SMALL ENOUGH, the GRADE never HIGH ENOUGH, the CALORIES were always TOO HIGH, my DANCE never GOOD ENOUGH. I wanted everything to be PERFECT, but it NEVER could be.

I was USELESS, HOPELESS, WORTHLESS. I was IMPRISONED in my MIND. All I wanted was to HELP PEOPLE. But I was a USELESS, SELFISH BITCH.

I deserved NO ONE. I deserved NOTHING. And SELFISHLY to end the PAIN, I saw DEATH as a door to PEACE.

The WORLD would be BETTER WITHOUT ME. Family, friends, the world would be better with me DEAD.

AFTER

AFTER 23 months, I am now understanding, truly, for I think the first time in my life, what "HAPPINESS" means.

I'm FREE. I'm SAFE. I'm INDEPENDENT. When I go for a walk, I DON'T wish I was under a car. When the SUN is out, I love the way the world looks. I LOVE my FRIENDS, I TRUST people and I have people who are so KIND to me.

I am so GRATEFUL I have people who UNDERSTAND me and KNOW the REAL ME.

I LOVE DANCING. I love going out for BREAKFAST or a LATTE. It's so fun to go for a *WALK* just because it's so beautiful outside. It's FUN to be SPONTANEOUS and to enjoy being SOCIABLE. To be honest, I do still feel like a burden and I worry that people feel obligated to take me out, but it DOESN'T rule my life, and is something I have to work on still.

EMOTIONS are *so* much STRONGER. I am NO LONGER numb or fighting to sub-exist. I'm NOT on drugs, and I'll NEVER have E.C.T. [electroconvulsive therapy] again, or have people threaten to lock me up.

When I SMILE, it's GENUINE.

When I LAUGH, I MEAN it.

I have ENERGY. I'm NOT in physical or emotional pain. I ENJOY MUSIC, I ALLOW MYSELF so much more. I DARE TO RISK. I LOOK FORWARD to making plans, I want to travel. I want to spend QUALITY TIME with my FAMILY, especially my FATHER and GOD-CHILD.

I'm so much more OBJECTIVE and can put things into PERSPECTIVE, quicker and easier or ask for help to.

I'm finding out who I am.

I'm discovering what I LIKE, and when I think of things I WANT TO DO, NOT everything and everyone I would never see again.

Now I go to bed because I have to sleep, NOT to escape, and I LOOK FORWARD to getting up in the morning and to TOMORROW. I don't know what TOMORROW will bring, but I DON'T fear it or worry. It's EXCITING and DIFFER-ENT, yet SECURE.

I know I will see or talk to people I CARE ABOUT. Not every day is a breeze, but I TRUST those I know and can now ASK FOR HELP.

I'm BEGINNING to find PEACE, and I'm very HAPPY.

It's a long road and it's not an easy one, but I like where it's taking me and it's incredibly WORTHWHILE.

I'm very HAPPY, LUCKY, AND GRATEFUL I'm still ALIVE. Now I have the chance to START to *LIVE* my life.

Ever since I can remember, I was a very caring person. I used to take every little thing that someone said about me personally. I was worried about my parents and felt badly about spending their money, taking their time. Four years ago, food started to become an issue; I stopped eating and felt good being hungry all the time. I used to care a lot about what other people ate, and I was always in the kitchen making food for others, but never for myself. I wanted to eat but I just couldn't. Something in my head was stronger than I was, and controlled the way I acted and what I ate or thought.

Now that I am better, I see life in a different way. I don't worry about little things, and I accept myself and my body the way I am. I am happy now and I have many interests and ideas. Food is not an issue anymore, and I can eat anything I ever wanted and was not allowed to have. This feeling is great.

Food was a dear friend from an early age. It was a steady chum to turn to; it was accessible, reliable and sweet, and after an hour in its company, I felt calm and sedated. Food was something controllable, and in a world that was spinning too fast to figure out, it was the eye of the hurricane.

But when, as a teenager, a burgeoning body led to a more mature world than I was prepared for, food became the enemy, and I was to continue a love/hate bulimic relationship with it for another twelve years.

There is a graphicness about anorexia and bulimia that only a guy like Oliver Stone could do justice to. Perhaps you have to experience it or witness it at close range to realize that it truly is a war. My friends and family had a lot of difficulty understanding why I'd enlisted. Trying to explain it to someone was always the most difficult part of intimacy.

Obsessed by my world of alcohol, cocaine, ipecac, and Dulcolax, I became equally compulsive about learning what I could about eating disorders, hoping I would discover the magic formula that would end the madness. I needed tools to apply my energy positively, rather than to my demise. My motivation to recover from bulimia was never lacking; however, my bleak financial picture from years of practicing my illness did little to encourage professionals to want to work with me.

My great fortune was in meeting people who understood my strange interior life without judgment and who, at a time when I didn't feel there was anything to live for, were there to lend me their vision and pull me through the grueling journey of recovery. I'd never been afraid of hard work and perhaps it's that "work ethic" that finally worked for me rather than against me. Recovery is arduous—coming back from being that far "out there" is a deep emotional and spiritual challenge.

I almost consider my struggle with bulimia an alchemical gift—I'm thankful for the opportunity it afforded me to take a cool, discerning stare into the contexts that were running my life and identity, contexts I didn't invent, but I went along with unconsciously. Driving the right car, wearing the right clothes, dating the right men, or impressing the right authority all seemed to matter when I was ill and trying to prove to the world that I had worth. The paradox was that when I stopped trying to prove myself externally, I realized I already had.

Now I look back on my illness without the veil of denial that is so characteristic of anorexia and bulimia, and I stagger when I think of what I did to my body, mind, and spirit for so many years. I now live a life where the important things are my husband, family, and friends and the comforting love we all share, not calories, exercise, secrecy, and shame. I gave up a life of chaos and drama, filled with constant thoughts of striving and achieving, for a gentle inner peace—traded the BMW mentality for a cardigan.

I hope someday to look back on this time in our history and only *read* about the curious phenomenon of anorexia and bulimia to be touched by it, not have to witness its destruction and ruin on the bodies and faces I pass on the street. Thank God one woman witnessed her daughters' pain, soothed it, and now tells others how she did it. I hope they'll listen. . . .

Everything in life is process; or at least it is in mine. I didn't become anorexic overnight. Nor is there a definite time when I can say I realized I was sick. It all happened gradually for me.

As long as I can remember I hadn't liked who I was in any facet or sense. To me, I was a terrible, despicable, and ugly human being who had been created simply due to negligence. I was a mistake from the beginning. I convinced myself that I didn't deserve anything, least of all love. I didn't allow myself to believe that I was loved, no matter what I was shown or told. I thought they must be lying, that I was unlovable. Over time, this negativity increased. I got to the point where I thought I didn't deserve to live. I thought I was such a terrible person that I deserved and was destined to die.

Food is one thing you definitely need to be alive. I didn't think I deserved anything that would facilitate life. I began to slowly starve myself. I slowly began to cut out things, but that wasn't enough. I deserved less and less every day. I eventually got to the point where I thought I shouldn't allow myself any food, that I had to get rid of it. This led to bulimia. Throughout this time, my opinion of myself plummeted even further. I thought I was a nobody and I hated myself for everything.

When I started getting better, I started believing that I deserved to be alive and happy. I no longer thought I was a terrible person who wasn't worthy of anything. I realized it was

okay to make mistakes, and that I didn't need to blame myself
for everything. I stopped focusing on imperfections and started
to focus on the good parts of myself. In letting go of all my
guilt for events in the past, I was able to start to like who I really
was. I allowed myself to be happy and have fun and soon it
became a natural thing.

I now look forward to getting up in the morning just because I enjoy being alive. I now like who I am as a person, and
that means everything to me. I know that I can deal with anything that may come my way. I know what is out there in the
world and what I can do, and what great fun it can all be.

No one should ever have to worry. I am a person who has
spent years worrying. I've been worried for everything from my
little sister's cold to the starving people in Africa and in my distress for every person, animal, and situation, I missed everything in life that is fun.

I am now sixteen and I finally feel like being a teenager can
be a happy experience; it's too bad it's taken me so long to accept myself, to be content. So many unfair things happen in this
world. I had wanted to fix everything, take away all pain, all
hate. Save everyone!

Now I know I can use this will to be strong so I can go out
in the world and just be happy. Instead of handling problems as
I always did before—hopelessly taking out the world's problems
on myself—I'm able to contribute a caring, but healthy and en-
ergetic personality to the people around me. At least I can actually get up in the morning looking forward to the day ahead of
me, knowing that though things won't be perfect, nor will
everything go exactly right, but I can do the best I can, and my
positivity will rub off on others.

I use my powerful determination to actually get things
done, instead of destroying my body in despair. With good

health, my outlook has become so different; I get so enthusiastic about things. I've also noticed this attracts others, from school friends to the neighbors next door—people just seem drawn to happiness. It's awesome!

I was sick with anorexia since the fifth grade. Even before that, I remember carrying everyone else's burdens along with my own load and slowly being crushed harder and harder into a person filled with self-hatred and depression. I thought that everything was my fault; I didn't deserve to live. After all the suffering, the eating disorder manifested, and I went through all the traumas that go along with anorexia in our society. I saw the end many times, in fact, I'm amazed that I'm here today after all I've been through. Now I can be glad I've made it!

Somehow a little flame flickered inside, even through the very toughest moments. A little part of me still had hope and wanted somehow, to live. Then, with the help of understanding and unconditional love, things started to be put back in perspective. Time and patience are the biggest and most difficult parts in fixing such a negative mindset, but life does get better, as I can attest to now. It's a relief when you realize it's true—no one should ever have to worry.

When bulimia started, I was about thirteen years old. I had always had a low self-image. As the condition took over, I started to lose everything; the ability to look at myself objectively, a sense of self, a positive perspective on life, and most importantly, the will to live. At sixteen, the condition had really taken over and at seventeen, I was out of school and all I did all day was write in my diary about how I wanted nothing but death. My soul had almost completely deteriorated and I was overtaken by the demons inside of me. All I could think about was how I was going to end my life.

Luckily, my friends and family exposed my condition, and I got help. I started seeing Peggy Claude-Pierre and found someone who really understood me and my condition. I went through a difficult process of gaining strength, confidence, and a sense of self. I am now twenty-one and I have regained my soul, my confidence, and my will to live. I love life and appreciate every pleasure it brings me. I love living without that negative feeling lingering around me constantly. When people used to look into my eyes, they would tell me how sad and distant they seemed. When people look into my eyes today, they say that they glow, as I glow. Life is definitely worth living, and now I know how much I have to offer this world, to the people around me, as well as to myself.

Anorexia is the most indescribable pain anyone can ever experience, as well as the toughest hurdle to overcome. I know this to be true because I had lived with the condition for five years, until I overcame it. Looking back, I can honestly say I had no life whatsoever. All I thought about every minute of the day was how unattractive I thought I was, at what time I would exercise, how I could get out of eating, what lies I would tell my parents and friends, how awful a person I was, etc., etc. These thoughts played like a broken record over and over in my head, to the point where all I wanted to do was to go to sleep and not wake up. I can remember getting so frustrated asking myself why I was going through such mental torture, that I would start screaming, pulling my hair, banging my head, anything to try to give myself a moment of peace.

The constant dictating or nagging to do what anorexia wanted me to do caused great loneliness and isolation. I withdrew from my family and friends and any social setting. I did not want to accept any help from anyone because I felt that I did not deserve it. I believed I was a horrible person for making my parents watch me slowly dying, thus, receiving help from them would be total selfishness.

Being able to see things realistically now, I can see that I did not purposely choose to be sick. Being overly sensitive from day one, feeling as though I had to take care of my family, feeling inferior to my friends, and having low self-esteem all contributed to my negative mindset. Thus, the act of starving myself not only from food, but of things that made me happy were the outlets or paths of my negativity. When I think about it today, how I treated my body and my mind, I am in complete shock and awe of how I survived. How I ate nothing for days on end, as well as not even drinking water, brings chills to my body when I think about it. However, feeling pain, hunger, fatigue, and weakness did not even cross my mind for many years, for it became my way of living.

I can now realize my true identity, separate from the condition, and what is normal for a 16-year-old girl. I promised myself I would overcome this hurdle, and I did. I feel like such a weight has been lifted off of me. No more do I base my worth on if I managed to exercise all day, eat nothing, my appearance, etc. I look at each day as a new one, and enjoy things again.

I was sick for most of the years of my adolescent life, with anorexia. Through my ninth year of school, I spent most of my days in hospitals and programs. I was a straight-A student, a dancer, involved in activities and in general, a pretty good kid; but inside I had a drowning feeling of worthlessness. I didn't know how to express my feelings and I strove to hurt myself instead of letting my emotions out. As I grew sicker, I began to have more hate for myself. I reached my goal; I was thin, but nearly dead, and I came to the realization that the thinner I became, the more unhappy I was.

One night, in the hospital, I had a dream where I was told by a heavenly power that I had a purpose to serve in life. The next day, I left the hospital and was on Peggy's doorstep. I made the choice—the choice to help myself. I learned to talk about my difficulties and work through them. Life is beautiful. Food isn't the issue, life is. When I stopped focusing my energy on food, I had so much more time for myself, for love and enjoyment of others. With the condition, I wasn't functioning to my full capacity. I now eat to be healthy and strong. The stronger I become, the more attractive I feel.

This year, my graduating class is the Class of the Phoenix. The Phoenix is a mythological bird that burns into ashes and transforms into a beautiful creature. I feel that the bird relates to us all; our struggles will help us grow, develop, and become stronger. I took the power within myself to help me transform.

Trying to recall the agony I went through when I was anorexic is at times easy because of the extreme state of torment it created. On the other hand, remembering becomes more difficult because I have not been in that negative frame of mind and body for over ten years. Over ten years without a hint of the anorexic condition left other than the understanding of what anorexia and bulimia means. This complex theory enables me to help any other victim of this horrible condition. . . . horrible though very reversible.

I am proof that you do not have to spend your life wondering if your heart will withstand one more evening or feel the desperation to torture yourself both physically and emotionally because you have made the wrong comment or perhaps have hurt someone's feelings. When I was ill with anorexia, I truly didn't think it was possible to be saved, I felt doomed 24 hours a day. I guess there must have been one percent of a seed of myself left to work with though it was not evident to me at the time. Now I know the road one must take to recovery, total recovery.

Coming though the painful tunnel to wellness has made me

a complete person. Once I conquered the negative mindset I was much more objective, gently confident and fully aware of my surroundings. By surroundings I mean society and its motives. The type of knowledge I now have makes me feel rich and fulfilled instead of diminished, hopeless, and frustrated. I once saw life through a different set of eyes.

I trust people and not an imaginary voice being repeatedly negative. I trust myself. Though I am inherently sensitive, interacting in any circumstance or situation is completely comfortable for me. I exude optimism without having high expectations of anyone or anything, including myself. I adore my position in life and the many, many people immediately surrounding my life. Because I respect my purpose for existence, I ultimately respect myself.

There was a time when I was young, eleven years old to be exact, that I came up with an idea of how to stay skinny. I decided that if I ate and then threw it up, I could eat whatever I wanted but never gain weight. At first it was just a little diet, then it became an everyday activity, then that diet became a web of terror, filled with anxiety, self-hate, and self-worthlessness, which I no longer controlled. I hated life, never believed I deserved to live, to be loved or to eat; in my eyes I was a fat, worthless, horrible person who deserved nothing, not even love. When my eating disorder was at its worst, I could no longer take the self-hate and pain, but I didn't know what to do because I believed anorexia was something I had to live with. I believed life would hold nothing amazing for me, nothing except misery.

I was wrong. Life was worth living and anorexia is nobody, it just feeds in the minds of those who are too nice to say no to its nastiness. I'm glad I listened to Peggy and my family and my special friends because [otherwise] I wouldn't have become a success—because I beat it and am living my life the way I always should have. It is strange how life is so pleasant and full of love once you are freed from the iron grips of anorexia. I can actually love myself for all of myself, no longer spitting at the image in the mirror. I cannot imagine if I had died because life began when I found my own self, a self who loves to be loved, a self who is the strongest she's ever been.

I am now fulfilling all of my dreams, dreams anorexia made me believe that I was too worthless to have. Anorexia was wrong; we are all worthy. I am living proof.

During my struggle with anorexia, I felt an overwhelming concern with my self-image. I felt I had to be perfect in all areas of my life, yet I didn't even know who I was. I tried in vain to be what I felt others expected me to be, but always fell short in my eyes.

I absorbed the pain and suffering of [all] I came in contact with, soaking up all the negativity around me, finally sinking into despair and depression.

Meanwhile, consuming food resulted in nausea and bloating, convincing me that I was allergic to most foods. Further, I still became ill after what little I did find safe to eat, causing me to question the value of eating at all. I often found myself lying on the kitchen floor, physically weak and emotionally pained.

Everything in life required great effort and I found myself losing hope and security in society, people and my ability to succeed in anything. I wanted to isolate myself, to disappear or cease to exist in an attempt to escape the despair, fear, self-hatred, and imperfections that I felt were so active and evident in my life.

Today my view of life has become one filled with hope, courage and joy. I find myself respecting and loving myself and accepting imperfections as a part of being human.

I enjoy a balanced lifestyle of enjoyment and responsibility. I am now married to a wonderful wife and we anxiously await the arrival of our first child.

All of my life I lived for other people—not out of choice, but because I didn't know any other way. It wasn't until years later that I found out that I didn't actually have a self. I became what other people liked, thought, said and did; without respect for myself, going day by day trying to please other people so that I could be good enough. The breaking point was when I displayed the manifestation of anorexia, because all of the self-hatred and worthlessness became too much, and I began a slow, subconscious suicide. My life became a living hell; isolating myself from anyone who cared while I destroyed myself; thinking that I was crazy and yet holding on for dear life; clinging to it because I felt that I had no other choice.

When I came to Montreux, all control was taken away from anorexia, and I felt sad, terrified, depressed and very panicked. I didn't know how I could live without my only so-called friend—my condition. Because I had no self, and the only idea I had of myself was the anorexia, I felt like there was nobody there; I had no personality, and this was really scary. In the environment of unconditional love and acceptance, my personality, locked deep inside for so long, began to emerge, growing stronger by the day, until it grew stronger than anorexia. I could fight what it told me, by myself. Now, anorexia has no control of me. I know who I am and I like myself—something I never thought possible. I enjoy my days, and other people don't scare me—I love being sociable and making friends. Going through this experience has given me so much knowledge and wisdom about the world; I don't regret having been sick because otherwise I wouldn't know what I know now. My only regret is for all of the wasted years when I was so miserable. I'm making up for it now, by being doubly happy. My life has just begun and I'm finally ready to live it.

For most of my life, I changed or interpreted situations until they caused me worry, anguish, and grief. It is extremely difficult to explain because a lot of what went on was in the subconscious mind. I didn't realize what I was doing until it became so obsessive and uncontrollable that I became severely anorexic. Let me start by giving you a brief synopsis of my childhood. I was a very intelligent, cheerful girl with supportive parents, tons of friends, vacations every year, a dog and a pool in the backyard. Everything I ever needed was provided for me, including much understanding, encouragement, and love. Looking back, I realize that even then, at a different degree, worry was always inside and sensitivity was a major factor. As the years went on, my self-acceptance and worth gradually deteriorated, causing negative thinking patterns and anorexia to enter my mind. Nothing was logical, yet everything was incomprehensible; for it felt like even though I had eyes, I couldn't actually "see," I had ears but I couldn't "hear," I could talk but not "listen," and I could think but not "understand." It felt as though I was incapable of doing anything because of how unreachable my true identity really was. If my life was in the form of a ladder, I was desperately grasping the last rung. Inside, my mind was a series of webs, entrapped and intertwined with negative thoughts, causing me to become greatly confused and upset. My anger and frustration would then get turned against me and I would harm myself even more. My mind, body, and soul were never at peace; even sleep was disturbed with evil nightmares and pains. Nothing in the world was of any importance to me, except suffering.

Now, years later, my life is incomparable to how it was then. I can actually live, go to school, make friends, interact with family and most importantly, I can truly laugh and be happy. I am able to be logical and look forward to making my future dreams into a reality. I often ask myself "why." The only answer I can come up with is this: Everything happens for a reason and with courage, determination, faith, love, and understanding from others, the top of the ladder can be reached.

Dear Peggy,

In the year that I have been here at the clinic I have learned more about myself and about others, and have finally begun to accept the joy of life, the goodness of so many, and the very miraculous gift you have given me. I want so much to be able to glean from you all the knowledge and guidance you have demonstrated and bestowed upon those who work with you. I have been graced with the chance to experience new thoughts [that are] no longer debilitating me with fear and [are] unable to plague me with hatred. I cannot express to you my sincere thanks for it would truly take the very wonderful lifetime you have helped me discover. I only wish to use all the wisdom and the progress to come in the future to aid another to realize the magnificence and contentment I know now. You gave me a miracle far greater than I could have ever imagined.

When I was young
My father told me
Smile
So they think you're happy
And my smile became a mask
That I hid behind, ashamed to come out.
I didn't realize until too late
That the mask had become
Stuck to my soul

I couldn't take it off
I didn't know how
Until I started learning
To smile with my heart
And the mask began to crack
And I could slow, slowly step outside.
I left the mask discarded
Cracked and broken on the pavement
So I could turn my face to the sun.

If someone had asked me four years ago where I would be today, I honestly would not have been able to answer. I suppose at that time I would have hoped that I would no longer be alive, because I could not have imagined living another year trying to battle bulimia. Every day I woke up hating myself more and more, convinced that I was a weak person unable to control a disease that ruling every minute of my day. I was purging at least five times a day, my face was swollen, my hair was falling out, and I was too ashamed to see my family and friends. I became withdrawn and secretly hoped that I would be diagnosed with some terminal disease so that I could finally end this torment. I had begun to think about suicide, but felt I could never disappoint my family with such a selfish action. I honestly thought that bulimia/anorexia was a part of my personality that I could never release and would have to learn to live with for the rest of my life. And then I met Peggy.

I remember walking out of my first meeting with Peggy and for the first time I had felt a small glimmer of hope. I had been to different physicians and counselors but had never experienced such a sense of compassion and understanding of eating disorders, not had I ever been told that I would one day be free from living like a prisoner in my own body. Well, I *am* free, and I *am* stronger than I could have ever imagined. I have learned to love myself and, along with this, have learned to be loved.

I know that whatever I am faced with in the future, I will succeed, and I will be happy, because I am a wonderful, intelligent,
beautiful individual who deserves the best that life can offer.
The road to recovery is never easy but I am so happy that I
have had all my experiences because they make me who I am
and I'm pretty happy to be me.

There was a time in my life when I thought that I would
never be freed from the "shackles" of anorexia. So powerful
were they, that I had inadvertently become a slave to an existence void of freedom by the obsessive darkness that controlled
my every thought and action. So heavy were they that I was
pulled further and further down into a state of despair. My
acute sensitivity and ultimately my great lack of self-esteem had
created a monster. Initially, this monster was my friend, my
comfort, and the one thing in my life that I could control. It
made me feel happy, strong, and safe from the disturbing injus-
tices of society that surrounded me. Before long, "it" had taken
over. "It" was no longer my friend; I no longer felt any joy,
safety, or strength. All that I can remember feeling is terribly
guilty, shameful, and powerless for having made my loving parents cry and suffer so.

I have been well for five years now, and rarely think of my
illness, as I know it was an isolated incident of the past. In retrospect, it was probably the most influential experience that I
could have gone through. The process of my recovery enabled
me to let go of my false sense of and need for control. I learned
how to love myself and how to live again. I feel empowered in a
way that I never thought was possible. I've taken responsibility
for my own happiness and future, as I have let go of all of the
elements that are beyond my control. I wake up smiling and always look forward to the wondrous adventures that lie ahead. I
feel strongly for those who are going through what I did, yet I
am convinced that however dark their reality may seem (forgive

the cliché), there is a light so brilliant at the end of the tunnel,
that the darkness (with the right help) will soon fade away.

I leap into the world
Embracing the sunlight
Fearlessly chasing the shadows
Which before I would run from
I laugh at myself
At the pure joy
The smiling faces
Children caught in a spider's web
Of wonder and delight
At a world still fresh and new
It's only a normal day
But only if I want it to be.

IO

A Final Message of Hope

A LETTER TO SOCIETY

Jesus Christ said, "Verily I say unto you, Inasmuch as ye have done it unto one of the least of these my brethren, ye have done it unto me."

Throughout history, societies stand by, time and time again, helpless, naive, or self-righteous, as human life becomes expendable; throughout history, death or murder are condoned or justified by mass inaction; boundaries of ethics are extended under the guise of morality to accept the unthinkable; societal desensitization evolves as a means of personal survival, and reason never did have a hand.

Throughout history, people have sought ways of identifying themselves by excluding others. Competition celebrates the individual or the few beyond the well-being of the whole. Race, religion, performance, or socioeconomic status decides who is valid in society and who is not. The natural imperfection of human nature is forever measured and made conditional.

Moreover, we humans cling to the traditional for the sake of stability, security, and continuity. We preserve kings beyond their time and create deities where none exist to validate our mores. Whichever way the trend, our perceived safety depends on our general adherence to the social norm. We bow to authority for its own sake sometimes, out of fear, confusion, or apathy. Doubt in our own abilities or acceptance of the status quo permits us to blind ourselves to questionable or inadequate leadership. We evade personal responsibility.

We naturally assume that society's members in some manner reflect it as a whole. Given the differences among people, it should be no surprise that many interpretations will develop from a seemingly equal premise. These many interpretations are not themselves the problem; it is our failure to understand and appreciate them that compromises the individual's sense of security and peaceful coexistence with his neighbor. If we do not understand another's motivation, at least let us not be unkind.

Fear that involvement in others' suffering might complicate our own forward movement can paralyze our inherent spontaneity to help those in need. Recall the case of Kitty Genovese, the woman beaten to death in New York City in 1964 as neighbors watched and heard her screams but did not come to her aid. (The term "bystander apathy" was coined at that time.) Cannot the same be said of people with eating disorders? We witness their ordeal and ignore their need for help. Not only do we not help, but we blame them for their plight.

My daughter Kirsten's poem, written while she had anorexia, speaks to that experience:

> . . . We are some, allowed error in minimum
> Depending on who we are
> Others would seem,
> Have free rein
> And with many disguises they strike and assume,
> Always looking to lay blame
>
> A title, a letter or two
> Borrowed from those who lie behind the mind
> Tools to flaunt
> Improvise and misuse.

My correspondent Edna also writes about society's misinterpretation of the anorexic's plight:

... If I were to choose
the finest words
available to man,
and sculpt
these baffling strifes
so fellow minds
might understand;

Assuredly,
those words would drown
in the tides
of interpretation;
the Truth
a victim of witlessness,
and confused evaluation.

We have allowed an unkind, sometimes inhuman interpretation of eating disorders to prevail, and that interpretation has permitted the deaths of countless innocents.

Life and the living of it are an unpredictable struggle for balance. That the human race survives as well as it does is perhaps commendable. The lamentable thing is that kindness and compassion have become rare, exceptional, even remarkable. Therefore, however well society feels it moves from each decade to the next, the concept of progress is always only that of interpretation.

Our successful interaction with others depends on the social contract of respect even when we do not always understand one another. Surely, survival of the human race depends on the inclusion of all. Why has not everyone's child become our own? Why do differences not bring enlightenment and curiosity but fear and disavowal? How can we turn our backs on a segment of society—those with eating disorders—unfairly announce that they have brought this calamity on themselves, and allow them to die?

Recently in a Western European country, a young girl with anorexia was granted permission to kill herself because she and her care team believed her condition was hopeless. That the sufferer of an eating disorder can be so mistaken and forsaken as to resort to the incredible loneliness of euthanasia makes me think we live in a psychological ice age. That a person who has lived a mere twenty-four years, albeit part of it in intense psychological misery, has been validated in her despair and hopelessness is a nasty comment on how society values such people. That we have come to condone despair, even promote it, leaves one to wonder at the purpose of "progress." If we do not embrace humanism, then what is the point?

I am deeply saddened by our indifference to the plight of those suffering from CNC. When do we become responsible for those who see no other avenue but euthanasia or suicide? How is this not condoning murder, especially when we see that eating disorders can be cured? When does bystander apathy or ego with regard to eating disorders become a crime against humanity as great as the others profiled in history books?

What has happened to tolerance, understanding, and compassion? Why is it so remarkable that any child is our responsibility? Modern society somehow adheres to a "survival of the fittest," a "kick him while he's down" attitude. Would we be so uncaring if it were an animal that was frightened and hurting rather than a child? Why? Perhaps because we have no expectations of animals, because they are less complicated, because there are not so many societal variables in interactions with them.

Could bystander apathy be a conditioned response? Could watching violent movies and television programming have furthered our inability to realize that we are not helpless when dire circumstances are real and not the product of someone's overheated imagination? Have we become so paralyzed that most of our actions are internal and therefore in need of sedation?

Could society have "progressed" to such a state of internalized turmoil and anxiety that it needs to be sedated in order to survive?

What part does the widespread use of prescription drugs play in our value systems? Granted, the value of these drugs is irrefutable. But has their usage become an unnecessary norm and a precursor to social acceptance of illicit use? Does the sedation of society create isolation and shame for those unable to survive without it? When we prescribe a pill for every emotion, do we seek to eliminate emotion and responsibility for others? Does this not suggest that emotions are expedient, that people and humanness are expendable for the sake of the greater cause of efficiency and productivity? A pill may address all of the symptoms, maybe, of an emotional problem, but the message conveyed is that the human condition, with all of its frailties and foibles, is not to be supported.

Do modern societies find it inexpedient to take time for nurturing? Do we expect too much of our children too soon? Do our children have the tools and support to construct their lives? Do our external values really represent our selfish desires? If so, how then can the true humanists, those predisposed to a CNC mindset, survive except by exclusion from such a society?

To comprehend the phenomenon of eating disorders, we must understand their origin—the platform of modernity. Eating disorders are a complex negative interpretation of one's role in life. CNC is the culmination of negative assumptions about oneself in the caring of and responsibility for the world. Because of the hallmarks of this mindset—sensitivity, above-average intelligence, caring, compassion, and commitment these children are sitting ducks for learning society too well for their own good.

How, then, can we castigate a segment of our population, who, being more caring and aware by virtue of their genetic endowments, have learned all they have been taught? They are guilty of the suggestibility and gullibility of the young trying to adapt to their environment. They are guilty of adapting without the maturity necessary for a proper perspective. Their sensitivity, caringness, and anxiety for their fellow man has created in them a subservience that precludes realistic existence. That these children are better equipped for learning society's lessons, are so vulnerable to sensationalism and marketing, has apparently worked as their worst enemy.

The victims of eating disorders are a devastating byproduct of modern society. The responsibility for this contemporary social issue is the responsibility of all of us, not of the victim! The attitude of "What are you going to do about your problem?" "When are you going to comply?" places the onus of blame and responsibility primarily on the victim. And ultimately that is incompatible with their healing. If we direct ourselves to nurturing the humanness within ourselves, we can drive out the scourge of eating disorders.

A LETTER TO PARENTS

Dearest Parents,

I write this letter to you in answer to the thousands of missives I have received from you and have been unable to respond to personally. You have much company. Your helplessness and desperation haunt my every moment. Your courage and dignity, even so, charge me with determination beyond what is sometimes humanly possible. Please pardon my limitations and realize that could I take into care every person I hear about, I would gladly.

But, I thank you for the gift you have given me—that of knowing what I have always hoped was true. The world is full of wonderful people, even in their moment of direst need and misery.

Know that you are not at fault for your child's condition. Know that she may at times attempt to alienate you. In her darkest hour she cannot bear the pain of the burden of her love for you and her sense that she has somehow failed you and

society. Be strong. Live the lesson *she* must learn for survival—
that of objectivity.

To understand the world, one must observe it from apart—
with compassion for the motivation, personality, and condition-
ing of each person, irregardless of how he or she behaves.

Love your child unconditionally. Talk to her with calm logic
to offset the negative tape running constantly in her brain. Do
not allow unkindness to her from any source. Try to teach
rather than to condemn those who do not understand. The end
of knowledge is wisdom; the end of wisdom, humility.

I have stood where you stand with my children; I stand
there yet, with yours.

A LETTER TO SUFFERERS

My Dearest Ones:

Every day I receive letters from you or your loved ones on
your behalf. Every day, my heart aches more for your pain.
Daily, I read testimonials of despair:

"My darling child has had anorexia for ten years. Her
organs are shutting down—she has been everywhere, she has
tried so hard—if she dies, my heart will be buried with her.
You are our last hope."

"Even the central venous catheter which always saved my
life when I was dangerously emaciated can no longer be used—
my veins are ruined. I am twenty-one and have had this for
twelve years. I cannot bear to live any longer like this. You are
my only and last hope."

"Our child is only eleven. How can he have become so sick
in two years? We don't know him anymore. How can he want
to die so young? He hasn't even lived yet. Please, please help us.
We are desperate. He is the hardest case they have ever seen."

"We were told to prepare for her death. They say that after
five years in hospitals, she is treatment-resistant. She is only
sixteen."

I hear cries from the shrinking self:

"No one can see me or
Watch me watching myself walking
Into walls."

I hear the despair:

"Scuffed faces stained with defeat observe
The still existence of themselves and others,
Everyone appears to be a watcher.
Watching life after life
Shuffle in their descent."

If I have one purpose on earth, it is to make your plight understood by the masses. With this book, I have attempted to clarify the nature of CNC to those who may wish to know. Of those, there are many—professionals, educators, parents—who would wish to study and to mitigate this societal calamity. The world is full of good people who care about you.

You are not failures at life, merely at understanding your own value. Soon professionals across the globe will discontinue treating the symptoms of eating disorders as the cause.

You are altruistic angels who care more for the well-being of the world than you do for yourselves. If there are those who cannot lend themselves to positive caring, give them compassion and understanding. Though ignorance will always exist, don't be afraid of it. Don't allow it to defeat you.

There are two parts to the living of life. Yes, the first you are masters of: to be kind, always. The second and the more difficult, however, is not to condone ignorance. We all have the opportunity to be teachers. In another discourse, it could be said, perhaps, that your purpose here is to teach the world what it is beginning to forget—patience, tolerance, kindness, and compassion.

A Final Message of Hope

A girl with anorexia wrote to me: "Know that my embrace of you is much larger than my arms are wide."
I couldn't say it better. You are always in my heart. My every thought begins with you. Much love from your forever kind of friend.

Peggy Claude-Pierre

Resources

THE CHOICE OF TREATMENT for eating disorders must be a personal decision. Let this resource guide be a first step in your search for information and support.

AMERICAN ANOREXIA/BULIMIA ASSOCIATION (AABA)
165 W. 46th St., Suite 1108
New York, NY 10036
(212) 575-6200

NATIONAL ASSOCIATION OF ANOREXIA NERVOSA AND ASSOCIATED DISORDERS (ANAD)
P.O. Box 7
Highland Park, IL 60035
(847) 831-3438

ANOREXIA NERVOSA AND RELATED EATING DISORDERS, INC. (ANRED)
P.O. Box 5102
Eugene, OR 97405
(541) 344-1144

NATIONAL EATING DISORDERS ORGANIZATION (NEDO)
6655 S. Yale Ave.
Tulsa, OK 74136
(918) 481-4044

NATIONAL INSTITUTE OF MENTAL HEALTH
U.S. Department of Health and Human Services
5600 Fishers Lane, Room 7C-02
Rockville, MD 20857
(800) 421-4211

There is also a wealth of information on the World Wide Web.

For Further Reading

The following is a list of some of the books on philosophy and psychology that have been powerful influences on my own thinking. I found these and others extremely helpful in shaping my own perspectives on eating disorders. I invite my patients to explore them for themselves.

Adler, Alfred, *Superiority and Social Interest.* Norton, New York, 1979.

Ansbacher, H. L., and R. R. Ansbacher, eds., *The Individual Psychology of Alfred Adler.* Harper & Row, New York, 1964.

Bruch, Hilda, *The Golden Cage—The Enigma of Anorexia Nervosa.* Vintage, New York, 1979.

———, *Eating Disorders—Obesity, Anorexia Nervosa, and the Person Within.* Basic Books, New York, 1973.

de Chardin, Teilhard, *The Future of Man.* Harper & Row, New York, 1964.

Foucault, Michel, *Mental Illness and Psychology,* Alan Sheridan, trans. Harper & Row, New York, 1987.

Fromm, Erich, *The Anatomy of Human Destructiveness.* Holt, New York, 1992.

———, *The Art of Being.* Continuum, New York, 1994.

———, *Man for Himself—An Inquiry Into the Psychology of Ethics.* Holt, New York, 1992.

Hegel, G. W. F., *The Phenomenology of Mind*, J. B. Baillie, trans. Allen & Unwin, London, 1966.

Horkheimer, M., *Eclipse of Reason.* Seabury Press, New York, 1974.

Koestler, Arthur, *The Sleepwalkers—A History of Man's Changing Vision of the Universe.* Penguin, Middlesex, 1982.

Lucács, Georg, *History and Class Consciousness*, Rodney Livingstone, trans. Merlin Press, London, 1983.

Marcuse, Herbert, *One-Dimensional Man.* Beacon Press, Boston, 1964.

Piaget, Jean, *The Construction of Reality in the Child.* Basic Books, New York, 1954.

Index

Actual Mind
  of acute patients, 93–94, 105
  and blame, 61–63
  characteristics of, 39–41
  and civil war in mind, 39–41,
    94–95, 148–49
  and getting help, 204, 210, 215,
    216
  and home environment, 185,
    191, 195
  and myths/misconceptions,
    83, 84, 86
  and reversing Negative Mind,
    113, 116–29, 138
  and unconditional love, 131
  See also Confirmed Negativity
    Condition; Logic; specific
    recovery stage
Acute patients
  Actual Mind of, 93–94, 105
  behavior of, 99–100, 102–3
  feeding of, 204–5, 208, 222
  getting help for, 203, 204–12, 215
  and home environment, 185,
    188

hospitalization for, 203,
    204–12, 240–41
  medication for, 212
  Negative Mind of, 89–90,
    92–99, 100, 101–3, 104–5,
    108–9
  physiology of, 90–92
  psychology of, 92–99
  social withdrawal of, 105–8
  and suicide, 97–99, 104–5
  trances of, 100–102
  See also Acute Stage
Acute Stage, 144, 146–49, 159, 163,
    169. See also Acute patients
Adolescence, 17, 23, 78, 158, 165,
    198–99
Altruism, 46, 54, 62, 173
  and asking for help, 40–41
  as manifestation of eating dis-
    orders/CNC, 7, 15, 33,
    55–56, 57–58
  and myths/misconceptions,
    80, 81, 84
  See also Caring for others; Self-
    lessness